Copyright ©
All righ

The characters and events portrayed in this book are fictitious. Any similarity to real persons, living or dead, is coincidental and not intended by the author.

No part of this book may be reproduced, or stored in a retrieval system, or transmitted in any form or by any means, electronic, mechanical, photocopying, recording, or otherwise, without express written permission of the publisher.

ISBN-13: 978-1-958456-05-7
Publisher: Moon Jumper Press

learn more at MoonJumperPress.com

Printed in the United States of America

SPECIAL THANKS TO:

Annika, for always wanting more pages, and without whose enthusiasm, this might never have been completed

Kari for always supporting my crazy dreams and taking great care of me along the way.

Melissa Smith and **Nate Heppner** for opening their classrooms and allowing me to present a number of candidate title/cover page options to my actual demographic

The **2023 8th Grade Language Arts Class at The Child's Primary School** and the **2023 8th Grade English Classes at La Jolla Country Day School** whose insight was invaluable in deciding on the final title and cover page

Ellen, thanks so much!

This page left Intentionally Blank....

(or was it?)

Table of Contents

Chapter 1: In which my English teacher completely loses it...................1

Chapter 2: In which my brilliant plan works brilliantly... but is still a complete fail..10

Chapter 3: If you lie with dogs, don't expect them to believe you later. Even with kittens...17

Chapter 4: In which I learn just enough to be driven really crazy.........21

Chapter 5: A life without dwarves is not a tall order............................31

Chapter 6: In case of emergency, break glass.......................................37

Chapter 7: In which something actually goes right. And that can't be good...41

Chapter 8: In which I discover a significant gap in my vocabulary......46

Chapter 9: In which I receive help from a surprising source................52

Chapter 10: In which Chocolate does, in fact, manage to defy description..58

Chapter 11: In which Not Dad Cracks the Code and I realize, yet again, that I can't do believable chilled vegetable impressions.......62

Chapter 12: In which I am reminded that I don't actually speak German..72

Chapter 13: In which the truth sets me free... from lying about something else..80

Chapter 14: In which the proverbial clock is ticking, yet nothing actually happens..83

Chapter 15: In which I realize yet again, I am never getting a pony.....84

Chapter 16: In which I discover that Mom's timing really sucks..........94

Chapter 17: In which life would have been more satisfying if I'd actually wanted tuna..100

Chapter 18: In which you have to choose whether to finally trust me. Or not..115

Chapter 19: In which I am introduced to Not Dad's 'Bowl of Balls' and another simple plan goes awry..121

Chapter 20: In which time passes. Excruciatingly slowly...................134

Chapter 21: In which I am reminded, once again, that Oprah is not Greek..143

Chapter 22: In which I discover religion..149

Chapter 23: In which I discover the downside of yet another brilliant plan...154

Chapter 24: In which I discover that I'm not missing any organs after all..160

Chapter 25: In which I am reminded to eat, for reasons best left to the imagination...166

Chapter 26: In which bovine end products feature prominently. (Though you'll have to wait to find out which end)...............173

Chapter 27: In which I make a grown man cry. And make him love it..183

Chapter 28: If it wasn't my blood, then why is my heart bleeding on the floor?..193

Chapter 29: In which the month of Thursday happens.....................202

Chapter 30: In hindsight, this was probably inevitable.......................211

Chapter 31: Two am...212

Chapter 32: 4 am..213

Chapter 33: Oh my god..214

Chapter 34: In which I realize that I might as well be in Oz................215

Chapter 35: In which I realize that knowing how to turn dead bodies into plastic might come in quite handy.....................221

Chapter 36: In which I have absolutely no idea what's going on........229

Chapter 37: In which I discover a terrible truth................................238

Chapter 38: In which I discover I might be the next Dalai Lama........251

Chapter 39: In which... well, things are good. Yeah, I know............264

BOOK BLOOPERS & OUTTAKES (or my murdered darlings)..........266

Chapter 1
In which my English teacher completely loses it

I can't believe he's still obsessed.

I don't know how long ago it was, but way back before it was even a "thing," my best friend—formerly known as Peter—started baking. Well, perhaps that's not exactly the right verb, because what comes out of his oven bears about as much resemblance to bread as it does to, say, reinforced concrete.

Now, why a teenage boy who's built like a refrigerator is baking bread in the first place is a whole other story. The short version is that it's my fault, because I was the one who gave him the book <u>The Hunger Games</u> for his birthday. If you've been living in a cave for the past couple of decades or are reading this in some far distant future where no one knows who Katnis Everdeen is, well, it kind of sucks to be you because it's a really great book.

The long version would probably require a panel of psychologists, years of intensive therapy, and a whole lot of dark chocolate to get through, but suffice it to say while the rest of the world was kind of fixated on the whole *kids-killing-kids* part of the book, what does Peter take from it? That boys can bake.

Yeah, go figure.

Oh, and of course, since the character in the book who bakes bread is named Peeta, Peter decided that was his new name. The only problem with this otherwise brilliant little plan is that we live here in Boston, home of the silent "R". You know, *Pahk the cah in Hahvahd Yahd* and all that. So insisting that he be called Peeta rather than, well, Petah, is kind of insane in its own right.

Now, you're probably asking yourself what a sixteen-year-old girl is doing with a boy as her best friend, or you would have, had I gotten around to telling you I was a sixteen year-old girl. Well, surprise! I am, my name's Gwen Pendergrass (and don't get me started on the baggage that last name comes with!), and he is, so you might as well just start dealing with the concept.

Or you could move on to some other book entirely, one which could perhaps be reasonably called "intelligible." And I wouldn't fault you; I mean, my mom's the writer anyway, as you might've guessed from all this incoherent ranting. She can't spell to save her life, but neither could Shakespeare, so there you go. Me, well, I'm not quite sure what I am, but I'm sixteen, so lay off, I'll figure it out eventually.

Okay. Start at the beginning, Mom always tells me, so here goes:

I was born. At the usual age and in the usual manner. Or at least so I've been told, as it's not like I actually remember it at all. Which is probably all for the best, what with all the squeezing, screaming and crying that I've heard goes on. In any case, it's always been just my mom and me, and since I'm not much of a believer in virgin birth or parthenogenesis (see Mom, I do pay attention in biology class! Well, at least sometimes...) I've always assumed Dad was out there somewhere.

I even have a small strip of pictures of him and Mom in some photo booth at a casino in Vegas. They both look kind of drunk but really happy, which I supposed explains a lot. Me in particular. Or at least my aforementioned birth nine months later.

But as I was saying, Dad's never been in the picture—or outside of the Vegas ones, if you take my meaning—and while I'm not thrilled with the idea, for the most part I don't dwell on it. It's just my life, such as it is.

If you've happened to do the math—which I can assure you I would *never* do in your place—you'll have figured out I'm a high school soph, which is just about as much fun as it sounds. In English class, we've just finished reading Oedipus Rex—you know, that timeless story of a boy who kills his father and marries his mother, something high school students throughout history have always deeply related to.

"...so, using Oedipus's failed relationship with his father as an inspiration," my English teacher, the inimitable Mrs. Beecham, tells us as we're scrambling to get all our stuff into our backpacks, "you're going to write about your earliest recollection of you and your father doing something meaningful together. Something other than going to his parole hearing, watching TV or playing video games."

My fellow students let out the traditional collective groan of dismay, which Mrs. Beecham, just as traditionally, ignores. "And make it good, people," she tells us. "Because if I get one more essay on my dad made me toast while momma was away, we're doing six weeks of James Joyce. Solid."

A Novel of Mystery, Love, and of Chocolate that Defies Description

James Joyce, in case you're fortunate enough not to know, is the Mount Everest of writers. You read him because it's such grueling, hard going that at the end you can plant a flag on the book and say I prevailed; I reached the summit of Mt. Joyce without the aid of Sherpas or oxygen tanks, and I lived to tell the tale.

However, as I bet there aren't more than two other people in the room who have any idea who the heck he is, the whole threat thing is kind of pointless. But as I said, Mom's a writer, so I know this stuff enough to shudder at the thought.

The rest of my classmates start filing out, scrambling to get to their next class before the bell rings.

"Three pages, typed," she calls after them. "And rough drafts by next Wednesday."

And then it's just me, standing in front of her desk. I want to ask if I can approach the bench, but I have a feeling it won't go over all that well.

"Yes, what is it?" Mrs. Beecham asks with a sigh. Actually, she adds a put-upon sigh as punctuation to every one-on-one interaction I've ever seen her have. She once even got so exasperated with us kids for "pestering her for clarifications" that she'd slammed a book down on her desk. "I'm here to teach," she'd told us in the resulting stunned silence. "Not to answer questions."

When the time comes, I'm going to push for getting that inscribed on her gravestone like a family motto.

"Um, I never knew my father," I tell her.

"Consider yourself lucky. Most of 'em are pigs anyway."

Not what I was expecting. But she's on a roll, now.

"If I hadn't met my kids' father, I would have been a whole lot better off, let me tell you. For one thing, I can guarantee I'd be doing something worthwhile with my life instead of being stuck here teaching the same junk year after year."

Well, okay, then. This is going well. I start to ask if I could write about my mom instead, but she's gone, lost in her own world.

"But they're classics..." she whines, presumably mimicking some member of the school administration. "Classics my ass," she tells me. "If you listened to those spineless worms on the school board, you'd think nothing worthwhile had been written since Mark Twain."

"Uh, that sounds pretty frustrating," I mumble. "But what should I do about this assignment?"

"Frustrating? You don't know the meaning of frustrating. You kid all whine and moan about the assignments. Three whole pages. Please. I've been doing this same curriculum twice a year for fifteen years. Fifteen years! At sixty, three-page papers a year, do you know how much I've read?"

I start doing the math in my head, but she's plowing onwards, saving me the effort.

"Twenty-seven hundred pages. Twenty-seven hundred pages of mostly incoherent drivel from you people! So don't you complain, Missy, don't you dare complain!"

"I wasn't," I protest. "I just need to know how to do the assignment without a dad."

"That's not really my problem, now, is it?"

"Excuse me?"

She looks down at me over her glasses. "This is a creative writing class. Be creative. Write about how the jerk broke your poor mother's heart, or about all the lies he told her."

"I really don't think it was like that, Mrs. Beecham."

"Yeah, right. Is he dead?" she demands. I suddenly remember there is no Mr. Beecham. Shocking, I know.

"I don't think so," I reply.

She smiles like she's just checkmated with me. "Then it was like that. Trust me."

"Hey, Pita Piper," I call, as I finally come out of school.

He's standing next to this massive oak tree in the school's front yard, and he doesn't dignify my adornment of his name with even the faintest of eye rolls. The tree doesn't react either, but given that it's a tree and he's Peter, neither of these events are particularly surprising.

By the way, have I mentioned how much I love this tree? It's just brilliant. It's supposedly been here since long before there *was* a here, here. And despite its size, it has somehow figured out how to offer no shade at all no matter where the sun is in the sky. I've never been able to work out how it manages this trick, but if I had to deal with people carving their names into me and covering me with TP on an annual basis, I wouldn't give them any shade either.

Peter steps away from the tree and matches strides with me as I pass.

"It's just Peeta," he tells me patiently. He's always patient with me, even when most people would want to throw me in front of a bus. Which may explain why he's my best friend, I suppose, because if your friends are trying to throw you in front of buses, something is seriously wrong with your life.

I'd met him when we moved into our current apartment building filled with double-income families. Unfortunately, the two incomes tend to both be earned by a single parent working two jobs that together pay in the low to starvation range. Peter's family is the exception in that he still has both parents, though with all the weed they smoke, you could mash their brains together and the resulting creature still wouldn't be as sharp as my mom. I wouldn't particularly want to meet it in a dark alley either, but I guess that's pretty much a given for anything created from two brains.

Don't get me wrong, they're nice enough and do their best to take care of Peter... it's just that their best isn't particularly good.

So where was I? Oh yeah, I was telling you how I met Peter. We've moved so many times that I can't remember where we were coming from, but my job is always to sit on the lawn of the new place and guard our stuff as Mom makes trip after trip in our old station wagon, moving our junk... sorry, our prized possessions... one carload at a time.

Of the two or three carloads, only two things are really mine: a huge box of books, and a ratty suitcase filled with hand-me-down clothes which are always somehow mostly smaller than I currently am, but which are insufficiently worn out to be replaced.

Of these, I only really care about my books and my clothes can go up in flames for all I care. Well, as long as I'm not wearing them at the time.

But back to yet another move. Mom was off on her second or third trip and there I was, bored out of my mind, so I decided to break open my book box and see if <u>Frankenstein</u> was anywhere close to the top. It is, without a doubt, one of my favorite books... and yes, I know, that makes me officially weird. Most of my generation don't want to have anything to do with something more than twenty minutes old and my favorite book just had its two-hundredth birthday.

If you've never read it, trust me, it's nothing like what you expect. In some ways, Dr Frankenstein is even more of a monster than his creation, and I can totally relate with the monster's perspective of having the world all around you, but being outside of it, only able to look in. Sure, being the poor kid on the free lunch program isn't exactly the same as being a reanimated creature too hideous to be gazed upon, but still, not being seen for yourself, can be pretty exhausting either way.

I had settled down and was in the middle of chapter four when the sun pretty much went away. I looked up and found myself in the shadow cast by this really big guy looking down at me.

"Hey," he said, then apparently realized he was blocking my sun, because he took a large step to his left and it all came streaming back in.

I blinked in the sudden light and tried to place him, but the only thing I could think of was that he could be the monster itself. Well, in size at least, because this guy was anything but hideous to look at.

"So, I was wondering," he said, "if I could borrow your copy of Frankenstein. When you're done with it, of course."

I had no idea who this kid was and considered the obvious questions that brought up, but decided to go straight for an even more basic one.

"Why?" I asked, looking up at him, innocently.

At this point in the conversation, most people will just stare at you blankly with a "that does not compute" glaze to their eyes. Like when a waiter bounces up to you and says, "If you need any help, my name is Candy" and you reply "What's your name if I don't need any?"

It kind of short-circuits their brain, and you can almost hear the gears whirring as they try to go back and make sense of what you said. And of course, this is exactly what I expected to happen to Peter. For yes, this is Peter, and this is the moment I've been talking about when I first met him.

"Because the rats ate my copy," he responded patiently, without even a hint of grinding gears, smoke, or glazed look at all. Impressive.

"Everyone's a critic," I told him, wondering if he'd follow my logic.

"Actually, they were pretty indiscriminate. They also ate one of my shoes."

I'm beginning to like this kid, not that I'd ever let him know. "Right or left?" I asked, as if it somehow mattered.

"Left definitely. I remember Mitch–that's my dad–saying it was ironic they ate the left shoe because with that one gone, now the right shoe is left."

Ouch. I did mention that his parents' brains are kind of cross-wired right? This sort of stuff comes out of their mouths all the time, and a lot of it is actually pretty funny. All the more so, as they have absolutely no idea that it is.

"You know," I mentioned casually, "lending a book to someone who has rats which eat them is kind of like lending money to someone with a gambling problem."

"They're not so much my rats, as rats who pretty much sublet the entire building."

Great, I'm just loving this new place already.

"If they bother you, though, you can always get coyote urine from predatorpee.com. Works like a charm. The downside, of course, is that your bedroom smells like a bunch of coyotes peed in it... or you could just embrace the rats as another marvel of nature's infinite adaptability, and anyway, what's a little black plague among friends?"

"One of these days," I commented to the universe at large, "I would really like to live in a place which didn't involve choosing among book-eating rats, coyote pee and the Black Death."

"Yeah, that would be nice, wouldn't it. So, can I borrow your book?"

Since the whole pee thing grossed me out, and having my precious books turned into rat turds was not something I wanted to risk, after we were all moved in he took me to this vacant lot where everyone dumps their junk and we found an old metal filing cabinet that he lugged up to our apartment for me. Must've been from the twenties or thirties because this sucker was made of real steel, nothing like that tin foil aluminum stuff they sell nowadays.

Weighed a ton, but it's been a life saver. Some people have gun safes. Me, I have a book safe. In return, I let him come and read any time he wants.

But back to me, Peter, and the shadeless oak tree that I started talking about like half a chapter ago.

"Can I borrow a memory?" I ask him as we start walking to the green line T-station to catch our train home. Sure, the orange line is closer and takes about a billion fewer stops but what can I say, I like green. And it's not like we have anything particularly exciting to do once we get to our luxury living accommodations anyway, so why hurry?

Life is the journey, not the destination. Therefore, the longer we can make the journey last, the longer we'll live. Or something like that.

By the way, for those of you outside of Boston, the "T" is the subway, short for the MTA, which stands for **M**ediocre **T**ransport **A**utocracy, or something like that. Some of the stations are actually pretty cool with art and bronzed clothing and stuff.

Ours isn't one of them.

"I mean it," I tell him. "I need a memory I can borrow for Mrs. Beecham's insipid Oedipus-inspired, father/relationships assignment."

He doesn't respond, just slowly turns and gives me The Look. You know the one: the look that says, "you didn't really just say that did you?" Which of course I just did, or he wouldn't have given me The Look in the first place.

So of course I hit him.

Remind me not to do that; the guy's made of concrete or something because it's like hitting a brick wall.

"Ow!"

As I shake my hand in the air to get some feeling back into it–or at least some feeling other than pain–I glare at him as it were all somehow his fault, but he shrugs, not buying it.

I rub my poor bruised hand as we descend into the open maw of Boylston station. It's cool and dim in there after the bright afternoon sun, and I fish in my backpack and we flash our Charlie Cards and head out to the platform. A train's already sitting there so we run for it, taking the stairs two at a time then dashing into the car, just as the doors... well, do nothing.

And they keep on doing nothing for about another ten minutes and we get to watch everyone else do exactly the same thing we just did: see the car from the top of the stairs and risk a broken neck running down to catch the train just before it doesn't leave.

"It doesn't have to be a good memory," I say as we continue to wait. "How about the one when Mitch thought he was the prophet David, or when you went camping and the raccoons found his stash...?"

The doors finally slide shut and the car lurches forwards. I plead all the way to our stop in Roxbury, the dissolved municipality we call home. Yep, some people get burgs or boroughs or townships, or even just cool neighborhoods like Angleside, Ravenswood or Pigeon Hill like they have over in Waltham.

Me, I get to live in a dissolved municipality. An alka-seltzer of a former town, whose old buildings often look like they've been sitting there dissolving away over the years ever since the proud city of Roxbury was eaten by Boston and dissolved into the melting pot of greater Bostburbia, relegated to a mere backwater of a neighborhood. But we will never forget!

Well, that's true, but mostly because nobody ever learns that stuff anymore, because it all happened about a hundred and fifty years ago. And it's kind of hard to forget what you never knew. But the principle is sound. And there's always Wikipedia.

Peter's still shaking his head 'no' as we climb up the four flights to our floor.

"Mitch is a bad enough influence in general," Peter tells me. "And you, in particular, don't need another one. Why don't you write about when your own dad was your imaginary friend?"

"I was about three. And it wasn't real."

"It was real to you."

"Yeah, so was the tooth fairy."

He looks at me, concerned. "What are you saying?"

"Nothing, I'm sure there are millions of cute little pixies out there who have nothing better to do than collect used teeth.

"They aren't pixies, they're fairies. And I'm pretty sure they're not all that cute. Probably more like Rosie the Riveter with wings."

I'm fairly sure he's putting me on, but when you look in the dictionary under deadpan it says: "see Peter." Well, at least it does since I whited out the old definition and penned that one in.

I know, me, the literary literalist, defacing a book. In my defense, I put a picture of Peter next to the entry which means I actually also face'd the book, so between that and the defacing, it should cancel itself out karmically speaking.

Aaaah, I'm turning into Mitch with his right shoe left thing…! Maybe Peter has a point about him being a bad influence after all.

Chapter 2
In which my brilliant plan works brilliantly... but is still a complete fail.

I drop my apartment keys in the Tibetan prayer bowl we keep by the door and rub Buddha's belly for luck. He takes a swipe at me but misses, due to my cat-like reflexes. Well, actually better than cat-like, I suppose, because he did miss, after all. And he is, of course, a cat. Probably two if you're counting purely by volume.

"You know, that's not a very Zen thing to do," I admonish him. If cats could shrug then Buddha would, as about all he and his namesake have in common is the big belly.

But back to me. I still have no clue what I'm going to do for the father/relationship assignment. As I see it, I have three options: 1) Make something up entirely, 2) Go weirdly existential about how Dad and I lived on this earth together, breathed the same air, coexisted in nearly the same space in that brief moment when he and my mom were, well, you know "making" me, or 3) Go get a snack.

Since the third option seems like the most achievable goal, I dump my school stuff in the corner and hike the grueling eight steps from the front door to the closet we call a kitchen. It's a truly brilliantly designed space where the non-functioning dishwasher blocks the cabinets, and opening the oven has to be done from the side unless you have very thin legs and don't mind having a drawer handle pressed painfully into the small of your back.

I personally think it was designed by the same guys who make those traffic car puzzles where you can only slide the cars forwards or back and you have to somehow get the one special car out of the gridlock.

Anyway, I rummage through the cabinets—a process which involves nearly getting brained by a can of stewed tomatoes that leaps out at me with absolutely no provocation on my part. Actually, the only food we ever keep in the cabinets are canned goods as the rats have literally chewed through the wall to get in there and nothing less than cold, hard steel will stop them.

However, while the cans themselves are rat-proof, the resident rodentia gnaw off all the can's labels, which made for some pretty, well, *interesting* meals until I got into the habit of writing each can's contents on their tops with a Sharpie®.

All unarmored food goes into the dishwasher if it doesn't need refrigeration, or the freezer if it does. Nothing goes into the refrigerator itself, for reasons that are best left to the imagination. And anyway, since the freezer hasn't gotten cold enough to produce ice since the mastodons last roamed the city, it all ends up as a fairly functionally dysfunctional system.

However, none of that matters as I still need a snack. Since neither the dishwasher nor the cabinets hold anything particularly enticing, I move on to the freezer. Hmmm... three hard boiled eggs left over from Easter—hopefully, the most recent one though you never know for sure—some chicken I know Mom's saving for pot-pies, a pair of carrots that are so rubbery they're fit for nothing but soup, ketchup and relish (but, of course, no hot dogs), tartar sauce, and a couple dozen packets of soy sauce.

I'm considering whether tartar sauce might be good on toast as I close the freezer door, revealing a shadowy apparition suddenly filling the doorway.

I let out a small scream, then jump back without thinking, my brilliant, super cat-like reflexes instinctively throwing me away from this apparition directly into that brilliantly placed drawer handle I mentioned earlier. Which slams into the small of my back, produces yet another scream, and as I spin around to escape, I, of course, manage to smash my hand into the 1970's Formica counter top that juts out over the dishwasher.

You know, even groovy flower-power patterned counters will hurt you given the chance. Trust me, I know.

Okay, adrenaline surge over, pain surge kicking in.

"Ow! Mom, how many times have I told you not to do that!" I glare at her as I rub my hand, and pointedly add another "Ow!"

Mom, of course, has seen me do this kind of thing plenty of times before, so she's not very impressed. If there's no blood and no bones protruding, the best I'm likely to get is "walk it off."

It sounds harsher than it is, but when you have a kid as accident prone as I am, I guess you learn pretty quick not to rush over at every scrape, collision, contusion, fall, slip, tumble, or non-concussive whack. Even seeing me being half-brained by the overly aggressive can of stewed tomatoes probably wouldn't have turned her from mild-mannered mom to Super Protecto-Mom. Still, I know if I really do need her, she'll be there in a flash, like when I took a nose-dive into the wet cement... another story also best left to the imagination.

Mom's wearing her waitress uniform with the blue stripes, and she's got her hair done up in that bun she hates, so I know she's going to (rather than coming from) Katie's Kountry Kitch'n. Yes, with three K's, an apostrophe, and one of the least thought out acronyms I know...

Anyway, she's looking at me kind of oddly, and she's holding an envelope in front of her, clearly presenting it as Exhibit A.

"Perhaps you'd like to tell me what this is?"

Her hand is over the return address so I can't see who it's from.

"Uh, at first guess, I'd say an envelope," I offer helpfully.

She rolls her eyes. Pretty well for an old person, actually. Most of them look like they're possessed or something when they try it, but my mom's cool that way even though she's over thirty. What she doesn't seem to realize, though, is that getting an eye roll from her is like eating a potato chip; you always want more.

"Oooh," I add enthusiastically. "Give me another, this is fun."

"The strange thing," she says, ignoring my scintillating wit, "is that it's addressed to me."

"That is odd. I mean, who writes letters anymore?"

"Also, it's from Yale," she says, eyeing me as if to see what kind of reaction she'll get. "From the admissions department."

She gets a big one. I'm sure my eyes widen to Disney-princess-like proportions and I'm fairly certain my mouth falls open. It's been so long, I'd completely forgotten about this.

"Did you open it? Did you get in?"

"What's really strange about it," she continues, ignoring my questions, "is that I don't remember actually applying to Yale. Or anywhere else for that matter."

"But you got in, right?"

"All of which makes me wonder," she goes on, ignoring both my new question and the fact that I'm nearly bouncing off the walls, "where they could have possibly gotten the idea that I wanted to go back to school..."

"Mom...!" I plead. "What did they say?"

I must have one of those veins pulsing madly in my forehead or am developing some kind of ominous nervous twitch because she gives in and silently hands me the letter. I snatch the folded paper out of the envelope and start skimming it.

Dear Applicant... blah, blah, blah, we're very pleased, blah blah, contingent upon proof of eligibility... we grant you the full Bloom-Wood scholarship for the humanities!

All I can think is "Oh, my god, Oh my god" over and over. I can feel myself grinning ear to ear. "Mom! You did it!"

I go for the big, congratulatory high-five, but for some reason Mom's not playing. She's still just looking at me with those oddly serious eyes.

"I didn't do anything," she says quietly.

"Sure you did. C'mon, Mom, this is great news! Fist bump."

No fist from Mom either, just that "you've got a lot of explaining to do" look that every mother seems to have. I've always imagined doctors handing newborns to their mothers along with a little laminated flyer with cute diagrams showing how to give this look. "Here you go, Mrs. Pendergrass. It's a girl. And by the way, you'll need this."

But laminated flyers notwithstanding, Mom's a grandmaster at this look and I crumble under her gaze in mere seconds. Good thing I don't know any nuclear launch codes, or Beyoncé's private cell phone number or anything, because they'd just have to look disapprovingly at me and I'd sing like a canary.

"Okay, okay... but can we at least not do this in the kitchen?"

She steps out of my way and waves me into the living / dining / entry hall / my bedroom room. We sit down on the rust colored futon sofa that doubles as my rust colored mattress from hell. Even unfolded, it's got a permanent crease down the middle and I either have to sleep in this crease, or squeeze all the way to one side and try to fight its black-hole like attraction all night. As I have yet to fully master the art of sleeping uphill, I inevitably wake up nose-down in the trench, which just does wonders for my dust mite allergies.

Have I mentioned that I have a tendency to get side-tracked? I think I probably have A.D.D., and I keep meaning to look up its symptoms on the Internet, but then I get distracted by some sidebar item and have never gotten far enough to even find out what the acronym stands for.

Right. Mom's still staring at me expectantly.

"A couple of months ago," I explain, "I was going through my old baby things, trying to find some good stuff to pass on as hand-me-downs to the Sloans up in 4B, and I found the first couple of chapters you wrote entitled The Care and Feeding of the Common New York Night Owl."

"You didn't."

Why do people say that? I mean, obviously I did, or we wouldn't be having this discussion.

Sigh. "I did."

Mom shakes her head, though I'm still not sure exactly what she's feeling. Normally I can read her like a book, but this is something new.

"I'd completely forgotten that," she says, half to herself, half to me, and half to the world in general. "I started it when I first took that night-shift bar tending job. You were about two, and back then I was still young and delusional and thought I could do everything."

"Mom, you still can."

"What? Be delusional?"

"No, do everything."

"Now you're the one who's being delusional. Honey, what you did was super sweet, but..."

"But nothing. This is your chance, Mom! This is Yale... this was your dream."

"Honey, you're my dream now."

My turn for the eye roll. And while Mom's good, I'm Olympic Team good. "Very Hallmark, Mom. You should write cards."

Mom takes my hand and squeezes it. "Gwen. Even if I wanted to do this—and I'm not saying I do—there's no way we could make the money work."

This isn't happening. It can't be. We're supposed to be jumping up and down, screaming our heads off in excitement and making the neighbors bang on the walls and tell us to shut up. We're supposed to be picking out her classes and figuring out what new school I'll be going to... oh, crap. New school equals no Peter. I push the thought away. This is important; this is Mom's moment and for some reason she's just not getting it.

I pick up the letter and hold it out to her. "What part of full scholarship don't you understand? This Bloom-Wood thing, it's like it was designed for you." I skim the letter. "Uh, here we go. It was established to enable exceptional students who had previously dropped out of college due to health, family or financial reasons to finish their degrees. That's you, Mom."

"I know but..."

"Some previous university education... check. Previously forced to leave school for health or family reasons... check. Currently in workforce... check and double-check. Desire to finish BFA or MFA in Humanities... duh, check. So, what's the problem?"

"The problem is that it says I have to focus exclusively on my studies and can't take a job while I'm on it."

"But they provide housing..."

She smiles at me sadly and shakes her head. "...shared housing, which you can't live in."

What? Mom points out the paragraph in the paper and I can feel it all unraveling... no, this was supposed to be her chance!

"But, but there's a stipend," I say, grasping at straws.

"Which would be enough if I could live in the housing, but it's nowhere close enough to pay for rent in New Haven."

"I could get a job," I say hopefully. I can usually get my way by being maddeningly reasonable, but she's not having any of it.

"No way."

"But you dropped out of college to raise me, I could just take..."

"Gwen. We are not having this discussion."

"But..."

"You are not dropping out of high school so I can go to college."

"But..."

"No. End of story."

"Fine," I say tightly, thrusting the letter back at her. She just got the Golden Ticket in the Wonka Bar and she's handing it off to some stranger, whoever is number two on their scholarship list. "They won't hold it for you, you know. This is your shot, Mom. All you have to do is seize the carp, and you can finally get your life back on track."

"Gwen, honey, it never got off track."

"Oh yeah. Your big dream was to be working two mindless, minimum-wage jobs. How could I have forgotten that?"

She smiles, conceding the point but not the argument. "No... of course not."

She tries to brush some hair that's fallen over my eyes, but I pull away. Why can't she be selfish just for once in her life?

She lets her hand drop. "I wouldn't give you up for all the career success in the world," she tells me.

I don't bother to reply because I know if I do, I'll say something I'll regret later.

Mom glances down at her watch and jumps up off the futon. "Oh crap. I'm going to be late. I really have to go."

She starts looking around for her purse, which is currently under Buddha.

"Sure. Go," I tell her as I push the big lug off the bag and hand it to her. The bag not the lug. "Wouldn't want to keep you from your destiny slinging the blue plate special."

"Gwen." She makes as if she's going to hug me, but I'm already tightly hugging myself, trying to keep from crying and she knows well enough to back off.

"Honey, thank you for trying," she tells me. "I know you just want to look out for me. But that's my job, not yours."

"Yeah, whatever," I reply, and she sighs, then turns and leaves because she has to. And I stare at the closed door after her in frustration because I have to.

And I know that "yeah, whatever" is not a particularly brilliant come-back, but screw it, Mom's the writer not me. Or she would be if I'd never been born.

Don't get me wrong; I like my life. Sure, it could use some improving, but I love my mom and I know she loves me. And I've got Peter and my books... but sometimes I think about what Mom's life would have been like if she hadn't had me when she did, and it's all I can do to keep from crying.

This is one of those times, and all I can do isn't enough.

Not anywhere close.

Chapter 3
If you lie with dogs, don't expect them to believe you later. Even with kittens.

I'm not exactly sure when I stopped crying and picked up my twelfth-hand netbook and started randomly clicking around online, but that's what I'm doing when Mom comes home. We can't afford Internet, of course, but there's this café across the street with an unsecured network and if I angle the netbook just right, I can get nearly one whole bar of signal.

Being online for me is a lot like rubber-necking at an accident. It's horrible and disturbing, but oddly fascinating. I saw a bumper sticker recently that said "Success is 3% perspiration and 97% not spending all day clicking around online." Truer words have never been stuck on chrome.

Still, in my mood, I need some distraction.

Which is why I'm reading about hundreds of dead people who are apparently voting from beyond the grave when she comes in. I was hoping for haunted polling stations or Ouija Boards or something, but it's apparently just people casting votes for their dead relatives, which is far less exciting. I guess they figure that if you were a lifelong democrat, you'd want to be a deathlong one too.

"Knock, knock."

Since my "bedroom" is also the entrance way, dining room, sitting room, library, mud room, and pretty much every other room you can imagine except Mom's bedroom, the kitchen, and bathroom, there's not exactly a lot of privacy in my life. Which is normally fine, but right now I'm still mad, so I don't bother to look up, hoping she'll just go to bed and leave me alone.

So of course she doesn't.

"What are you still doing up?" she asks as she comes over and sits on the futon next to me.

I shrug and keep clicking around aimlessly. The Deadliest Shoes in the World. Aw, they're not even real, it's just a painting. World's Greatest Public Bathrooms? Yech...

"You want to talk about it?" she asks, trying to get my attention.

"What's the point?" I say, still without looking up. I click on an advertisement for "Mom Whose Secret Makes Botox Doctors Furious" but my heart's not in it, even though the "Furious at Mom" combo sounds appealing.

"Honey?" She gently takes the netbook from me, and I let her have it without resistance. "Talk to me. I know you're mad at me for not wanting to go to Yale..."

"But you do want to. I know you do!"

"Well, sure. Of course a part of me does. But I'd also like a little house with a garden filled with crickets and fireflies, somewhere out where you can still see the night sky. But just because I want it doesn't mean I can have it."

"But this is how you get that house. You go to Yale, graduate, sell a zillion books, and bang! we're there. We can make it work, Mom, somehow... but you have to at least try."

She shakes her head sadly, her eyes bright with the hint of tears.

"Honey, we can't. When I first opened that letter I thought it must have been a mistake or a joke, or even some kind of scam. But when I finally realized it was real, I tried to figure out how we could do it. I really did. But even if we ate just rice and beans for a year, we still couldn't stretch my stipend far enough. It's just math."

She's smiling at me, but her eyes are still too bright and I suddenly realize I've just made things worse. She'd been going along, making the best of a bad situation, and I was stupid enough to hold out real hope of something better, only to have it smashed by the ogre of our poverty.

"I'm sorry, Mom," I say, all choked up. "I only wanted to help."

"I know, Gwen."

She hugs me and we have a little cry together, after which I feel a bit better. All the way up from utterly miserable to merely wretched.

You know how I said I was mostly fine with not having a dad? Yeah, well this is one of those times where it really sucks. If he were here, even if we weren't rich, we'd probably be at least a *little* richer, and that's all we'd need to make this whole Yale thing fly.

"So what kind of lies did Dad tell you?" I blurt out, my mouth apparently deciding that it couldn't just let it be.

"Why would you think he told me lies?" Mom asks, but before I can formulate an answer, I see the light dawn in her eyes. "Oh. I bet Mrs. Beecham gave you an assignment. That sounds like her."

I guess I must have nodded in confirmation because she gets a wry smile on her face as if the question is somehow funny. "Lies..." she says to herself, clearly caught up in some memory.

"No, he didn't tell me any lies," she finally tells me. "Not a one."

"So what kind of truths did he say? Was he married? Chased by the mob? Had only twenty-four hours to live?"

She smiles and shakes her head. "No, nothing like that."

"Then what? Why didn't you try and find him? Why won't you even tell me his name?"

"Gwen, honey, we've gone over this all before. It was just a couple of days in Vegas; he didn't sign on to raising a kid."

"You didn't even give him a chance to make that decision."

"No, I didn't. But having you was my choice. And I couldn't tell him, Honey, I just couldn't."

"You mean you wouldn't. Oh, just forget it; I'm tired of having this conversation over and over and getting nowhere. You should have just lied to me, Mom. You should have told me he died and made up some fake name and a good story."

I turn away from her and pull up the covers like I'm going to sleep, but my dramatic exit from the conversation is kind of spoiled by my immediate slide into The Trench. God, I hate this bed.

She sighs and leans over and turns off the light by my head. She kisses the top of my head but oddly doesn't leave, just sitting there in the darkness next to me. I crack one eye and see that she's staring off into nowhere.

Then, without turning to look at me, she begins to talk in a low whisper.

"I did. I made up a great fake name and one hell of a story."

Oh my god... she's finally going to tell me something. I've been dreaming about this moment for as long as I can remember, and my heart rate goes up to about a billion beats a minute but I don't move. I feel like she's a wild animal who's just taken a single hesitant, tentative step towards me and I have to stay completely still or she'll run.

I'm barely breathing, waiting for more, but she seems to have stopped there. So, after a long moment of silence, I take a leap of faith and whisper back to her. "I've never heard them."

"Yeah, kiddo, that's because I told them to him."

Chapter 4
In which I learn just enough to be driven really crazy.

Oh, come on!

She can't stop there, she just can't...

I don't know how long I wait for her to continue after that one astonishing sentence, because time is going kind of screwy. The echo of those words *that's because I told them to him* are bouncing around inside my head like an endlessly ricocheting bullet, but the silence that followed is going on for so long now that it's beginning to acquire a sound of its own, a hissing nothingness filling my ears.

She's staring off into space and I know that if I do anything to break the fragility of this moment, this tiny window into my past will shatter. She'll lean over and kiss me on the forehead like she does most nights, then get up as if nothing had happened and head off to bed, the story once more snatched out of my reach.

But she just sits there, not leaving, not speaking, lost in some memory I'm desperate for her to share.

I think I've forgotten to breath because the room is beginning to go a little fuzzy around the edges when I finally hear the whisper of her voice issuing from the darkness.

"My first year college roommate," she says, her soft words barely audible over the sound of my blood pounding through my ears, "was this crazy girl named Cheryl.

"I loved her," Mom goes on as I slowly ease myself into a more upright position, forcing air past the iron bars wrapped around my chest.

"Probably because she was everything I wasn't. Outgoing, confident... beautiful. And when Spring Break came around, she convinced me to go with her to Vegas. She'd been going every year since she'd turned eighteen, and each time she'd invent some new name and persona and be that person the entire time she was there."

"I mean, I'd never even considered going to Vegas," Mom says, still staring out into space as if the only way she can tell this is to pretend I'm not there. "But somehow Cheryl convinced me I had to go with her, and

I had to be someone else as well. So I became Yvette, a French chef de patisserie who was opening a new bistro/bakery at the Bellagio Casino, which had itself just opened earlier that year..."

Despite the dimness of the room, I can see Mom shaking her head, almost as if she still couldn't quite believe she'd done it.

"I know... Yvette," she says, giving it her best French flair. "But I didn't care about actually fooling anyone. I just wanted to be exotic, and French was about the only accent I could do.

"I had budgeted a whole thirty dollars to lose, but was actually having a hard time doing it. Just as I'd get down to five dollars or so, I'd have a big win and shoot back up to thirty or forty again.

"At about 1am, I was finally down to four dollars and seventy-five cents. Cheryl had gone through her whopping budget of forty-five dollars, but had just found a quarter someone had dropped and was debating which machine to feed it to when an excited yell drew my eye to the roulette table. Someone had just won something and the croupier was sliding over a stack of chips.

"It was like something out of a James Bond movie and if we pooled our money we could just make the minimum $5 bet. Cheryl thought it was fate, her finding that quarter, that guy winning just then. We had to do it.

"So she dragged me over to the roulette table just as the guy was calling for last bets. There were a lot more options than I expected, odd, even, black, red, numbers and some other ones I don't remember. Cheryl was telling me to go on, that this was the one we were fated to win so I put it all on the green double-zero..."

"Go big or go home..." I say, then immediately wince. Oh crap. For a moment I'm sure I've broken the spell, but she finally takes a deep breath and then goes on.

"I knew it was a sucker bet but I figured we might as well go out with a bang. They spin the wheel one way but then send the little silver ball going the other direction so it bounces around all over the place. Cheryl was crushing my hand so hard I almost didn't realize it when the ball finally stopped.

"I still don't remember who started screaming first, me or Cheryl, but we were hugging each other and jumping around. People must have thought we'd won thousands of dollars, but all that mattered to us was that we'd won."

I can see the picture in my mind. Two college age girls jumping up and down screaming, the croupier probably looking amused, everyone else wondering what the heck was going on.

But I can't put Mom in that picture. Steady Mom. Practical and competent and calm Mom.

I realize now that I'd somehow expected to get that crazy, screaming-happy Mom when she got into Yale, but I have no clue what I'd been thinking. I mean, I've never actually seen her like that, though somehow, deep down, I'd still known it was possible.

Crap. This is one of those rare cases when being right pretty much sucks the big one. Because between this story and the Vegas one, something took that wild, unbridled excitement away from her. Maybe it's just part of growing up, of becoming an adult, but I don't think so.

I have this sinking feeling it was me.

So despite the nearly overwhelming excitement of finally hearing *the story,* I can't help but think what her life would have been like if she hadn't taken that trip, if she'd never had me.

"When we'd finally settled down," Mom says, dragging me out of my growing sinkhole of self-pity, "we collected our massive $175 payout and I turned and walked right into a guy standing behind me, literally knocking him down. I still remember it in slow motion: him rocking backwards, reaching out with one hand, his eyes widening as he crashed backwards to the floor, blood splattering everywhere..."

"What?!" The words slip out before I can stop them. But Mom turns to me, a small smile at my apparently shocked expression.

"At least that's what I saw," she says. "It wasn't until Cheryl starting laughing hysterically that I saw the glass in his hand and noticed the overpowering smell of tomatoes and vodka. His shirt was just covered with it.

"I was mortified, and Cheryl's continued laughter wasn't helping. I helped him up and started babbling apologies. I have no idea what I said other than repeatedly turning to Cheryl to tell her to shut up, but she kept laughing and pointing at his shirt, finally choking out something about 'his pocket.' It wasn't until he started laughing as well that I actually looked, and saw that somehow the celery stalk from his drink had somehow landed directly into his breast pocket.

"And that," Mom tells me, her eyes bright. "Is how I met your dad."

Now, as you've probably guessed, since Mom had just won the princely sum of $175, she insisted on buying him a new shirt, and wouldn't take no for an answer. And, because this is Vegas, where everything is possible—though most of it highly unlikely—buying a dress shirt at two in the morning is no problem at all.

After the new shirt expedition, Dad insisted they go out for drinks because he'd never actually gotten to enjoy his Bloody Mary. One thing led to another, which of course led to another, and if you don't see where this is going, you should go watch Animal Planet or the Discovery Channel and I'm sure you'll figure it out eventually.

Mom said he was like something out of a fairy tale. Not the prince mind you, more like a frog who'd been enchanted into a prince and who didn't know how to do it quite right. I can't do the story justice, but apparently at some point either before or after the Making of Me, they went to some restaurant and he was talking so enthusiastically that when he made a particularly dramatic gesture, he ended up accidentally impaling his fork on a palm tree next to him.

Thanks, Dad. Now I know where I got my amazing grace and style.

However as you may or may not remember, at this point in the story Mom isn't Mom. And I don't just mean in the existential sense that she isn't Mom because I'm not there yet. She isn't Mom because she's Yvette, the French pastry chef. And in like fashion, Dad-to-be is this writer who'd just signed a huge movie deal based on this novel he'd written. So there they were, two peas in a pod, both playing outrageous characters and loving the hell out of it.

Mom wipes away a tear as she's telling me this. But she's smiling too.

"It was so amazing being someone else," she says. "And knowing he was playing exactly the same game. And Yvette got a little crazier than I normally would have. But you know those French girls…"

I'm not entirely sure that I do, but Mom's already moved on.

"For the record," she adds, looking at me seriously, "when they say that birth control is only about 98% effective, they mean it. My green double-zero wasn't the only incredible odds I beat that night."

I nod. I can't say I'm generally a big fan of birth control failure, but in this case, I guess I have to make an exception.

"Anyway," she goes on, "when it was time to say goodbye, he gave me his number and Yvette gave him hers."

"Let me guess," I say as I sit up in bed, all pretense of trying to sleep abandoned. "He never called."

Mom shrugs. "He may have. But it was Yvette's number; I'd made it up."

"What?! But why? It sounds like you really liked him."

"I did. It was three of the most amazing days I'd ever had. But it was all a game, an escape from the real world where we were both pretending to be other people. And I didn't want the memory ruined by giving him my number and then having him not call... or worse, have him call and finding out that the real him was actually an accountant or taxidermist or something."

"So you both gave each other bogus numbers, and then you found out you were pregnant with me."

"Not right away, of course. And I'm fairly sure we didn't both give each other bogus numbers."

"So, you called him?"

She shakes her head again. "I couldn't. See, while I'd been telling him my crazy made-up story, it turns out he was telling me the absolute truth."

"What?!" I didn't see that coming, even though I suppose I should have given that she'd already told me he hadn't lied to her.

Darn. Foreshadowing and everything, and I still missed it.

"After I found out that I was having you," Mom continued. "I went to a bookstore to buy a book on pregnancy, and right in the front they had a shelf of the store's staff picks. And there at number one, was his book."

"But how did you know it was really him?"

"That was my first thought too. But his picture was on the back cover. It was him."

"But if he'd given you his real name and phone number, why didn't you call?"

"Think about it. Everything I'd told him, and I mean everything, was a total fabrication. A complete and utter lie. He was a multi-millionaire. Can you imagine me calling and trying to explain that um, Yvette didn't really exist and oh, by the way, I'm pregnant with your child?"

"Oh, Mom."

"But it's all okay. We made it through. You and me. And I don't regret a second of it."

"So what's his name? My dad's?"

You can almost hear the conversation slam to a screeching halt, its wheels throwing sparks as they lock against the momentum we've built up. In that instant, even before she actually says anything else, I know she's turned back into my old Mom, the one who won't tell me a thing.

On cue, Mom shakes her head, no. "Just let it go, Gwen. It doesn't matter. It's ancient history."

I want to scream, but I know logic's my only hope, slim as it is.

"Ancient history? Excuse me. I'm right here, right now. I'm still living my life and as far as I'm concerned, this is what we call the Present. And he's out there in it somewhere. Mom, you've got to tell me," I say in my most reasonable voice.

"Okay, okay. It's Thor. God of Thunder. Happy now?"

"What do you think?" I ask sarcastically.

But Mom's gone all tight-lipped on me again.

I still want to scream. I can't believe I've come this far only to have the window into my past slam shut, the wall go back up, the curtain come down, the microphone cut, and her lips sealed. Her silence is so final that I'm half expecting that cartoon pig to show up and stutter our "That's all, Folks."

While the universe mercifully spares me that indignity, all my begging and logic and puppy dog eyes are just useless. Mom just shakes her head through it all, and when I've finally run out of pleas, she kisses me gently on the forehead and finally gets up from my bed.

"I love you, honey," she says as she heads for the bathroom. "Sleep well."

Yeah, like that's going to happen. I grunt something noncommittal and roll over as she shuts the bathroom door.

A car drives by with its highs on, and the headlights sweep across the room like a lighthouse beacon, briefly illuminating the photo strip from Vegas I told you about. The only pictures I have of Mystery Dad with Mom, or should I say Yvette.

"I'll find you," I whisper to the picture. And though I know I must have imagined it, in the dim light, it seemed like his smile got even bigger.

And the next thing I know, it's morning.

"This is a terrible idea," Peter tells me.

I've just finished recounting the whole shebang: Yale, Vegas, fork-impaled palm trees, Mom's refusal to name names, and how I'm going to find my dad. Admittedly, at the moment it isn't so much a "how" how, like how I'm actually going to actually find him, as it is a "see how," like see how convoluted a sentence I can write about the word "how."

But it doesn't matter. I'm going to find him.

I am.

Really.

Somehow.

Yes, I know, repeating something over and over doesn't make it true. Unless, of course, you're a politician in which case it doesn't matter as long as people believe it. Mom says I'm too young to be this cynical, but last I knew there wasn't an age or height requirement for cynicism.

"You do realize he probably doesn't even remember your mom... sorry, Yvette," Peter points out as we walk along a street to nowhere. Or at least nowhere in particular. "Remember, she got you as a souvenir of the visit. All he got was a new shirt."

I know he's right, but in my world that doesn't matter. It's something I Have To Do, even though in the pit of my stomach, I have this sick feeling it is not going to end well. Like that poor salmon I'm sure you've seen in this photograph with a bear. It's heroically fought the river's current to get back to its spawning place and is leaping out of the water over one last mini-waterfall... only to throw itself right into some bear's open mouth.

Talk about your "Agony of Defeat" moments.

We stop at a street corner for the usual reasons: we have a **Do Not Cross** light and, even more importantly, Bostonians drive like they're in a giant video game, one where speeding around like a lunatic is somehow considered a "good idea."

As we wait at the traffic light for our walk guy to go green, Peter turns to me with those cool, unblinking eyes of his.

"Are you really sure you want to do this?" he asks.

Peter, being far more level headed than I am, is still trying to talk me out of the whole "finding Dad" thing.

I nod, and he frowns, considering for a moment, then shrugs. "Okay, what can I do?"

Well, I never said he was trying that hard.

"So what do we know?" Peter asks as we cross the street, still wary of the hurtling tons of steel heading our way.

"Dad had some book published probably the year before I was born, and it was made into a movie."

He frowns again "I thought your mom said he'd just signed this big movie deal... that doesn't mean it actually got made."

Crap. I hadn't thought of that. I thought we'd just be able to list all the fiction books published that year, cross-reference them with ones made into films and voilà, instant Dad, no water necessary.

"And even the ones that do," he continued, "they can take years and years to get produced."

"You're not helping. And why do you know this stuff anyway?"

"Guy below us about three apartments ago used to go on and on how he was going to be this big director, and he told me all this movie stuff. Like whom a gaffer is, and what the Best Boy does."

"So did he? Become a big director?"

Peter shrugs. "When we left, he was still driving a cab. So, do you know what a Best Boy does?"

"Yeah, he helps his poor fatherless friend track down her missing dad. And maybe gives good shoulder rubs if he's the Very Best Boy."

"Nope. First assistant to the gaffer."

I know he wants me to ask him what the heck a gaffer is, but I refuse to give him the satisfaction. I'll just look it up on Wikipedia later.

"Focus," I tell him.

"Nope, lights."

I resist the urge to roll my eyes and instead just give him a slow, steady blink along with a small, put-upon sigh. Not a full-on mouth sigh, mind you, as that would show he got to me, just a little one through my nose. The kind of sigh that says "I heard, but I'm ignoring you."

Which is precisely what I'm trying to do.

"We also know," I say, "from examining the Vegas Picture, that he was probably twenty-two to twenty-five at the time."

"Plus or minus ten years. Well, not so much the minus I guess, as that would make him twelve."

I glare at him. He's supposed to be helping, not poking holes in everything I thought I knew.

But he goes on despite it. "Don't people get you and your Mom confused sometimes? And she's, what, twenty years older than you?"

"Nineteen."

He's right, much as I hate to admit it. These days Mom and I are beginning to look so similar that I've actually had one or two adults (who obviously don't know her all that well, or who are severely myopic) come up to me and start talking, thinking I'm her. I generally correct them unless they want to talk to her about me, in which case I see no need to bother them with trivialities like my actual identity.

But I do hate it when other people are right. Mostly because it often means I'm not, which I hate even more. But I'm a big girl, I'll admit it when I'm wrong. Just not necessarily to them.

Sadly, however, Peter does have a real point. I could be way off on my age guess for Dad, particularly trying to judge it from the small photo strip from Vegas. If people can think a sixteen year old is thirty-five, then Dad could have been anywhere from his late teens to his mid-thirties too.

Now, admittedly, you wouldn't confuse most teenagers with someone in their thirties, but I am pretty well developed for a girl my age—which I can tell you right now is a heck of a mixed blessing—and Mom just looks great. None of this, however, brings me one step closer to finding Dad, and this whole discussion with Peter is just getting me down.

We cross another street of hurtling death when I suddenly notice we're in front of a bookstore. Yes, they still exist, hard as that is to believe. And this isn't just any bookstore, this is the bookstore that Mom works at part-time. I guess my feet had more of a plan than I did.

I always call it the Pretentious Page because it's a small discount bookstore with delusions of grandeur. Its real name is the Pampered Page, which always conjures up images of rare texts, lovingly laid out on crushed velvet pillows; instead, you get used text-books in discount bins.

But standing here gives me an idea.

You know how in TV shows, the cops, or some crooks, or some cops who are crooks, are tearing apart someone's place looking for something, and the owner, while indignantly proclaiming their innocence, always has that one crucial moment when their gaze flicks to the object's hiding place and gives it away?

Well, Mom, your bookstore is about to get "searched."

Chapter 5
A life without dwarves is not a tall order.

"Mom, I have a question."

"So do I. Why aren't you two in school?"

"Mom, it's Saturday," I say in my most pained teenage voice... you know, the one that says "how did you even manage to survive to reproduce when you're so clueless?"

Mom fires back with the steady gaze and half-cocked head that says "Young lady, don't be a Smart-Alec."

I reply with the grin that says... well, I don't want to give it all away. We've just spent so much time together, just the two of us, that we can have whole conversations of just glances and sighs, grins and snorts and shrugs, all with deep layers of meaning if you know how to read them.

"You remember weekends, right?" I say, still grinning exactly like a Smart-Alec. "Those two days everyone gets off from work." Dramatic Pause. "Well, almost everyone."

In my defense, my snarkiness is not just to be mean; I'm trying to throw her off her game so that when the big moment comes, she won't have the self-control to avoid that guilty glance.

In her defense, she decides to ignore me.

"Peter," she says, looking past me. "You were right about the coyote pee, ever since I started putting a cup of it in the laundry, the rats have stopped chewing on Gwen's clothes completely."

EWWWW! No, she wouldn't have... would she?

"No problem, Ms. P. Glad I could help," he says, all innocent and helpful.

Traitor. I shoot a glare at Peter but it bounces off him, or would if glares could bounce. I know they're messing with me but I can still feel my entire body turning into one big goose bump. I'm sure I can smell it on me now and it's all I can do to keep from ripping off my clothes and running away screaming.

I am not covered in coyote pee. I am not.

I must be going a little white around the eyes because finally Mom takes pity on me.

"Gwen, honey, I wouldn't do that to you. Really."

I shrug, though I can still feel it on my skin. "I know," I say as if I hadn't just had a major attack of the creeps. Or at least, I hope it comes off that way.

"Especially," she adds, "because Peter told me ferret pee works just as well at about half the price."

Everyone's a comedian.

The bookstore has a little coffee counter in it with the usual Costco pastries and muffins, and a real Italian espresso machine. It's all brass and copper with enough tubing and valves that I could easily imagine it powering a steam locomotive. That, or it getting stuck with all its gauges pegged firmly in the red, clouds of scalding steam forcing billowing forth, then ultimately exploding like some steam-powered bomb.

Still, steamy death notwithstanding, it's a pretty impressive device. What's far less impressive, however, is that the kid who usually mans the counter always calls what it makes eXpresso.

Yeah, I know. I don't even drink coffee, but it still makes me want to strangle him. The only reason I don't is that he makes a pretty mean frothed hot chocolate which, with Mom's employee discount, I can actually sometimes afford. Also, I'm not really ready for the whole life-on-the-run thing that usually follows strangling someone, no matter how deserving.

He's not here today, however, which means Mom has to pick up the slack, and if she's behind the coffee counter, she's facing the entire store, perfect for that guilty, revealing glance.

"Can we get some hot chocolates?" I ask innocently. Maybe too innocently as Mom looks at me a bit skeptically. "Sorry. Please?" I add hastily as if that were the cause of her expression.

She looks around the store, which is pretty empty right now, and apparently decides there are no potentially paying customers who particularly needs her help at the moment.

"Sure," she says and heads over behind the counter.

I hop up on a stool and shoo Peter over to the side so he can see exactly where she's looking when she gives that inevitable Big Glance.

"Thanks, Ms. P.," he says, politer than me, as always.

"Yeah, thanks, Mom."

She nods and gets out the gallon jug of milk from the little fridge below the counter and pours a generous amount into the silver milk-steaming carafe, then adds a long, double-squeeze of Midnight Moo, Trader Joe's brand of chocolate syrup.

Now that's a good name, Midnight Moo. Alliterative, yet still relevant and evocative of the product's purpose. It's a name that conjures up images of little feet padding softly downstairs in search of that irresistible hit of choco-milk, just as the grandfather clock strikes midnight in the background. Or cows who slip silently from their barns to conduct strange, mystical rituals under the light of a full harvest moon.

Midnight Moo.

Midnight. Moo.

Midnight.

Moo.

Plus, it's just good, tasty stuff.

The high pitched squeal of the frother jolts me back to the bookstore. Mom has already finished assembling the two cups and is using the espresso machine's frother to turn them into hot foamy chocolate.

"So, you said you had a question," Mom says then lets the frother rip again with another squeal of hot, high pressured steam.

When she shuts it off and turns to us with the two cups, I know my moment's here. "Well, Mom, I've been thinking about what you told me last night and I wanted to know the name of Dad's book."

Nothing. She just blinks at me, nonplussed.

"Could you at least tell me what section it's in?"

Her eyes are boring into me, no furtive movement at all. She doesn't look all that happy about my continued obsession, but I've come this far and I'm not ready to concede just yet.

"Young adult? General Fiction?" Crap. She might as well be the Mona Lisa for all the eye movement I'm getting. "Science Fiction? Humor?"

She coolly looks from me to Peter, still without any nervous glances to the bookstore beyond. "I assume you know what she's talking about, right?"

"I think so."

"Hey," I protest. "I'm right here..."

Mom goes on talking to Peter, ignoring me. "You've got a pretty good head on your shoulders, Peter. Will you please tell her to drop this, as she doesn't seem willing to listen to me."

"I already tried."

I'm tempted to tell her how hard he tried, but she turns and looks at me with such gentle sadness that the words dry up.

"Gwen, honey. If you keep picking at a wound it will never heal."

For a moment I feel really bad about putting her through all this, but then I remember how much she's given up for me, and I tell myself that I'm doing this for her as much as I am for me. And I think I'm not lying to myself about it... at least not too much.

Sure, intellectually I know that even if I can find him, he may not remember Mom, and he'll probably think I'm just after his money. Which, to be fair, is not entirely untrue if it'll make the difference between Mom going to Yale or not. But all my life I've been staring at his picture, seeing how happy they were in Vegas, and maybe, just maybe, Mom was his "one that got away" and he'll swoop back into our lives like Prince Charming.

Minus the dwarves and wicked step mother, of course.

We leave Mom in peace and take our hot chocolates elsewhere. Peter's still pretty lukewarm on this whole "finding Dad" endeavor, and seems intent on shooting down all of my ideas like he's in some cheap carnival shooting gallery, trying to win the Big Prize. Pop. Pop. Pop.

Congratulations, you've won the giant, inflatable albatross.

We go to the BU library and do some quick research on fiction books published about eighteen years ago. Only about 70,000 per year in the US, and nearly the same in England. Per year. And oddly enough there's no simple list of books written by men in their twenties... or nineteens... or early thirties or any other particular age group for that matter. And you know how many movies are based on books? Or, I should say, you know how few of them aren't?

So after about three hours of online searches and attempts at cross-referencing, I'm exactly back where I started, which is to say nowhere.

All I've really learned today is that if I need someone who can hide a body and not give it away, Mom's the one to call.

At about the two hour point, Peter decides to call it quits and goes home to bake something which I'm sure will look and smell very much like bread, but which will have a crust so thick it could probably save your life in a shoot-out. And that will still be a lot more productive than what I'm doing.

I woke up this morning with a mission, a goal, and the only thing I've been able to accomplish is to show how utterly impossible it is. No, I also managed to make Mom sad.

I just don't know what to do next. All I have is that strip of Vegas photos and what I really need is some semi-magical facial recognition software to feed it to, and have it spit out his identity.

I idly type in online facial recognition search and nearly fall off my chair. I thought I was kidding, but it's even built into Google, which lets you upload an image then will find every page that uses it.

The whole thing is just creepy, if you ask me, but if it can help me find Dad, then send in the creeps.

Now all I need to do is figure out some way of uploading the photo.

I hurry back home because I want to get there before Mom does, so I don't have to explain why I'm taking the strip of Vegas pictures out of the frame that it's lived in for the last sixteen or so years. I know she wouldn't like my real reason, and I always try to keep my lying to a bare minimum as it can really turn around and bite you if you aren't careful—as evidenced perfectly by the story of Mom and Dad in case you haven't been paying attention.

Also, I'm really bad at it.

As I come into the lobby I notice an envelope in the outgoing mail basket, and something about it draws my attention. As I get closer, I realize it's addressed to the Yale Fellowship Department and it's in Mom's handwriting. Crap.

I know it can be saying only one thing. So, I quickly look around to make sure no one's watching, then pluck it out of the basket and stuff it into my backpack. No way am I letting her mail this.

A shiver overtakes me as I realize how close I'd come to missing the letter, and how close she'd come to throwing away her dream. If they get a letter from her officially declining the scholarship they'll move onto the next candidate and that'll be it, no going back.

I hurry into the apartment and toss my backpack onto my futon/sofa-bed from hell, and then plop down next to it. Young Mom and Mystery Dad stare out at me from the framed Vegas photo strip, and I stare back at them.

I'm still not exactly sure how I'll upload his picture to the image search engines, but I've turned putting-difficult-problems-off-into-the-future into a true art form. Mom has threatened to tattoo "we'll cross that bridge when we come to it" on my forehead, but she's missing the point entirely. I'm all for avoiding the bridges completely, and I figure if I ever do come to one, I'll just swim the darn river.

In any case, my problem at the moment is how to liberate Dad from his glass prison without the warden—aka Mom—noticing.

As I pick up the framed photo strip, I find myself smiling at the thought that here I was, about to free my mom's very own Prince Charming from his little glass coffin and bring him back to life, or at least back into our lives, which from my point of view, amounts to pretty much the same thing.

Still, there's something odd about this particular frame and I stare at it for a long moment before I realize what it is. There's no way to open it.

The frame is one solid piece, with neat little nails in all four corners, sealing the glass and back alike in the frame's little wooden embrace. I look the corners over again and see that at the bottom, the nails are a slightly different color, brass instead of silver, and they aren't quite as evenly placed as the ones on the top. Someone, probably Mom, has nailed this shut... either in some existential idea of sealing the past away, or because there's something on the other side of the photo that she doesn't want me to see.

Now, I absolutely have to get it out, but I'm baffled how I can do it without destroying the frame, which would kind of be a dead give-away to Mom that I was still digging.

Chapter 6
In case of emergency, break glass.

Peter comes to the door in a long apron well sprinkled with flour.

The rich scent of baking bread wafts from the kitchen, taunting my nostrils with the false promise of light, yeasty goodness... a promise that I know better than to believe, though my mouth instantly starts salivating.

Way to go, mouth; haven't you learned anything?

Peter silently steps aside from the door, and I come into his apartment, carrying the mysteriously sealed frame. Peter glances down at it and frowns slightly. He slowly looks back up to meet my eyes, raising just one eyebrow as he does so. Show-off.

"I take it you're still on the trail of the rare and reclusive DNA source that is your father."

"He's more than just DNA," I protest.

"If you say so," he says, then he turns and we walk into his kitchen.

"What I don't get," he says, slapping a big wad of dough on the wooden board in front of him, "is why you think it will be a good idea to essentially walk up to a complete stranger and say 'I belong in your life because we have twenty-three chromosomes in common'."

He folds the dough over and presses down on it, forcing out an air bubble which escapes with an audible sigh. I know exactly how it feels.

"He's my dad," I say. "He's part of me... my family; that's got to count for something."

"Why? What if he didn't exist? What if your Mom had you cloned and you're 100% all her. Or at least 95% her and 5% sheep if they forgot to clean out the test-tube well enough."

"And you think that's a particularly likely scenario?"

He shrugs, apparently unwilling to commit either way. "But the real question is: would that make you any less the you who you currently think you are?"

"No... though I don't think I'd ever think about science class the same way again."

"Or what if you do have a dad but you are some freak of nature and somehow got twenty-six chromosomes from your mom and only twenty from your dad? Is he any less your dad?"

"Um... I don't think so."

"How about if he doesn't remember your mom and he's one of a set of identical triplet circus acrobats, so there's no way you could tell which one was your dad, even with genetic testing?"

"Circus acrobats?"

"Okay, fine. Lion tamers. It really doesn't matter."

"Do they have to work in a circus?"

"What, you'd prefer a set of identical triplet dentists?"

"If it's up to me, I'll just stick with a singular novelist dad."

"But it's not up to you," he says, pounding the dough like he was a boxer preparing for the Big Fight. "That's my point. And don't avoid the question. What do you do with your three dads, any of whom could have done the deed? Do you try and have the same father-daughter relationship with all of them? Do you arbitrarily pick one and say you, you're the one?

"Or what if one of them comes forward as your dad and you settle down happily into a good father-daughter relationship. Then, ten years later you both discover that he was confusing your mom with some other girl in Vegas and he's the wrong triplet? Does he suddenly unbecome Dad, and you move on to the triplet with the next weakest alibi for where they were on the fateful weekend you were conceived?"

I don't have a good answer and frankly, I hate the realities he's trying to get me to acknowledge. Intellectually, I get what he's saying, and I can't argue it, which really pisses me off. Sure, Mom could tell me that any guy out there who is about the right age is Dad, but somehow it does matter if it's really him, in the same way it matters if you call my cat Buddha "she." I mean, it's not like he cares, but it somehow matters to me.

"Did my mom put you up to this?"

"No."

I watch him doubtfully. To the best of my knowledge, Peter has never lied to me, though he doesn't always correct my erroneous assumptions.

"You know," I tell him, wincing in sympathy as his hands continue to push and squeeze with all the tenderness of a threshing machine, "I don't think that dough's ever going to talk, no matter what you do to it."

He looks up at me coolly, never once stopping the brutal kneading.

"You still haven't said which triplet you're moving in with."

"Your powers of observation never fail to astound me."

He sighs. "You're going to keep looking for him, aren't you?"

"I have to."

He doesn't say anything for a long moment, his hands continuing to torment the bread dough. Or brick dough, depending on your acceptance of reality.

"So, hand it over," Peter tells me as he wipes his floury hands on his apron.

"Hand what exactly?" I ask warily.

"The pictures. That's why you came over, wasn't it?"

He and Mom should do a mentalist act sometime, as both of them can be so incredibly perceptive that it just gives me the creeps. I consider denying it out of a matter of principle, but it is what I came over for, and if I claim that it isn't, I can't exactly ask for his help. Not that I'm sure he'll give it to me anyway, after that whole triplet rant of his, but at least there's still a chance.

So I hand him the picture frame. He looks it over, rubbing his finger along the nails in the bottom of the frame and peering at it closely. I watch him as he silently examines it from a number of angles, and gently tugs on the bottom part of the frame.

As you may have noticed, Peter is usually in one of two modes: (a) babbling his head off about something like, say, circus acrobats, or (b) doing the tall, dark and silent routine. When he gets into that second mode, it can be hours between verbal communication, and I can't wait that long.

"I was hoping you might have some needle-nose pliers or something," I say to break the silence. "So we can pull out those bottom nails."

"Won't help," he says, still examining it.

"Why not?"

"Glue."

"Uh, can I buy a verb?"

"Glued. Past tense. As in, 'the frame is.'"

"Thank you, Yoda," I reply sarcastically.

He shrugs. "And why do you want the pictures out?"

Since I know he's with my mom on this being a Bad Idea, I consider lying, but as I start to construct some elaborate pseudo-truth, he looks at me thoughtfully.

"You probably want to run this through some facial recognition software, don't you?"

Why do I even bother?

"Yes," I say, exasperated that I can't get anything by anyone. So much for my career as a con artist... or used car salesman, for that matter.

"How were you going to upload it?"

I give him my "we'll avoid coming to that bridge for as long as humanly possible" look.

"You don't have a clue, do you?"

I glare at him.

"You know," he says, "you could use the camera on your netbook, and then you wouldn't even have to take it out."

I stare at him, nonplussed. That's so brilliantly obvious that I feel like I've just been bashed upside the head with one of his brick-like bread creations.

Peter offers me back the picture frame, but as I take it, Fate decides to step in. Or, if not Fate, at least Gravity.

Chapter 7
In which something actually goes right.
And that can't be good.

The picture frame crashes into the floor like a flat wooden box with a sheet of glass in it. Which, is not all that surprising, considering that's exactly what it is. Equally unsurprising is that the glass shatters as glass has done since time immemorial. Into tiny, razor-sharp pieces.

Lots of them.

"Oops" is another thing Mom's threatened to tattoo on my forehead, but as she doesn't know any tattoo artists, I think I'm fairly safe. I do, however, sleep with all the Sharpies in the house under my pillow, but that's a whole other story.

"Or you could do that," Peter says dryly.

"I'll get the broom," he says, heading for the clean-up supplies as I bend down to see what I can salvage.

I gingerly pick up the frame, glass shards raining down from it. I give it a gentle shake to release any other glass fragments that might be still clinging to their former home. As I do so, a long strip of glossy paper drifts free as well.

Now I'm fairly sure the celestial chorus going "Aaaah" doesn't actually happen, nor does the paper strip float down in slow motion, spiraling slowly to the floor. Still, who am I to argue with my brain, which, by the way, grinds to a complete halt as soon as I see the back of the photo. For there, in faded but legible felt-tip pen, it says:

> *I've never had pastries half so sweet as you...*
>
> -H

And underneath that is a phone number with a 617 area code.

617! That's greater Bostburbia's area code... He's local, or at least he was sixteen some odd years ago.

OhMyGodOhMyGodOhMyGodOhMyGodOhMyGod.

Peter returns and looks down at the photo strip lying amid the pile of viciously sharp glass. He tilts his head to one side, so he can read the note right side up, and we stare at the mysterious H.

H.

Ahh, he has an initial. And it's H.

Not the one I would have necessarily chosen, but I'll take it nevertheless. Mystery Dad is slowly, quietly, becoming less of a mystery.

I feel like I'm assembling him like a jigsaw puzzle, piece by piece. First a picture, then a name—or at least the start of one—and a phone number. I'll find his book, and then he's sure to have written others; maybe Mom's a character in one of the later ones, a literary shout-out into the world to reunite with his long-lost love.

Back in my apartment, I do a quick online search for book titles with Yvette in them, and aside from a billion hits on Guy de Maupassant, the only one which looks even possible is what looks like a really trashy romance novel whose cover needs a PG-13 rating, and whose description starts with *After being kidnapped by a vampire hunter, vampire bodyguard Yvette's first instinct is to kill the bastard.*

All I can say is that I hope to God this isn't Dad writing under a pseudonym. After I finish shuddering over that horrible thought, I get out our phone and stare at it.

For a long time.

Now, of course that wasn't my plan. I mean, I wasn't trying to catch it in the act of morphing into some mechanical alien toy franchise or waiting for it to ring or something. I was planning on picking up the handset and making THE CALL, but my body isn't cooperating.

You know how you sometimes wake up in the morning and you're lying there, staring at the ceiling, telling yourself you should get up. Really, you should. Now. Go on, body, you can do it. Up, up... go on...

It's like there's a disconnect between the Mental You who's feeling guilty or pressured, or—god forbid—responsible, and the Physical You who is just quietly going ahead and proving the first law of Newtonian physics: a body at rest tends to say at rest, unless the body is compelled to change its state.

Which means, of course, that the next time your mom yells at you for not getting out of bed, you should reply: "Don't blame me, it's physics."

Anyway, that's the state I'm in, staring at the phone, willing my arm to pick it up but without even a twitch. Go arm, you can do it... hello, there? Arm?

The truth of the matter is that my body's no dummy, notwithstanding its salivary glands and Peter's enticingly dreadful bread. And whether I'm willing to admit it or not, my arm knows that the phone number I want it to dial is over sixteen years old, and will almost certainly be disconnected or reassigned to someone else who, with my luck, will be a completely different writer named H., and I'll have to go through Peter's circus acrobat scenario of bonding and then later ungluing.

Peter, of course, will be there for me through all of it, and he'll studiously avoid showing any smugness which will only make it all the more galling.

Sigh.

Enough of this. Mom always says, "when the going gets tough, the tough get going." So, for once, I'll follow her advice. Body, you win this round, let's get going... back to the library.

"I'd like to see a phone book, please."

"Here you go."

"Um, thanks, but I need one from about sixteen-and-a-half years ago."

"Time travel project in school?"

"Something like that."

"I'm afraid we only have it back to... hmm, let me check on that for you... okay, here it is. The oldest phone books we have date back to the one I just gave you."

"That's not back at all. That's the current phone book."

"True."

"But this is a library! You collect books, don't you? And phone books actually have the word book in it. How many of your other books can say that?"

"Well, none, I'm sure. But expired phone books are just not something we get a lot of call for... as it were. Maybe you should talk to the phone company and see if they have any."

So I did. And they did, but then I remembered how phone books worked, so I didn't.

I mean, even if I could find the right one, the only way to find Father H.'s phone number would be to read the entire thing. And as much as I love books, I know how this one ends: with Zygmunt Zywicki's phone number and my eyes melting because I've just scanned over three million phone numbers and missed the single one I was looking for.

Yeah, I know. Just shoot me now.

I get home and find myself right back where I started: staring at the phone and willing my arm to pick up the handset and dial. This time, however, I refuse to give up and manage to use my incredible powers of mind-over-matter to finally get my arm to comply.

I dial slowly and carefully, drawing the process out as if the phone were a bomb and entering one wrong number would make it explode and take out half the building. By the time I press the last number and hold the phone up to my ear, I'm clenching it so tightly that I'm sure there will be finger shaped indentations in the handset's plastic when I put it down.

There is a long series of clicks and pops as if it's routing the call through Eastern Mongolia via Pittsburgh. Finally, the phone starts to ring. I almost hang up immediately, but I power through the panicked urge and listen as the phone continues to ring and ring and ring and ring for what must be the greater part of a century.

With each unpicked-up ring my heart beats faster and faster and climbs higher up my throat. At this rate it will probably climb out all together and explode high over my head, and then the coroner will have to come and try to figure out why a sixteen year old girl is covered with exploded heart bits. And somehow, I don't think "no one picked up the phone" will be high on their list of explanations.

As I continue to await my doom, I try to lower my expectations.

I tell myself it's probably a pay phone on a street corner somewhere. Or it's ringing in the house of some ninety year-old great grandmother who's frantically getting out of the shower to answer it because she's of an age that still doesn't believe in answering machines or voicemail.

I can almost see her as she struggles to put on a robe while soaking wet, the phone ringing and ringing. And there's just no way this is going to end well. Even if she does answer the phone, it's not like it's going to do either of us any good. And she's probably far more likely to slip in her hurry to answer my call, and crash to her death on the wet tile. And it will all be my fault.

I'm so deep in my macabre fantasy that I almost don't hear the voice on the other end.

"Hello? Hello? Is there anybody there?"

Chapter 8
In which I discover a significant gap in my vocabulary.

My mouth goes so dry, I could put that special dissolving paper that spies use in there and nothing would happen. For the guy on the other end of the phone line could actually be a viable contender for the role of Dad. From his voice, I'd guess he's somewhere in his mid-thirties, and though he's slightly out of breath from running for the phone, he still has a pleasant tone with a hint of a smile. Good teeth, that twinkle in his eye, I know so well...

Stop it brain! It's probably not him. It can't be.

"Hello." I force out.

"Hi," he says, and I can hear the unspoken question in the single word. In my mind's eye, I can see him in a bookshelf-lined room, light and airy, with the comforting warm smell of comfy leather chairs. He's sitting in one such chair, looking off into space, his forehead wrinkled as he tries to place my voice.

"I'm sorry, can I ask who's calling?" he finally says.

"Of course," I reply out of force of habit, before I can stop myself. But the silence at the other end of the line isn't the good silence of a baffled telemarketer, but is rather a thick silence with the man who might be my Dad, and I hurry to fill it.

"I know this is going to sound completely odd," I say, trying to keep the nervous excitement from my voice. "But does your name begin with H, and did you ever have a fling with a girl named Yvette in Vegas?"

"Yes..." he starts to reply, and the blood rushes to my head so fast that all I can hear is it pumping past my eardrums like a dam broke. It's him. I found him! I really found him!

OhMyGodOhMyGodOhMyGodOhMyGodOhMyGod.

"...and my middle name is Harry, is that good enough?"

His words slowly penetrate my excitement, and as I struggle to make sense of them, I can feel it all unraveling. A moment ago I was sky high, and now it's like someone's pouring ice-water down my back.

"Sorry, what did you say?" I ask, finally unfreezing my tongue.

"I wanted to know if my middle name was good enough. It begins with an H."

"What do you mean good enough?" I ask, already knowing I'm not going to like the answer.

"For Yvette. I mean, I've never dated anyone who cared what letter my name started with, so I don't know the rules. Did she already go through A thru G and now she's on to H? Is that it?"

"Not exactly," I say, trying to figure out exactly when this conversation fell down the rabbit hole and ended up in in Wonderland.

"I'm confused," I continue, stating the obvious. "Did you or didn't you sign a photo with the letter H to a pastry chef named Yvette?"

"Pastry chef, huh? This is sounding better and better. But no, I've never really used Harry or H or anything like that. But I'm flexible, I can sign my name any way she likes."

"Okay…" I say, though it's really about as far from okay as I can imagine. Every word out of his mouth screams that this is NOT Dad, but I can't let go of the fantasy just yet. "Can we back up for a moment.?"

"Sure. But could you first tell me if this fling has to be in Vegas, or would Yvette be willing to meet in Reno instead?"

I suddenly know how all those telemarketers feel when I completely throw them off their memorized little scripts. "Hold on." I protest. "Why did you say 'yes' when I asked you if you'd had a fling with a woman named Yvette in Vegas?"

"No, I said 'yes, that sounds completely odd, but interesting.' I thought you were asking if I wanted to have a fling with some chick named Yvette in Vegas, provided my name began with H."

"Is someone likely to call you up asking you that?"

"I hope so."

Huh. Either he's clinically delusional, or I'm still missing something. Or possibly both, of course.

"Where did you think I'm calling from?" I ask, dreading the answer.

"IWannaFling.com. You know, the website."

Ew…!

"So let me get this straight," he went on. "You're trying to find someone who has already had a fling with this Yvette. And his name begins with H."

"Pretty much. Could you tell me how long you've had this number?" Even as I ask, I'm not sure why I'm bothering, as I have no clue what good any answer he could give me would do.

"Um, sure. I guess 25 or 26 years."

Wait a minute, that can't be right. That's definitely way before Mom's Vegas trip.

"Are you sure?" I demand, and even to my ears, I sound a bit shrill.

"Yeah, I got it when I moved here for college. So who's this Yvette anyway? Oh, it's you, isn't it?"

I panic and hang up, slamming the handset back into the cradle. Something is wrong, something is very wrong, like I walked through a door and ended up in a parallel universe where everything's almost the same, but not quite. Like we all drive on the other side of the road, or Justin Bieber was never discovered, or, if he was discovered, it wasn't really him but some girl named Larry. Or maybe what we call yellow is blue, and blue is red, and red is called twinkie.

Pull it together, I tell myself.

I stare at the phone number on the back of the photo strip. The digits are really clear, written in a firm, eminently legible handwriting; none of the them are even marginally ambiguous.

Could I have misdialed?

Just then the phone rings, and my super cat-like reflexes kick in with a massive burst of adrenaline that causes all my limbs to try and simultaneously run off in different directions—even my arms, which shouldn't be trying to run in any case—the net result of which is a complete spaz-out that ends as I smash the back of my hand against the table.

Why nature decided that wildly flailing all of your limbs is some kind of great survival strategy is beyond me. Unless, of course, the goal of the strategy is to make the predator that's attacking you burst out laughing at how ridiculous you look, thus allowing you time to sneak away. Hey, I suppose whatever works.

I look at the caller ID and nearly lose it. Oh crap, it's the number I'd just called. I quickly hang up again, but not before I double-check the caller ID against the number written on the back of the Vegas photo strip. Double-crap with a cherry on top. It's the right number, the one written (I assume) in my father's own hand. But it's not right. It's not right at all.

After all this time, could Mom be wrong? Could his stories and phone number have been just as fictitious as hers?

RING!

After I peel myself off the ceiling I pick up the phone and answer it.

"Stop calling," I hiss at the guy, and hang up again.

My heart's pumping like I just ran a marathon... [1]

Breathe, I tell myself. Just breathe.

I manage to calm myself down somewhat by focusing on the blindingly obvious—that breathing is a good thing— and I am just starting to think that I will actually survive this experience without my heart exploding (which I've decided would be a Bad Thing, regardless as to whether it happens high above my head or in my chest), when the phone rings again.

Aaaah! I snatch it off its cradle before it can even finish its first full ring.

"What do you want from me?" I demand.

"Well, a pleasant hello might be a good start," Mom replies on the phone.

I really need to learn some new swear words because Oh, Crap and Ah, Drat just don't have the punch to capture these sudden, gut-wrenching feelings of impending disaster that I seem to be experiencing with greater and greater frequency.

"Um, hello," I reply lamely.

---

[1] Hopefully, however, without the sudden death at the end. See in case you don't know, people run marathons, because some 2,500 years ago, after a big battle at Marathon, a Greek soldier ran about 26 miles to Athens to spread the good news of the Greek victory. When he finally arrived, he cried something like "we won!" then keeled over dead, thus becoming one of the first people to literally *kill the messenger*.

Now, you'd think the moral of the story was fairly obvious. But no. Apparently, the average person's reaction to hearing this heart-warming (and heart-exploding) story of exhaustion and death was: *oh, that sounds like a good idea; let's run 26 miles too!*

"Do I want to know what that was about?"

"Not really."

"Just to be clear, the question was, do *I* want to know what that was about, not do *you* want me to know about it."

"Yeah, Mom, I got it." Surprisingly, her questioning is actually calming me down. The utter Mom-ness of it is like a comforting hug, assuring me that everything's going to be okay, even if it isn't right now. And implicit in her question is a kind of trust in me that I'm not altogether sure I deserve, but which buoys me up, just the same.

"It's nothing," I tell her. "I just dialed a wrong number, and the guy won't stop calling me back."

"Lovely." She puts such a feeling of exasperated frustration into those two syllables that I can see her expression even through the phone.

"I got it." I tell her. "If he calls again, I'll tell him I'll give his number to the cops and say he's making harassing phone calls, smells bad, has a stupid haircut and looks funny."

"Isn't having a stupid haircut part of looking funny?"

I roll my eyes. While this is not normally a useful thing to do in a phone conversation, Mom knows me so well, I know she saw them.

"Drop off the last three," she says. "But otherwise, perfect."

"Killjoy. So, mother of mine, what can I do for you?"

"Oh, that list is so long, I think I should give it to you in writing."

I can practically hear the rim shot: ba-da-bum, (cymbal crash).

"Very funny," I tell her. "So, is there a purpose to this call, or are you just practicing your stand-up routine?"

"There's a purpose. I just got an extra shift tonight filling in for Charlene at Katie's Kountry Kitch'n, so you're on your own for dinner."

"Oh, lucky me."

"You can always come down and have dinner here on my employee discount."

I'm briefly tempted, especially as I hear in her voice that she'd like me to, but it's nearly a half-hour T-ride either way and I still have to figure out what I'm going to say to her about Dad's broken glass, not to mention making sure that Fling-boy really isn't going to call again. Especially when Mom's here.

So I decline, and after the traditional reminders not to stay up too late, to brush my teeth, eat my veggies, wash behind my ears, avoid burning down the apartment, don't have wild parties, don't run with scissors, look both way before you cross, and always flush, I'm finally free.

And the phone rings again.

"What did you forget?" I ask, "Never eat yellow snow?"

"I'd never forget that," Not Dad replies on the other end. "So, I've been thinking. You can't be Yvette."

"Brilliant deduction, Sherlock. How about you deduce what's going to happen if you don't stop calling me? I'll give you a hint. It involves cops and me calling them."

"My guess is that you don't want to do that, because then your mom would know you called this number. And SHE is Yvette."

I really need some new swear words.

Chapter 9
In which I receive help from a surprising source.

"My name's Dave, by the way," Not Dad says. "David Harry Fitzgerald, in case you need my full name for the police complaint. Do you need me to spell Fitzgerald?"

"I need you to stop bothering me."

"No, you need me to help you."

"Thanks, but I'm doing fine. Or I was, until you started calling back."

"See, I got to thinking," he said, ignoring me. "If you were Yvette, as I first thought, then you'd already know what name "H" stood for. Someone might sign a card or a note with just a first initial, but they'd never introduce themselves that way. Unless, of course, they just used that first letter as a name like "L" in which case there still wouldn't be a question as to what it stood for as it's just their name."

"This is all very fascinating..." I say, trying to interrupt him, but he just interrupts my interruption.

"I think so too," he replies enthusiastically, and I can tell he's just getting warmed up.

"So that gives me three pieces of information," he continues. "The first is that you are not Yvette, the second is that you've only read a note from the mysterious H, and the third is that this note probably had this phone number on it, as you clearly expected, or at least hoped, H would answer when you called."

Who is this guy? And why can't I pull anything over anyone? It's like I have one of those comic-strip thought balloons floating over my head, and everyone can read what I'm thinking as I think it. And apparently it works over the phone too, as this guy's going through my life story as if he had it on cue cards.

My thoughts immediately shift into high gear, but as they consist solely of "Oh, crap, oh, crap, oh crap," all that produces is a thick cloud of black smoke that pours out of my ears as my brain cells all ignite. Or, at least it feels that way.

Since I have absolutely no clue what I can say to derail his chain of dead-on conjecture, I don't respond, hoping my silence will pass for disinterest. Unfortunately he doesn't seem to care either way, continuing on unstoppably like some movie detective building up his chain of deduction before spinning around with an outstretched finger and dramatically revealing the killer. And while we're currently missing a body, between my burning brain and exploding heart, I'm fairly sure I'll be able to accommodate him soon enough.

"Now despite your protests to the contrary," he continues confidently. "We both know that you called to find the man who had a fling with Yvette. And, since you became upset when I told you I've had this number since before you were born, I have to assume Yvette's little tête-à-tête with H happened sometime after that time."

"Tête-à-tête? Really?" I put all the teenage, eye-rolling disdain I can muster into the really, hoping I can slow his steamroller of a monologue.

"It's French," he offers cheerfully. "Or would you prefer the Japanese pillowing? Or, my absolutely favorite euphemism: making feet for children's shoes?"

"What? Oh."

Under different circumstances I might even like this guy, but right now he is messing with my life big-time, and I prefer to be the one doing the messing, thank you very much. Being the 'messee' doesn't have the same charm at all.

"Or I could go Anglo-Saxon, if you really insist."

This is just spiraling out of control. I wrack my brain, trying to come up with any way I can get this guy to just go away. But I've got nada.

"Anyway," he continues, "given that (a) you're trying to contact H; (b) you reacted, shall I say, rather strongly when I told you how long I've had this number; and (c) nobody puts a date on love notes, I'm forced to conclude that you know the date of their... union... because you yourself are the product of it.

"This, of course, makes H your father. Additionally, since I'm sure you've been interested in your dad for your entire life, but you've only called just now, I expect you recently found the love note, and with it my phone number."

"Nope, it was Colonel Mustard in the Kitchen with a Candlestick. But thanks for playing."

Neither of us is fooled by my scintillating wit. He's ripped the curtain away, and I know it, and he knows that I know it, and he knows that I know that he knows it. None of which makes it any more likely that I'll admit it.

"Now that you've gotten that delightful little fantasy off your chest," I tell him, trying to bluster my way through this, despite the fact that it's clearly hopeless. Still, persistent and repetitive denial of reality, despite any amount of evidence to the contrary, seems to be the cornerstone of our political system, and who am I to argue with the wisdom of the founding fathers?

"Please put me on your 'no call' list," I go on, trying to be as unstoppable as he's been. "And forget you ever called me."

"Actually, you called me."

"Forget that too."

"I could... but then neither of us will ever find out who H was..."

"Is," I correct without thinking, refusing to thrust the idea of Dad into the cobweb infested corridors of the past.

"Very well, 'is.'" he says, and I can hear the self-satisfied smile in his voice. "But if I do, Gwen, then you'll never learn what I realized after you hung up on me... and it could make the difference between finding Daddy H., and not."

This is the definition of not good. No, make that very not good. I mean sure, he could be bluffing about knowing something, but after that tea leaf reading of my life over the phone, I don't think so. And as much as this guy gives me the creeps, without some brilliant new insight, my search for Dad has pretty much slammed into a brick wa...

WAIT A MINUTE!

"How did you know my name was Gwen? Did my mom put you up to this?!"

He laughs, not unpleasantly, though I'm in no mood to appreciate it.

"I've never met your mom," he assures me.

"What about other types of communication? Letters, voice-mail, texts, newspaper classifieds..."

"Nope, not even international semaphore. The first I heard of her was when I did a reverse phone look-up on your number."

"And why would you do that?"

"It was one of the oddest phone calls I've gotten in a while, and it intrigued me."

"I don't buy it. Even if you were that desperately bored, our phone number listing wouldn't tell you anything about me as my name's not on any of the phone records."

"True," he says, clearly amused. "But those aren't the only kind of records out there. When I figured out that you couldn't be Yvette, I started working backwards and got your mom's name from the reverse phone look-up which I'm sure you know about."

"Yeah, you plug in a number and get a name and address out."

"Exactly," he says as if I were some cute pet who'd just done a trick. "From her name, it was a simple matter of pulling up public birth records, which gave me you along with your birth date, all of which was completely consistent with the rest of my theory."

My birth record! I suddenly flash on the idea that maybe Mom listed Dad's real name on the form. But before I can ask, Not Dad interrupts my thoughts.

"No, she just put down 'Father Unknown'," he says, sounding genuinely regretful, apparently still reading all my thought bubbles. "But, I have a theory about what his phone number really is, or at least was."

"Yeah, right. And how could you possibly know that?"

"Now, that's the trick isn't it? I'll tell you what; meet me for coffee —or hot chocolate, whatever you drink—and I'll tell you, and promise to never call you again. And I'll even treat."

"Forget it, not going to happen. Look, I don't know what kind of sicko you are…"

"You've got it all wrong. I'm a P.I., a Private Investigator."

"Right, and I'm Jamie Bond, Secret Agent. Look, even if you are, I can't afford you."

"I am. And you can. Look me up on the Internet, Fitzgerald Investigations. And my entire price is that you'll join me for a coffee, or hot drink of any kind. And you should bring a friend. In fact I insist on it."

"Yeah, and what do you get out of it?"

"Now we're getting somewhere. It's simple. Most of my cases are incredibly dull, doing background checks for employers which inevitably means spending hours on Facebook documenting all the incredibly stupid things people put online, or going through people's trash to find out what some cheating husband's been up to so a soon-to-be-ex-wife can get even more out of the divorce settlement. Frankly, I need a vacation from all that, and your story sounds interesting."

"Oh, thanks." My life has just been relegated to the adult all-purpose adjective "interesting," which we all know is code for that's really hideous but I love you so I'll say something that at least sounds positive. For example, what do you say when your child brings home some artwork that looks like a dog barfed on it? Oh, Honey, that's really interesting.

"Anyway," Not Dad says, "I've enough paying work that I can afford to treat myself to a real mystery. So what do you say? How about tomorrow at noon at L.A. Burdicks in Harvard Square? They've got a single-source Madagascan hot chocolate that defies description."

My mouth starts watering at the thought, but I tell it to shut up or I'll give it more of Peter's bread and it reluctantly complies.

"I'll check you out," I tell him, trying to sound calm, but the possibility of getting Dad's phone number and killer hot chocolate is distracting, to say the least. "But if I do come, I'm going to bring a friend whose father is a cop, and if you try to follow us back home or do anything at all dicey, I'll report you and deal with whatever fallout there is from my mother."

"Fair enough. But tell your friend's dad to ask Sergeant O'Brien at the sixth precinct about me, I just got off doing a consulting gig for them. And if you do come, I'll be the bald guy with the red beard. You can't miss me."

"No promises," I tell him, even though I know I've already decided to go. Assuming I can drag Peter along and this guy's story checks out, that is. I mean, I may be desperate to contact my dad, but I'm not completely stupid. Even when there's chocolate involved.

Peter's surprisingly easy to convince, which leads me to once again question Not Dad's story. I mean, if this is some elaborate scheme by Mom—or Peter himself for that matter—to teach me a life lesson worthy of a Hallmark card or Motivational Poster, I can't say I'll be all that surprised. Still, what choice do I have but to play it out and see where it takes me?

And maybe both Not Dad and Peter are just what they claim to be, a P.I. looking for fun, and a friend who's highly motivated by the opportunity to (a) meet a real-live private investigator; (b) finally learn who my dad was so I'll stop driving him crazy; and (c) drink hot chocolate that defies description... though quite possibly in reverse order.

Since Peter's voice is much more convincingly adult over the phone, he calls Sergeant O'Brien for me and pretends to be someone considering hiring Mr. Fitzgerald, which lets him pepper O'Brien with questions about him. In a very traditional Irish-Boston accent, O'Brien heaps praise on Fitzgerald so deeply that had he been standing in it, it would probably have covered him completely.

After Peter finally extracts himself from the talkative O'Brien, I get online and run a whole bunch of searches, all of which come up pretty much exactly as expected: he's a P.I., he's not on any watch lists, and his company's been around for well over 20 years.

All in all, it seems like a safe bet, so we decide to chance it and meet.

Chapter 10
In which Chocolate does, in fact, manage to defy description.

We get to Burdicks early so we can scope the place out, plan our escape routes... you know, as they say in those crime and detective novels, case the joint. But one step into the place and all that goes out the window. Normally I'd never even enter an establishment like this—and trust me, this is an establishment, not merely a store—as I always knew it would just be torture.

And, yay me, I get to be right again.

I can't even describe how out-of-place I feel being here. It's all paneled in pale wood with touches of brass, the entrance lined with airy display cases filled with little hand-crafted delicacies, each one probably costing more than my Mom spends for dinner on the two of us. And it's not all chocolate, either. There are heaping trays of little hamburger shaped cookies in yellow, pink and purple pastels.

What's more, the narrow room is filled with darkly elegant men wearing tuxedos and silk top-hats, women in long, flowing ball gowns. Ten there's me and Peter, grubby little street urchins with grime-covered faces, intruding where we don't belong.

Well, that's how it feels, at least.

Okay, breathe.

I try to take a deep, calming breath, but the air is so infused with the amazing scent of rich, dark chocolate that my heart only starts racing faster. It's like a contact high, subtle and complex, and so utterly unlike any chocolate I've ever smelled.

Well, I mean, of course it's like other chocolate. But only in the same way that guppies are like Great White Sharks. Or these ramblings are like the musings of an ordered brain. Same galaxy, different solar system altogether.

My feet seem to have more courage than I do, leading me deeper in, past the display cabinets, leaving me facing row upon row of LA Burdicks apparently world-famous chocolate mice and I almost lose it.

When I was looking this place up online, I stumbled on a photo of President Obama eating one of these mice, and now here they were, staring me in the face. And I mean that literally. They stare up at you with such a look of such wide-eyed innocence that you can't help but both smile and salivate at the same time.

Still, at over three dollars each, there's a lot more than just glass between me and those so enticing little morsels.

I want to stay there forever, inhaling the scent of the place, devouring it all with my eyes, but I also want to turn and run from these glass cases filled with wonders that I can never afford. And so I do nothing but stand there immobile, vibrating from my conflicting desires like an aspen leaf in the wind.

"Can I help you?"

I turn to find a clerk looking at me as if she's wondering if she should call the Center for Disease Control, like I might suddenly start frothing at the mouth or have some kind of fit. She's just a couple of years older than I am, probably going to one of the hundreds of colleges that permeate greater Bostburbia like the holes in Swiss cheese.

She's got short, mousy brown hair, and her round, wire-rimmed glasses frame dark pupils, open wide in the comfortable dimness of the room, turning them into the shiny black eyes of a rodent. Between her looks and the veritable army of delectable chocolate mice, I feel a nervous giggle coming on that I know isn't going to be pretty.

Peter apparently senses it too and casually takes my hand, squeezing it painfully enough to stop the giggle before it can escape. "We're waiting for someone," he tells her confidently, and she nods, still looking a bit doubtful, but then heads off to help someone apparently less psychotic than I'm sure I appear.

"Ow," I tell Peter after she's out of earshot, and he loosens his grip on my hand so it's merely firm, not crushingly vice-like. It feels a little strange to be standing holding hands with him, but kind of nice too. I know he's holding on simply to be ready to keep me from causing some kind of a scene that will get us thrown out before Not Dad arrives, but at the moment I don't care. I need his steady solidity, and while the distraction of his touch causes another kind of turmoil in my brain, it's more confused than panicked, and that will have to do.

"And you two must be Gwen and Peter."

Only Peter's firm grip on my hand keeps my über-cat-like reflexes from throwing me through the glass case behind me. We turn, and there, smiling ear to ear, is clearly Not Dad.

I know I'm staring but I can't help myself. I mean, you know what it's like. You hear someone on the radio, or a podcast, or something, and you kind of feel like you know them. But then, if you actually ever see them, they always look nothing like what you expected.

So, what do you think of when you think Private Investigator? Me, I think late forties, kind of balding, probably too short and out-of-shape for the police force, and, of course, wearing an old tie pulled loose around his neck under a seedy, rumbled, out-of-fashion suit coat that smells of cigarettes and stale whiskey.

So, of course, I'd expected him to look like anything but that... but there he stands, ripped straight from my imagination and plopped down in front of me. I mean, he's so impossibly, exactly like I pictured him, I'm tempted to reach out and poke him to make sure he's real, but Peter gives me a warning squeeze on my hand, which tells me he sees him too.

It also reminds me that we're still holding hands and I quickly yank mine free as I feel my cheeks beginning to burn.

Now I'm a big believer in Darwin's Theory of Evolution, but really? Blushing? Can anyone tell me what the possible survival value of having a big neon sign go off every time you're nervous or embarrassed could be? Anyone?

Peter elbows me in the ribs—either that or an invisible mule is walking around taking pot shots at people—and I realize Not Dad's holding his hand out for me to shake. I take it and it's surprisingly cool, not the hot sweaty grasp of my imagined P.I. at all. We shake and he leads us over to the little order counter in the back and tells us we can have whatever we want.

Oh yeah, if it only it were that easy. I'm tempted to start in on my wish lists of wants, one that is roughly the length of all the Harry Potter books put together, but I manage to restrain myself. I figure I should keep the snarkiness to a minimum until the promised hot chocolate is in hand, and who knows, if I'm really restrained, maybe I'll get a mouse thrown in as well.

The menu's on a blackboard on the wall and they offer single-source hot chocolate, sorry, single-source drinking chocolate from five different countries with descriptions about hints of this flavor and notes of that aroma with cacao percentages and I feel like I've just been given a final in a class I forgot to take. Quick quiz: where the heck is the Dominican Republic? When describing pretentious chocolate, what is the difference between a hint, a note, overtones and highlights? And, of course, for bonus points, how many Ecuadorians does it take to screw in a light bulb?

Still, I'm nothing if not decisive so I promptly say "Grenada." Mostly because it sounds like grenade and my head feels like it's about to explode, but you work with what you've got.

There aren't a lot of tables and a couple is just leaving so I dash over and snatch theirs. The serving guy come over with the drinks after a couple of minutes and I have to confess I'm kind of disappointed. The cups are really small, probably half the size of the hot chocolates we get at mom's bookstore.

Not Dad's looking at me, amused, which makes me pretty sure he knows what I'm thinking. Sigh. Just for once I'd like to be the tall, dark and mysterious type. However, since I completely lack all three of those salient qualities, I think I'm stuck with medium, dirty-blond and completely transparent. Doesn't quite have the same zing, does it?

To cover my annoyance, I take a sip of the hot chocolate and... oh.

Now I understand why the cup is so small. This stuff bears as much similarity to hot chocolate as I do to tall, dark and mysterious. I thought "drinking" in drinking chocolate was an adjective, but it's not. It's a verb.

I could try to describe it further, but I won't because (a) I know I won't do it justice and (b) I think it will come out sounding like a badly written sex scene. Even the smallest sip infuses me with the purest essence of primal chocolate, saturating my taste buds with flavor, and sending my heart pounding... yeah, definitely bad sex-scene material.

Let me put it this way. There's a series of books called The Chronicles of Amber, and the premise is that there are a continuum of dimensions with Amber being the one true dimension. All the other dimensions (including our own) are just "shadows" of Amber, degraded copies if you would. The royal family of Amber can cross from one dimension to the next and the farther from Amber they get, the more degraded the dimension is from the true ideal. Like if you make xeroxes of xeroxes, they just get worse and worse. Our dimension is maybe a couple dozen dimensions away...

And this small cup is from Amber.

Chapter 11
In which Not Dad Cracks the Code and I realize, yet again, that I can't do believable chilled vegetable impressions.

"So, you do know our parents don't have any money for ransom," I tell him. "Just in case you had any ideas."

"Good to know."

"And Peter knows Kung Fu."

Out of the corner of my eye, I see Peter shaking his head in denial.

"Did you set up a dead-man switch as well?" Not Dad asks.

I look blank. I'm hoping it's poker-face-blank like I'm not giving anything away, but I have this sneaking feeling it's just deer-in-the-headlights blank, like I have no clue what he's talking about. Which wouldn't be all that surprising as, sadly, it happens to be absolutely true.

"You know," he continues. "You hire a lawyer or set up a website, and if you don't call or log in every hour, he/she/it shouts to the world that you were last seen with some creepy guy who can't shut up about your mom's sex life."

When he puts it that way... ew.

"So what can you tell us about her dad?" Peter asks, thankfully derailing my run-away train of thought.

"Ah, now that is the question," Not Dad says, leaning back in his chair and smiling.

"And what is the answer?" Peter asks calmly.

"Well, I think I have his phone number."

"We've already been through that," I interrupt. "Remember, I called you?"

"So you did. No, by have, I meant know, or at least knew..."

Great. He's not only kind of round and balding, apparently he's related to Humpty Dumpty as well. Which is oddly appropriate, if you think about it, as my whole life story has that kind of skewed Wonderland-esque quality about it. Without the whole size-changing bit... well, excluding puberty, of course.

He's still smiling, clearly pleased by his deductive prowess and waiting for us to ask how he figured out the number so he can walk us through his brilliant deductions one-by-one, and have us ooh and ahhh at the appropriate moments like he was some fourth of July fireworks display. But I'm not going to give him the satisfaction. He was the one who wanted to meet us here, and I've got a cup of steaming chocolate nirvana in front of me, so I just lean back in my chair and do my very best to look as cool as a cucumber.

"So what is it?" I hear my mouth blurt out.

Crap. Just like when I try to warn it about Peter's bread, my mouth apparently doesn't get the memo.

"I'll give you an answer for an answer," Not Dad says.

"Do my answers have to be to your questions?"

"If you want mine to be, then yes."

Hmmm. So, "forty-two" is probably out.

He smiles again. He's enjoying this waaay too much. This is my life we're talking about and he's turning it into a game show.

"So, what do you want to know?" I ask.

"Where did you find my phone number, well, his really."

"On the back of his head."

Peter cocks his own head, clearly thinking over where we found the number, then slowly nods to himself. "Marginal, but I suppose it's technically accurate."

I was just born in the wrong mythos. I mean, I would have made a great genie. "I wish I were rich." POOF, you're a chocolate cake. "I wish I could live forever." POOF, you die at the usual age. Well, you *could* have lived forever had I not messed with you but well, I did, and you didn't.

"I wish you'd give me lots of gold with the following caveats: 1) it can't be stolen, cursed or otherwise bring me bad luck; 2) I will not be buried in it, turned into it, or harmed by it in any way; 3) It is the element gold, atomic number 79, not merely something gold colored, and 4) No harm will come to me, my friends, family or anyone else either directly or indirectly due to this wish or effects caused by the implementation thereof."

POOF, you're now the proud owner of asteroid (337) Fortuna which contains about 8.5 metric tons of gold. Go get it, cowboy.

He rolls his eyes, strictly amateur stuff, but not bad for an old guy.

"My turn." I say. "So what's his phone number?"

"A series of ten digits, starting with an area code, then a local exchange and the four final digits. Where did he write his phone number down?"

"Las Vegas. What are the numbers of his phone number?"

"Zero through Nine. Hmmm, wait a second, I don't think there's a three. Yeah, zero through nine excluding three. Describe the material on which the phone number was written in sufficient detail that I could positively identify it in a box of randomly chosen items."

"Forfeit. Not a question. What are the numbers of his phone number in the order you would dial them?"

He rattles off the number I found on the back of the photo.

"That's your number," I protest. "How can it be both your number and his unless you were rooming together? Oh, my god, you weren't..."

"That's two questions out of turn. But no, I wasn't, and it can't. Or vice-versa."

"You know," Peter interrupts conversationally, "you guys could be at this all day. Or we could actually get on with our lives."

Much as I hate to admit it, he's got a point.

"But I have a question for you," Peter says to Not Dad.

"Shoot." Not Dad replies. Someone should probably tell him that's not the best expression to hear from someone who I expect is carrying a gun.

"Why are we here?"

"I assume you mean here as in LA Burdicks, not here in the larger metaphysical sense..."

Peter just stares at him, so still his face could have been carved out of marble. Now, that boy has some mad chilled vegetable skills.

"It's like I told Gwen on the phone," Not Dad says. "I'm bored. Look, I grew up reading Sherlock Holmes and Inspector Morse novels, and I became a P.I. because I like solving puzzles."

"Have you tried Sudoku?" I offer helpfully.

He sighs. "You know the last time I had a really interesting case? One that actually required deductive reasoning instead of just stalking some poor schmuck to prove he is or isn't having an affair?"

"You can't prove a negative."

"Sure I can. If someone thinks an employee is embezzling money, for example—you know, taking money from the company and then cooking the books, uh, manipulating the accounting, to keep it from being noticed—I could prove that the accounting was, in fact, correct and there's actually no money missing, the company's just doing really badly, then I've proved a negative. The employee is not embezzling."

"Or you're in on it, and are just part of the cover up."

Not Dad turns to Peter. "Is she always like this?"

"Pretty much."

"It's part of my charm," I protest.

"Is that what you call it?" Peter asks.

"Whose side are you on, anyway?"

"Do there have to be sides?"

"Unless you want to live in a one dimensional world, then yes."

"Well, if I did, at least I'd know my life wouldn't be pointless."

I give him my best *we are not amused expression,* but his deadpan expression doesn't budge.

"Because all there would be were points," he helpfully, well, points out.

"Yeah, I got it."

Peter turns back to Not Dad. "So you were talking about the last time you had a Sherlock Holmes worthy case?"

"That's the thing," Not Dad says. "I've never had one. Ever. And then out of the blue I get one of the weirdest phone calls I've ever received."

"One of the weirdest phone calls?" I demand.

"Well, there was the time this guy called me up and said he thought he'd accidentally killed himself during an episode of Lost, and now he can't get cable."

Peter nods, impressed, then turns to me. "I think he's got you there."

"Hmph."

"So, anyway," Not Dad continues. "You call and I've finally gotten a real-live mystery... so, of course I want to be involved. And here we are."

I'm still a little miffed that mine wasn't the weirdest call he'd ever gotten, but Peter's satisfied with the story. And for someone who's been trying to derail me at every turn, he seems oddly invested in moving this forward.

He turns to me. "Are you going to answer his questions, or should I?"

"Go ahead," I tell him, and he proceeds to relate the whole story as I've told it to him. Not Dad listens quietly, jotting down some notes now and then in a small notebook with a real-live pencil, or at least the end of one.

It's short and stubby, kind of like his fingers, with a whole bunch of deep teeth marks from where he's obviously been chewing on it. I can relate. In fact, Mom even started calling me Madam Beaver once in a misguided attempt to get me to stop. Of course it...

My train of thought jumps off the tracks. Hold on... what about the dead guy who couldn't get cable?

Once Peter finishes the whole story to date, Not Dad closes his notebook. "So, do you want to know how I could have had this number since before you were born, and it still be your dad's number?"

I give him my best teenage "Really?" look and he smiles.

"The answer," he says, still grinning. "Is that I can't."

I can't process what he's saying for a moment, but when I do, I feel like he's just punched me.

"What?! Are you kidding me?" I demand. "You promised, you promised you had this great theory..."

"Gwen, slow down."

I guess I must be pretty loud because out of the corner of my eye I see people start to look at our table with something other than the usual predatory desire for it when we leave. But I really don't care.

"I'm not going to slow down! I'm on a chocolate high that you put me on, and you said you knew Dad's, my real Dad's, phone number."

"I do."

"But you just said you can't tell me!"

"No, I meant I couldn't have had this number all that time and it still have also been your dad's. I didn't mean I couldn't tell you."

"Oh." I realize I'm leaning over the table on the very edge of my seat, and I slump back into it sheepishly. Well, not so much like a sheep would do it, were one sitting in my place, but you get the picture.

"See, when I got to really thinking about the problem I suddenly realized that what I think of as my number is really just the last seven digits. I've had those numbers for nearly twenty years, and I had it transferred when I moved to Boston from Western Mass about ten years ago."

"That's just fascinating."

"Actually it is. See, when it was transferred, the area code changed to 617. So, although I've had what I think of as my phone number long before you were born, I've only had the exact number you called for the past five or six years."

I'm not getting it.

"How about you pretend Peter's stupid and explain it again."

Peter looks at me.

"I said pretend." I protest.

"Okay, let's go back about sixteen years. Your dad gives your mom his phone number with the 617 area code. I'm happily living in Western Mass with the same phone number but with a 413 area code. Then all those new-fangled cell phones and fax machines and modems come along..."

I have no idea what a modem is, but for once I don't interrupt.

"... and they start running out of phone numbers. So, what they did was split up the 617 area code into five or six different regions, each with their own new area code and only a tiny area right around the heart of Boston keeps 617."

The light bulb over my head finally illuminates.

"Okay, so Dad's number goes from 617 to one of the new area codes," I say. "And his number with the 617 becomes available for reuse."

"Exactly! When I moved to Boston, it was after this whole area code split. So when I asked if they could transfer my old 413 area code number—which was the same as your Dad's—they could because the 617 version now wasn't being used, and suddenly I have his old phone number."

"So all I need to do is call his old number but with all the new area codes and see if he answers any of them."

"Unfortunately, I already tried that."

"And...?" I demand, though I know it's pointless. The whole "Unfortunately" business kind of gives it away.

"Nobody had heard of him. So I used the reverse phone lookup again to get the addresses associated with these numbers, and then checked public land sale records to see if I could find a likely candidate who owned one of the properties during the right time period."

"And...?" I ask, dreading the answer, my chest tight.

"Nobody with a first name starting with H but a Henrietta Mills. So I started looking at last names and found Richard Hochins."

"And that's him? That's my dad?!"

He shakes his head no. "He apparently died a couple of years later at the age of 83, leaving behind his wife and two daughters. So it couldn't have been him or a son living at home either, as he didn't have any."

"What about a cousin or nephew or someone living with them.? Who also was a Hochins..."

I know I'm grasping at straws but when you're falling off a cliff, you'll grasp at anything. Or at least I imagine I would, having never actually fallen off a cliff. Tell that to my stomach, though, as it is currently in the process of plummeting to the floor like it had a dead weight in it.

"Nope. There weren't any Hochins writing best-selling books back then. Or any books at all for that matter."

"So all this brilliant deduction was useless," I say dully.

I should have expected this, but it still leaves me feeling hollow. It's over, and believing anything else would be just kidding myself.

Even with Peter's help I'm sure we couldn't have gotten half as far as Not Dad did. He seems to really know his stuff, and if he couldn't track Dad down, then what chance do we have?

I know I should probably be angry at Not Dad for putting me through all this and getting my hopes up, but that would take too much energy right now.

So Peter gets angry on my behalf. "That was a pretty shitty thing to do, you know."

I look up sharply. I don't think I've ever heard him swear before, and that he did so for me is about one of the nicest things anyone's done. He takes my hand and hauls me to my feet.

"I hope you're proud of yourself, asshole," Peter tells him, then turns away as if Not Dad wasn't even worth his time. His hand's really hot in mine and I'm feeling really confused. Half of me is still numb from the whole search-for-Dad ending in a brick wall; half of me is still marveling at having Peter swear for me; and half of me is kind of watching the whole thing unfold like a movie.

"Come on, Gwen, we're done here."

I follow his lead and we start towards the door when Not Dad jumps up, almost spilling the hot chocolate left on the table.

"Wait!" he calls out. "You kids don't get it. When one trail ends you just pick up another one."

"And have you?" Peter asks slowly.

"Yes, yes, of course."

"And does this one end just as uselessly as the other two?"

"They weren't useless at all. They were pieces in the chain..."

"Which I'm very tempted to wrap around your neck at this point," Peter tells him quietly.

Not Dad looks back and forth between us, shaking his head. Then he turns to me.

"You've got one heck of a boyfriend here, Gwen. I hope you appreciate that."

"He's not my boyfriend."

"Okay," Not Dad says, clearly not believing me as I'm still clutching Peter's hand. We both seem to realize it at the same time, and we let go, my hand still tingling from his grasp. I cross my arms over my chest because now that I'm not holding his hand, I suddenly feel like I need to do something with them, and I don't know what else there is.

"So, do you know something or not?" I ask flatly.

"I think I do… I can't promise anything, but I really think I do."

"Then why did we just go through that whole area code and property title song and dance?"

"Because it was cool."

A half-laugh/half-sob climbs out of my chest. Through my mouth, mind you, but it started in my chest, somewhere deep inside me. Not Dad's eyes are shining with his passion for the puzzle of it all, and I can't really blame him. I mean, it was pretty cool how he worked it all out and if it weren't so important to me, I would probably appreciate it. But right now I don't want cool, I want answers.

"I can't take much more of this," I tell Not Dad. "Can you just cut to the chase and tell me what you've figured out?"

"It'll make a lot more sense if you let me tell you how I think I found him."

"It'll be a lot faster if you don't," Peter replies. "And, as you may have gathered by now, Gwen and sense are not always on speaking terms."

Not Dad sighs.

"Fine, but you're missing the most interesting part," he protests, but like so many other things, his protest collides with Peter and bounces off without eliciting a reaction.

Not Dad sighs again, then gives up and starts talking. "I think he's got a house on Barret's Island just off the coast. It's a small private island with only one home on it. Owned by Holden Baxter, author of The View from Midnight and Down the Rabbit Hole."

I don't know either of those books but trust me, I will.

"If he has a phone number, it must be unlisted because I can't find one. Still, with all the other information I could dig up, property taxes, utilities and so on," Not Dad continues, "it appears he's still living there."

I can feel my eyes widening to the size of dinner plates and I squeeze Peter's hand so hard my own goes numb.

Holden Baxter.

Dad.

My dad's name is Holden... My dad.

I'll never read <u>Catcher in the Rye</u> the same way again.

Chapter 12
In which I am reminded that
I don't actually speak German.

Peter and I leave Not Dad after promising to keep him informed if anything else happens with Real Dad, then we head for the T Station at Harvard Square, passing the ever-present clumps of people standing around the entrance. They never seem to be doing anything, nor do they seem to be waiting for anyone either. They're just there. Hanging around.

And no, I know they aren't Harvard students because they don't have that annoying, burning aura filled with the certainty of their own intellectual (and future financial) superiority that Harvard admissions seems to require in their student body.

They used to creep me out—both the guys just hanging around and the Harvard students, each in their own special way—but now I ignore them just like I used to ignore "the world's only Curious George store" that for decades sat right across the street from them. Why the world ever needed any Curious George stores, much less one right in the heart of Harvard Square, is a question best left to people with far less on their minds than me... like the ones who apparently have nothing better to do than hang around a subway entrance.

Mind you, none of this is going through my mind at the moment. I'm just trying to set the scene because otherwise I know you'll be imagining me walking through a formless gray fog without anything to latch onto. And that's what's going on in my head right now, not in the world around me.

Dad, his books, his name, Peter's hand... they're all chasing each other like that Norse snake that's eating its own tail and I'm running along with them, trapped in an endless loop of raw, unprocessed thought.

As we head into the station, we can see there's a train waiting at the platform, a flight of stairs below us. Normally we'd run to catch it, but I'm still stuck in my head and anyway, whenever we do, we always end up just sitting in the subway car for an extra ten minutes.

So of course it leaves just as we reach the platform.

"Are you alright?" Peter asks.

I'm not sure how to answer him. I mean, I'm great, I'm confused, I'm anxious, I'm excited, I'm scared, I'm in shock... well, you get the picture.

I really do want to answer him. I want him to help me make sense of these crazy conflicting feelings, but some of them involve him, so instead I shrug, just the smallest lift of my shoulders.

"I guess so," I finally say.

Yeah, real eloquent, I know.

He doesn't ask me if I want to talk about it because he knows me too well. If I wanted to talk about it, I would, and he knows it and I know he knows it.

Still, I kind of wish he would ask, because for some reason I can't start this on my own. So we just stand there side-by-side on the platform, and I'm hoping he'll ask, or take my hand again, or swear at someone for me, but he doesn't move. Great. The one time I want the thought bubble over my head to work, it doesn't. Either that or it's just showing that hourglass cursor you get on your computer, flipping over and over and over, just like my racing thoughts.

Holden Baxter.

His name keeps bouncing around in my head like it's in a pinball machine, careening into this emotion, then that one, triggering them one after another with the requisite flashing lights and loud ringing bells. Peter keeps glancing at me like he's worried I might not be breathing or something, which, given that I'm not talking, would normally be a legitimate concern. But I'm fine. Well, sort of.

The train finally arrives and we shuffle in and find a couple of free seats, but the moment the doors shut, I know I've made a terrible mistake.

Can anyone please explain to me why our brains work this way, always remembering things the moment after you could have actually done something about it? Like when you walk out to get the mail and the second you hear the door latch behind you, you realize you've locked yourself out.

Or when you have a quiz coming up that you've completely forgotten about. Yet somehow it's always the first thought you have when you jerk awake the next morning, your body flooded with adrenaline at the sudden panicked realization that you've completely forgotten to study.

Anyway, my oh crap realization when the doors shut is that the Cambridge public library is only a couple of blocks away from the Harvard Square T Station... from which we are now currently departing. And I need to go to the library to get Dad's books.

Now.

So Peter patiently lets me drag him out at the next stop to get on the train going in the other direction, back to where we just left. And this time, we do run to catch it.

With, of course, the fully predictable results.

A quick interlude:

I don't know about you, but I've got a lot to take in, and frankly, I could take a break from all this Daddy and Peter angst. So let me introduce you to my favorite library.

Sure, Cambridge Public doesn't have lions, but the historic part of it looks like a small castle. It's set back from the street in a park and the first thing you see coming up to it is this massive central turret, capped with open archways and a steep cone made out of some pinkish-red hammered metal. The cone rises up nearly half as high again as the turret itself, and it's tipped with a big blob of something white, making it look like a dunce cap or one of those plastic cheerleader megaphones.

Surrounding the turret are sharply steepled red tile roofs interrupted by dark brown, cathedral-framed dormer windows thrusting out to the very edge of the eaves. The walls and turret are made of white mortared stone, and if you know where to look, you can find a whole bunch of little medieval people in robes carved into this stonework.

They are all tucked into deeply incised niches quietly reading books, or striding somewhere carrying books, or lazily reading an unfurled scroll, and there's even one little guy in the process of dropping a stacks of books taller than he is.

Forget Disneyland, this is my happiest place on earth.

Now, back to my breakdown previously in progress.

I'm breathless when we arrive in the library and I can see one of the librarians glancing up at me, annoyed at my exasperatingly loud breathing. Still, I'm apparently not yet shush-worthy and he goes back to doing whatever it is librarians do when they aren't checking out or reshelving books. I know what I'd be doing in their place, but somehow you never see librarians sitting at their desks reading. Go figure.

We find a free computer terminal and I slide into the chair. It's still warm from someone else's butt, which feels kind of nice as long as you don't think about it too much. The prompt on screen is asking for author, title or keywords and I freeze.

"What if they don't have them? Or what if he doesn't really exist?" I whisper to Peter. Or at least I try to whisper but apparently it comes out louder than I'd intended as the librarian looks at me again.

"What if they do?" he replies, whispering back more successfully than I. When I still don't move, he leans over and types in Dad's name: Baxter, Holden, then leans back, leaving it to me to click the submit button.

I can do this, I tell myself, and to my surprise my hand actually agrees with me and clicks the mouse. The screen goes gray as the search starts, and at that moment, I'm absolutely convinced it's going to come back with no hits whatsoever. That Not Dad just made up Holden Baxter as some kind of practical joke and I swallowed it hook, line and sinker along with the fishing pole itself.

Then it comes back with three listings:

A View From Midnight	Available
Down the Rabbit Hole	Checked Out
Hinunter In den Kaninchenbau	Available

OhMyGoOhMyGodOhMyGodOhMyGod. It's real. It's really real. He's really real!

Without thinking about it, I take Peter's hand and squeeze it really hard.

"Can I help you?"

It's the librarian who kept glaring at me and I guiltily drop Peter's hand. Up close, however, the librarian doesn't seem as annoyed as I thought he'd be.

"Um, I think we're okay," I start to say but Peter overrides me.

"Actually, we're looking for these books."

The librarian peers down at the screen. "Holden Baxter," he mumbles to himself. "Don't think I've ever heard of him."

"At least one of these was a best-selling novel," I tell him defensively, already protective of Dad.

"Okay. Well, one of these it checked out, and it looks like the third one is the German translation of it. You should be able to find <u>A View From Midnight</u> in the novels section down that aisle. It looks like it should be on shelf 2B, though if you don't see it there, look on the shelves above and below it because people are always reshelving things in the wrong places."

"So, it's either 2B or not 2B," Peter says innocently, but the librarian just nods and keeps on talking, though I can't help but wince inwardly.

"The German edition would be in our foreign language section," he says, "but I'm guessing you don't want that one."

Are you kidding me? "No, I'll take both."

The librarian shrugs and gives us directions to the foreign language section as well but I drag Peter over to the novel section first. With my luck someone will grab the only copy just as we get there. But the universe is apparently amused enough watching me scramble around in a panic and no one else is in the aisle when we arrive. My heart starts pounding as I scan the titles... it's got to be here, it's got to... and then, there it is.

The angelic choir descends, and I can't hear what Peter's saying over the chorus.

"Earth to Gwen... hello."

I turn to him, the angels breaking for coffee or something.

"Are you going to get it down," he asks, "or are we just going to stare at it all day?"

"I'm savoring the moment."

"Well, could you savor it faster? I've got to pee."

"Really? And since when do you need me for that?"

"I don't. But this... it's your Dad's book and I want to be here."

I sigh. "Okay, okay... the moment's kind of gone anyhow."

I turn back and gaze at my prize. It's a hardback copy with a deep black spine, standing stately and tall among its brightly colored, paperback companions.

I reach up and gingerly pull it down from the shelf like it might be booby trapped, or the whole aisle was going to come crashing down like some giant game of Jenga® if I remove it too quickly. When it finally comes loose from the press of its neighbors, I realize I've been holding my breath. I let it out about as slowly as I'd removed the book, all the while staring down at the work of my father sitting there in my hands.

I suppose my hands are, in their own way, also the work of my father, but since it doesn't seem to rip apart the space-time continuum, I think we're okay. The book feels so solid, so real, I can't believe it. Its cover is pitch black, as are the title and his name, but they're embossed and appear back-lit by the full moon that graces the cover's upper left corner, making them look like they're almost floating in front of the book.

It looks pretty dog-eared which makes me very happy as it means it's been read and read despite that hired shusher never having heard of Dad. True, I'd never heard of Dad nor his books until this afternoon but hey, it's been a big dark secret that's been deliberately kept from me. What's his excuse?

I turn the book over and find myself staring down at Dad. He's wearing a different shirt, but otherwise he looks almost exactly like he does in the Vegas photos. It's so weird seeing him without Mom next to him and I'm suddenly sobbing, clutching the book as if it were him I was hugging.

Then I feel Peter's arms around me, and I'm pressed up against his chest, tears streaming down my face. I try to pull away—I know I'm balling and I don't want to soak his shirt with my tears—but he holds on tightly, and I give up, relaxing into his comforting solidity.

I finally get my tears under control and this time when I pull away, Peter gently lets me go.

I rummage through my backpack for some tissues and blow my nose, then look up at Peter. He's got this huge wet spot on his chest, but despite the way my nose is running, I amazingly didn't get any snot on him. Thank god for little favors.

"I got your shirt all wet," I say, apologetically stating the obvious.

"I'll send you the dry cleaning bill."

I give him a small smile and blow my nose again. "I must look terrible."

He looks my face over, carefully appraising the situation. "Yeah, pretty much," he tells me.

I wipe my eyes, knowing he's telling me the absolute truth but I can also see in his face that he doesn't care, which is almost as nice as swearing for me.

"It's him. It's really him," I tell Peter, showing him Dad's picture on the back of the book.

"I know. I saw. Just before you got all that dust in your eyes."

I nod, my face still struggling to decide between crying and grinning like maniac.

"Still, good thing you had a human tissue on hand."

"Yeah." I try a small smile.

"But I still really need to pee."

I smile even wider.

"You go do that," I tell him, my face having made a decision. "And I'll get..." I have to read it off the slip of paper the librarian gave me, sounding it out. "<u>Hinunter In den Kaninchenbau</u>. Can-inchen-bow. Can-IN-chen-bow..."

"Now you're making it sound Japanese."

I try again. "Kahnin-shen-bau."

"Not to belabor it, but you do realize you don't speak German, right?"

"And your point is...?"

"Nothing, just thought I'd mention it."

I collect <u>Hinunter In den Kaninchenbau</u> while Peter relieves himself, and I even manage to do it without the previous waterworks. He meets me as I'm checking them out, and even though there's plenty of room in my backpack, I need to carry them. They're like talismans of my dad, and I need to see them, actually hold them, to keep proving to myself this is all really happening.

So, for the second time in less than an hour, we catch the T at Harvard Square, and my face is beginning to hurt, probably because I'm grinning like a madman. The entire ride home, I just stare at Dad's picture on the back of <u>A View From Midnight</u>. I can so completely see him as a Holden, kind of geeky-cute, impaling palm trees with forks and sweeping my mom off her feet.

Holden Baxter.

It's got a great sound to it, and with that name, you could be just about anyone. I mean, Holden Baxter could just as easily be a plumber as an international jewel thief. Try doing that with Gwen Pendergrass.

Hey, wait a minute. If my dad's name is Holden Baxter, then I could be a Baxter too. Gwen Baxter. I could rock that. Or Gwendolyn Baxter, even. I'm already mentally reprinting the business cards that I don't have with my new name. Hey, I'm a high school student... why would I have business cards? But if I did...

Mom's not home when I get there, and I know I should invite Peter in after everything he's done for me this afternoon, but I kind of want to be alone with my dad. Apparently my thought balloon is working again as he tells me he promised Mitch he'd help him out with his "garden" when he got home. So we say our goodbyes and then I slip inside and shut the door, leaning against it, holding the prized books tight against my chest.

"I'm going to find you," I whisper to the books, but they don't reply. Which, all things considered, is probably a good thing.

I dump my backpack in its official backpack corner behind the understuffed armchair, and am about to walk away when I notice a piece of paper sticking out of one of my textbooks. I pull it out and realize it's the letter I intercepted from Mom to Yale.

Oh crap, I'd completely forgotten. What the heck am I going to do about Yale?

Chapter 13
In which the truth sets me free...
from lying about something else.

I'm awakened by the sound of keys in the front door and for a second I think I'm lying on the floor, and it was all a dream. But the hard thing under my face isn't the floor, it's one of Dad's books from the library.

I'm filled with relief until I realize that Mom can't see them or she'll know what I've been up to, and I'm <u>not</u> ready for that, because she'll want me to stop. So, I frantically stuff the books under my blanket and grab my physics textbook from my backpack as the door opens.

Mom comes in with some groceries and pushes the door closed with her foot.

"Hey Gwen, did you..." she interrupts herself when she sees me. "Good Lord, what happened to your face?"

My hand flashes to my face and I can feel the ridge the corner of the book has left on my cheek.

"Um, I fell asleep on a book."

I'm sure the title's been imprinted along with it and I'm frantically thinking how I can explain why my cheek says Kaninchenbau, but Mom just shakes her head and walks the requisite few steps into what passes for our kitchen.

"You must be exhausted," she says as she starts putting the groceries into the freezer.[2] "I don't think I've ever seen you fall asleep while you were reading."

"I wasn't reading," I say indignantly.

"So, you were just using a book as a pillow?"

"More or less."

"And you were doing this because...?""

"Mom, does everything always have to have a reason?"

"Generally speaking, yes."

---

[2] Yes, the freezer. If you don't remember why then you'll never pass the quiz on this book, and trust me, there will be a quiz. There's always a quiz.

"Well, I guess I was tired. And then there's this whole gravity thing going on around here."

She looks at me suspiciously. "You haven't been eating over at Mitch's again, have you?"

"No, Mom. I learned about the brownies."

She abandons the groceries and comes over and sits on the bed, narrowly missing sitting on one of Dad's hidden books, and thus narrowly missing giving me a heart attack.

"So, what's going on," she asks.

"Why does there have to be something going on?"

She gives me her look that basically says Really? Are we going to have to do this the hard way because I'm not going away, and I'm not buying the innocent Bambi eyes.

Crap. I get up, hoping she'll follow me before she leans back onto one of the hidden books, but no such luck.

"Peter held my hand today."

She raises an eyebrow, "And...?"

"And... uh, I think I liked it."

Mom bursts out laughing.

"Hey! It's not funny."

She gets up—finally!—and crosses to me. "I'm sorry, honey... I shouldn't have laughed."

"Really? You think so?" I demand.

"Really," she tells me seriously. "You were just acting so guilty that I thought you might have done another Yale or something."

Hmmm. I'm still mad at her for laughing, but it's kind of hard to be righteously indignant when you've done exactly the thing that you've been accused of.

"You're sixteen, Gwen. I think it's nice you like a boy."

"I never said I liked Peter. I said I liked his hand."

"Well, that's a start. And he's got pretty nice arms too."

"Mom!"

"You do know he's crazy about you?"

"We're just friends," I protest, though I'm not as entirely sure as I would have been yesterday. I'm also not entirely sure if I think that's a good thing or not. Basically I'm not entirely sure about anything right now, so just cut me some slack.

"Is that what you want?" she asks gently. "To just be friends?"

"I don't know."

"Peter's a good kid, sorry, young man. And if you like him, you should let him know."

"But what if you're wrong? What if I like him and he... doesn't. At least not that way."

"That's a risk we all have to take, one way or another."

"You aren't."

She sighs. "I'm not always the best role model in the world."

"I didn't mean it that way..."

"No, you're right. But with you and the jobs, I just haven't had room for anyone else."

"Oh, Mom."

We hug and shed a few tears together, then after a while she pulls away and holds me at arm's length, looking me in the eyes. "Just promise me you aren't going to run off now and fill out a profile for me at one of these online dating services."

"Not one," I agree.

"Nor two or three, or any number of them."

I grin.

"Really, Gwen, I mean it."

"Okay, okay."

She gives me one last I mean it look, then wipes the few remaining tears off her face. "Come on, let's go make dinner."

We walk towards the kitchen, and she puts her arm around my shoulders and gives me a little squeeze. "Well, honey, whatever you decide to do about Peter, you can always talk to me about it. And I promise I won't laugh."

"I know. I love you, Mom."

"I know." She grins. "And I love you even more."

Chapter 14
**In which the proverbial clock is
ticking, yet nothing actually happens.**

Sigh.

Chapter 15
In which I realize yet again,
I am never getting a pony.

I know I'm running out of time.

Mom's bound to notice that the Las Vegas pictures are missing at some point. Yale's bound to notice she hasn't responded to their offer. Peter's bound to notice that I'm acting really weird around him, and my head's bound to explode from staring at Dad's books without ever opening them.

Working backwards. I know I said I was going to get to know his books really well, but the truth is, I'm terrified. I haven't even had the nerve to open them to read the liner notes. What if I don't like them? What if <u>A View From Midnight</u> is some bodice-ripping, vampire bodyguard, romance novel? Peter's offered to pre-read it for me, but that's just too pathetic for words. He's my Dad, my problem.

I'm like this for days, basically paralyzed about moving forwards with any of it. Dad, Peter, his books, Yale. And normally when I get in this kind of state, Mom is my go-to shoulder to cry on, but for obvious reasons, that's not an option either.

She, of course, thinks my more-than-averagely high-strung state is all due to Peter. And, as I don't disabuse her of the notion, it only adds guilt to the whole cocktail of emotions swirling around inside me.

I know I have to break this cycle of inaction... but to do so would require me to actually perform an action, which is precisely the problem in the first place.

Okay, focus. Whenever I start feeling overwhelmed by my school assignments, Mom always tells me to break it into small, manageable pieces. So, what do I have to deal with?

Yale.

Okay, next. Dad. At first glance, this one appears possibly solvable, so I start to break it up into steps in my mind.

Step One: Find out where he lives. Check.

Step Two: Show up at his door with the Vegas photos.

Step Three: Have him remember Mom and actually be pleased to see me.

Step Four: Have him not get a restraining order against me, and have Mom not kill me when she discovers Steps One through Three.

Step Five: Have Mom remain in a non-homicidal state while convincing her to accept Dad's generous offer of financial help so she can go to Yale.

Step Six: Somehow bend the space-time continuum so that Yale and Boston are actually next to one another, so I don't have to lose Peter in the process.

Step Seven: Bring peace to the Middle East, cure world hunger, and get a pony.

Well, I figure if I'm dreaming, I might as well go for the big stuff, and I never did get a pony. Not that anyone I've ever known has gotten a pony—nor do I know what I'd do with one should it magically appear—but as it always seems high on the wish list, I figure I might as well go for the gold.

Oh, yeah. I feel so much better now that I've worked that out.

But perhaps the worst part about it is that I have absolutely no clue how to even begin accomplishing Step Two: showing up on his doorstep. I mean, how do you drop in on someone who lives on a private island and has an unlisted phone number? Swim?

Peter's in his living room reading this historical/fantasy that our favorite librarian insisted we just had to read.

Peter's really gotten into it and tried to explain the plot to me, but all I got out of it was that it was something about King Edward, and Elves, and Edward's uncle trying to kill him in order to steal the throne.

Anyway, he loves it, so I don't say anything to drag him away from it, and just plop down on the sofa that Mitch dragged in from somewhere when it fell off a moving truck and they just kept on going... or so the story goes.

Peter doesn't look up, so I just fidget around on the sofa, making my very best impression of looking bored. I pull out the copy of <u>A View From Midnight</u> from my backpack and idly trace the embossed title with my finger. For a brief moment I consider actually opening it, but the urge passes.

"You trying to learn Braille?"

Peter's looking at me over the top of his book.

"How long have you been watching me?" I demand.

He smiles. "Pretty much ever since you moved in."

Now that I notice it, he's got a great smile.

Which only makes me feel worse. I'm just his messed-up, klutzy next-door neighbor with my dirty-blonde hair, and he probably only hangs out with me because he's afraid what will happen if he leaves me on my own. I can feel tears threatening, but I threaten them right back.

I will not cry again, I won't.

He puts his book down and comes over to sit next to me on the couch.

"What's wrong?" he asks, his knee incredibly warm where it touches mine.

"You mean other than me being completely mental?"

"Yeah, other than that."

I don't respond, still arguing with my overly enthusiastic tear ducts.

He looks down at the book in my hand, then looks back up at my face suddenly, his eyes widening in concern. "Oh my god, you hated it."

I shake my head mutely and he lets out a sigh of relief. Yeah, I know. *I* wouldn't want to be around me if I hated it, and I can only imagine how bad it would be for him.

"You still haven't read it." It's not so much a question as a knowing observation.

"So, what?" he continues. "Did your Mom ask you about the missing Vegas photos?"

I shake my head, no.

"Okay. Is an asteroid headed for us that will wipe out all life on earth?"

"It would certainly make things simpler."

"True. But a heck of a lot less interesting."

"And this is interesting?"

"With you around, life is always interesting."

God, I hate that adjective.

"Hold on a sec," he tells me, then gets up and walks over to his bedroom and vanishes inside. And yes, Peter has his very own bedroom, and you have no idea how jealous that makes me.

Still, I don't understand why he suddenly walked off. I can hear him rummaging around in there and I'm beginning to feel a little miffed until he comes back in with a long strip of toilet paper which he's trying to fold into a neat little packet.

"I couldn't find any tissues," he says apologetically as he sits back down next to me and hands me the toilet paper. "And no, you don't have anything disgusting hanging off your nose... I just thought you looked like you might want to have them."

"I'm that obvious?"

"Yeah, pretty much."

Now that I have the toilet paper in hand, my tear ducts finally back down off their threat of opening the flood gates.

"So, does this mean you don't want me crying on your shoulder again?"

"Actually, you were kind of lower than that. More like..."

"Nipple height?" my mouth offers helpfully. I cringe; I can't believe I just said that.

Peter actually looks a little embarrassed. "Um, I was going to say chest. But I suppose the other is technically accurate as well."

We both look down, suddenly uncomfortable. Hmmm, I can't imagine why.

"I should go," I say as I start to get up, but Peter gets up as well.

"No, stay," he tells me. "What's going on?"

"Nothing."

"Nothing? Come on, Gwen, talk to me."

I'm still looking at the floor, so he bends down to get in my line of sight. "I'll bring you some fresh bread," he offers, looking me in the eyes.

"Okay, I'll talk, I'll talk!"

He smiles, satisfied with himself, and leads me back to the couch where we sit.

"Okay then," he says. "So what's the tissue-worthy occasion?"

Since, I can't admit that it's him that's getting me all teary—and yes, that sounds even worse now that I've put it down on paper—I instead explain all about my "solving Dad" seven-step program and my utter inability to get past step one. After over sixteen years, I finally know where he lives, it isn't even that far away, but it still might as well be on the moon for all my ability to act on it.

As I talk, the utter frustration of it all threatens to bring the tears back. So, in some, strange, perverse way, I don't end up completely lying to him about why I'm teary after all... will wonders never cease?

Peter doesn't interrupt me through my entire rant, though he nods here and there at appropriate spots. With a lot of people, that could mean they're thinking about something completely different, like what they're going to have for dinner, or whether their favorite TV show is going to be on tonight, or wondering what they'll have to do to get this girl to stop babbling so they can stop nodding mindlessly. I think I get a lot of the latter, but with Peter, you know he's present.

Well, at his size, it's kind of hard to not know he's present, but I mean you know he's actually listening to you. At first, I found it kind of unnerving, that kind of intense focus, but I'm used to it now and at times like these I really appreciate it. Like they said in the movie Avatar, he *sees* me.

When I finally wind down, Peter looks thoughtful for a moment, then gets up and starts rummaging through an ancient roll-top desk, looking for something. Wait a minute. Didn't he get the whole "he sees me" instruction manual? He's not supposed to just *see* me, he's supposed to respond to me, and I have no idea what could be in that desk that's so important right now.

Or maybe he wasn't paying that much attention after all.

"Well, now that I've got that out of my system," I say, getting up from the couch, "I'll be next door putting my head in the oven."

Peter moves over to an old Chinese style medicine cabinet with a couple dozen little drawers in it and starts opening them one by one.

"That only works with gas ovens," he says over his shoulder. "And yours is both electric and never really comes to temp anyway."

"You're so helpful."

"And while ours does work better than yours, it's also electric, so you're pretty much out of luck."

"I think you're missing the point."

"Aha," he says triumphantly. He turns around, holding up a photograph of the Atlantic City boardwalk at night. For those of you unfamiliar with Atlantic City, it's the East Coast's Las Vegas wannabe. In New Jersey.

I think you get the picture.

"Well," I say sarcastically, "now that you've finally been reunited with your long-lost photograph, I'll leave the two of you alone to get 'reacquainted.'"

"It's not a photograph, it's a postcard. And it's never been used, either."

"The poor thing, all dressed up with the lights and all, and nowhere to go."

"Until now," he says, clearly pleased with himself.

"And exactly what part of my life story gave you the sudden, irresistible urge to write a postcard?"

I know I'm missing something and normally I love bantering with Peter but right now, I just can't do it. "Could you please just tell me what you're thinking."

He cocks his head, just a tiny fraction of a degree, but then I feel him seeing me again and I just want to curl up and hide. I know I'm being bitchy and prickly and all-around obsessive, and he's just being normal Peter and getting crap for it.

"It's for Step Two," he says gently.

A Quick Digression that's Totally Relevant, if not actually Quick.
(Trust me on this one, it will all make sense at the end)

You know about Stonehenge, right? Big bunch of simply massive stones standing up on their ends, many of them with equally large stones as crosspieces extending from the top of one standing stone to its neighbor, creating a kind of roofed circle? It dates back to the paleolithic era, something on the order of 2,500 years before Christ.

Currently we're only a little more than 2,000 years after Christ, which means Stonehenge was already 500 years further away in the past to him, than he is to us. Or to put it in your average Englishman's terms, the thing is bloody old.

It also is mind-boggling to think that some 4,500 years ago (which is way before the Internet, in case you were wondering) people moved these multi-ton rocks from distances upwards of 250 miles away. And then, once they got them there, they stood a bunch of them upright and then lifted a whole bunch more on top. And then, and only then, did they get the pizza and beer.

I can only imagine the proposal discussion.

"Okay, Mr. Grood, it says here on your application you want eighty bluestones, each weighing four to six tons from a quarry in Preseli Hills, in what I understand is someday going to be Wales."

"Yes, sir, that's correct."

"You do realize that this is about 250 miles away, and across the water from your worksite, which I see will be Avesbury."

"Yes, that's why we have that budget item for rafts."

"Ah, yes, I see. And are you aware, Mr. Grood, that I've been advised that even the newly invented Whill won't be..." One of the other men whispers in the speaker's ear.

The speaker looks at the whisperer doubtfully. "Really? But I thought their slogan was 'Where there's a Whill there's a Way?'" More whispering.

"Well, if you're sure." He turns back to Mr. Grood. "I've been informed that it's being called a Wheel. But in any case, with the weight of the stones you're proposing, we've determined that even this new *wheel* won't help you because we have no roads. Poor forethought, as I see it, inventing a wheel with nowhere to use it, but nobody asked me."

"Yes, sir, that's been taken into account. We intend to roll them on logs."

"But really, there aren't any closer large stones you could use?"

"Not that turn kind of bluish when they get wet."

"Ah, well then. Of course."

"And what exactly, Mr. Grood, is your monetization plan for this construction?"

"That's an excellent question. As you'll see on the last page, by our estimates, in roughly five thousand years we'll be able to charge about $20 per head to visitors."

"Excellent."

Okay, so Mr. Grood now has his funding, and he and several hundred of his closest friends drag, roll, float and otherwise transport eighty of these bluestones (each weighing about as much as two full-size pickup trucks) to Avesbury. And those are the small stones. The larger ones come from only about twenty-five miles away, and those are the bad boys of the outer circle and they weigh two to six times as much. Which brings us to the question, how the heck do you lift a ten ton rock fifteen feet up to place it across a pair of other rocks without the use of any modern technology?

In one word: carefully.

There have been, needless to say, dozens and dozens of theories how they managed it, ranging from aliens, to tripod cranes, to burying and then digging out the standing stones, and so on. At some point, however, one researcher actually got permission from the British Heritage Site people to test out his theory of using massive levers to incrementally lift one end a tiny amount, at which point you slip a piece of wood under it to maintain the gain in height, then repeat on the other side. You keep alternating sides and slipping in pieces of wood, basically building a crisscrossing stack of wood underneath the stone until it is high enough to move onto the upright standing stones.

So, this researcher got all his grad students and a bunch of volunteers, and they took one of the lintels that had fallen down and started the laborious task of incrementally levering it up the fifteen feet or so to return it back to its rightful place atop two of the outer circle's stones.

After some days or weeks, they'd successfully gotten it more than half-way up, thus proving it was feasible for our Paleolithic builders to have raised these ten ton stones without the aid of aliens. Which, of course, doesn't actually *prove* they didn't have help from aliens, it only proved that it wasn't *necessary*.

Anyway, once the efficacy of this technique had been thoroughly demonstrated, the British Heritage Site people said something to the effect of "good job, old chaps, we'll take it from here." They then brought in a tried and true building crane to quickly finish the job in good ol' twentieth century fashion.

The crane fell over.

All of which goes to show that sometimes the old ways are the best ways. A postcard it is then.

I take the proffered postcard and look it over. Now that I think of it, it's actually kind of appropriate that it's Atlantic City considering they met in Vegas and all.

"I can really have this?" I ask Peter.

He nods. "You said it yourself: you know his address but can't show up at his door because he lives on a private island, and you can't call him because he has an unlisted number. But you do have his address and if you hurry, the US Postal Service will still be in business by the time you send it."

"But what if he doesn't respond?"

"Well, to quote someone I know: we'll cross that bridge when... well, you know the rest. Also, by sending a postcard, there's no letter to open, it's eye-catching, and he's pretty much guaranteed to read it, so I think there's a really good chance he will. Respond that is."

I'm still not convinced.

"As I see it," he continues, "there are three possibilities. 1) He responds, and then either arranges to meet with you, or he tells you he doesn't want you to contact him again."

"Was that one possibility or two?"

"One. No, I guess it's really two. Okay there are four possibilities: 1) He responds and arranges to meet with you; 2) He responds and says to go away; 3) He doesn't respond at all; and 4) he..." Peter trails off. "Hmm, maybe there are just three possibilities. I was sure there was another one."

"But what would I say?"

"Well, I'd hold off on the 'Dear Dad,' for the moment."

"Point taken."

"I think you just have to make it intriguing. I know, let's paste a xerox of the note he wrote on the back of the Vegas photo strip onto the postcard and say something like: "Your number's changed since that weekend in Vegas. Please call.""

"Don't you think we should mention it was over 16 years ago?"

"Nope."

I wait, but he isn't forthcoming. "Uh, any reason why not?" I finally ask.

"Well, he'll either remember it so it won't matter, or he won't remember it but will recognize his own handwriting and old phone number. And I imagine this will make him curious enough that he'll want to at least find out who sent it. But if you put the year and he doesn't remember, then it might be so far in the past that he won't care."

"Okay. But we can't put my number; what if Mom answers?"

"We could put mine, but who knows what Mitch or my Mom would say if they answer. And even if I tell them what's going on, there's no guarantee they'd remember to give us any messages."

"If I had thirty bucks I could get one of those pre-paid cell phones."

"Or would be thirty dollars closer to buying a pony."

"I don't want to buy my own pony. I told you, I want to be given a pony. But regardless, I still don't have thirty bucks."

Peter suddenly gets a big grin on his face.

"What?" I demand.

"I think I have an idea who might give you a pony. Or at least a cheap, pre-paid cell phone."

Chapter 16
In which I discover that
Mom's timing really sucks.

Peter won't tell me who he thinks my phony fairy godmother might be—and that is phony as in tele-phony, not phony as in, well phony—but he does tell me he has a cousin who works in the copy shop just down the street. The relevance of this is that Peter's sure he can talk this cousin into making a copy of Dad's note from the back of the Vegas photos so we can tape it the postcard I'm going to send.

And since the sooner we get this into the mail, the sooner I can find out whether I have a real live Dad, or if I should just settle for a sock puppet and get over it. I'm sorry if I'm babbling, but I'm stressed because I let Peter take the photo strip with him down to the copy shop.

Away from me. Out of sight. Where anything could happen.

Sure, I trust Peter more than anyone other than Mom, but that photo strip is literally irreplaceable. To date, it's my only real connection to Dad, and letting Peter take it is one of the harder things I've done lately. Sure, intellectually I know he understands how important it is to me, but things happen. What if he's hit by a bus, or a particularly aggressive pigeon decides it's just the thing it needs to finish off its nest? Or maybe his cousin is a klutz and accidentally knocks it into their shredder, or there's a toner spill that covers it in black?

This is why I never do aerobics. I can get my heart-rate way up there just by catastrophizing, and you don't even need a gym membership for that. Maybe I should market this on YouTube like that Prancercize® Lady did, and then I can get a national commercial selling pistachios too. I could call it AeroboPhobics™; fear your way to better health.

In case you're wondering why I'm sitting here planning the Next Big Thing rather than going with Peter to his cousin's copy shop with the photo strip in a briefcase handcuffed to my wrist, it's because A) I have neither a briefcase nor handcuffs, and B) tonight's my night to make dinner and I've got to boil me some water.

Admittedly, boiling water and opening tomato sauce cans are about the limit of my culinary expertise, but I am really quite excellent at both.

And while I imagine you are not terribly impressed by these skills, you obviously have never tried boiling water in my apartment. And if you have tried it, I want to know how you got in, what you think you were doing, and why in God's name you bothered to commit breaking-and-entering just to boil water?!

The reason that boiling water is an art form in our household is that we have a gas stove–though not (as you would know if you've been paying attention) a gas oven. But what makes this stove so exciting to use is that the gas never actually comes out of its burners with quite as much gusto as it was designed for, which means that the slightest breeze can turn your high heat into a wonderful source of explosively asphyxiating gas at a moment's notice.

So while a watched pot on our stove will eventually boil after an excruciatingly long time, an unwatched pot might very well kill me. Just like my mother when she figures out everything I've been up to recently.

"Hey, honey. Are you in the kitchen?"

The sound of me slamming my hand into the cabinet as I jerk in surprise is all the answer she needs.

"Owwww..." I complain to the world at large. And speaking of "at large," Buddha rushes in just then, presumably to see whether I'd dropped anything he'd be interested in eating.

However, seeing nothing exciting on the floor, he decides to rub up against my legs for brownie points, then bats at me as if I were bothering him and leaves in a huff. For those of you without cats in your lives, this may seem rather schizophrenic. But trust me, it's typical and I think I've finally figured out why. All cats are sociopaths.

Mom appears in the doorway, wearing her Katie's Kountry Kitch'n uniform but looking oddly exhilarated, which is not an adjective I get to apply to her very often.

"So, what's for dinner?" she asks, though of course she knows the entirety of my dinner repertoire full-well.

I almost immediately go into my normal spiel of something like "Beef Wellington with a port wine reduction served over baby broccolini sautéed in yak butter," but decide to fake her out with the truth.

"Pasta."

She raises an eyebrow. "No truffle oil or caviar?"

"Nope. Tomato sauce."

"Well, I've got pie."

"Five second rule, or burnt?"

She shakes her head. "Neither. Yesterday's."

"Cool."

The stink of unburned gas tells me the burner's gone out again and I relight it. It bursts into blue flame with a small whoosh, but I manage to avoid singeing my hair and eyebrows, something I've not always been quite so adept at.

When I turn back to her, Mom's still standing in the doorway looking disconcertingly non-exhausted. Don't get me wrong, I'm not saying that Mom still having energy after working two jobs is a bad thing, it's just nearly unprecedented.

"And how much Red Bull® have you had?" I ask her.

"Excuse me?"

"You know, Red Bull®, the energy drink? Or was it triple shots of espresso?"

"Um, neither. Where's this coming from?"

"That's what I want to know," I say, knowing it will confuse her, but instead she looks a bit concerned.

"Is everything okay, Gwen? Did you talk to Peter?"

"Yes, and yes," I tell her. She begins to look excited, so I hastily add "Though not about... the thing."

"Ah. The thing." She sighs. "You know you'll never find out what might happen if you don't take any risks."

"You're changing the subject. I want to know what happened today to make you so..." I look her up and down, trying to find the words to encapsulate her unusual state. But I'm not very good under pressure as we've already determined. Multiple times.

"So... so... this." I finish lamely, waving at her.

"Ah. It's that obvious? My this-ness?"

"Would we be having this discussion if it weren't?"

"Personally, I've always thought a discussion required a topic. And I've yet to find one."

I smell gas again and relight the stove. The water's bubbling sluggishly, which is about as good as it gets around here, so I dump in the pasta, which again snuffs the flame.

"Mom, the topic is you," I say as I relight the stove for about the fifth time since I started.

"And what about me?"

I can't tell if she's honestly confused or if she's just messing with me, and of course both are about equally possible.

"You seem, I don't know, happy or something."

She raises an eyebrow. "We really need to work on your vocabulary. This, The Thing, Happy or Something... You sound like a teenager."

"And your point is? No, don't answer that question. Look, normally you come home and you're exhausted, kind of hunched over and slumpy..."

"I'm not that bad," she interrupts.

"No, really, you are. I mean, I get it, I'm not complaining or anything, but you normally do look like something the cat dragged in."

"You're saying I look like a dead mouse."

"No, not dead. Just one that's been run over once or twice."

"And what do I look like tonight?" she asks.

"I don't know, normal I guess. Well, not weekday normal for you, maybe Sunday afternoon normal. No, maybe even a little happier than that."

She looks thoughtful for a moment. "Well, I wasn't planning to tell you like this..."

"Tell me what?" I interrupt. "Did you figure out how you can go to Yale?"

"No one's going to Yale."

"Someone is, lots of someones. And one of them could be you. Should be you."

"Honey, that door has closed. Let it go."

I have to bite my tongue to stop it from telling her that I intercepted her letter, and the door was still wide open. But I stop myself in time. Barely.

"So what then?" I ask her.

She looks the slightest bit embarrassed. "I got asked out on a date."

My emotion cocktail overflows.

Now if you'd asked me five minutes ago, I would have bet you cold hard cash that my adrenaline glands were pretty much squeezed dry by now, but the jolt they give me tells me otherwise.

I almost blurt out But what about dad? but am saved by the fact that I'm still reeling from the basic idea of Mom on a date, and my brain is shouting so many contradictory things that my mouth can't figure out which of them to say, so I end up just staring at her.

Pretty much every thought you can imagine is racing through my head, struggling to be the defining thought on the subject. What if she really likes him? What if I like him? What if he's a scum but she can't see it? What if he's not a he? What about Dad? Why, now? How can she suddenly start dating just as I'm about to find Dad?

I suddenly realize I've been building a whole sappy movie story in my mind where Mom and Dad get back together, and we move into his castle, and everything is happily ever after. I know this is ridiculous, that it's the plot of almost every bad Hallmark movie out there. But I can't help myself.

"So, are you going to say anything?" She asks me gently. "You know you can, anything at all."

"Why now?" I demand, more forcefully than I'd intended.

"Well... I've been asked out over the years, but it never felt right. Leaving you with some babysitter. Bringing someone new into our little 'us.' But then our talk about Peter got me thinking... and I meant it, I haven't always been the best role model."

"Mom, you're a great role model. I don't think I've seen anyone do a better croissant impression."

She just blinks at me.

"Seriously, Mom you don't have to go out on a date for me."

She laughs. "I'm not. I'm doing it for me. And don't worry, Gwen, it's not much of a date anyway. We're just going out for some coffee."

"Hmmm. So who is the lucky fellow?"

"You don't know him. Just a guy who's come into the restaurant a couple of times. And I promise I won't do anything without your approval."

"So where's he taking you? It's someplace pretty public, right?"

She smiles at me indulgently. "Yes, 'mom.' It's right in Harvard Square, and Katie started raving about it when I asked if she knew it. Apparently, it's known for its single source hot chocolates."

Oh, no. He wouldn't have.

"I think it's called Ella Birdrocks."

My heart sinks. "Burdicks," I tell her numbly. "It's L.A. Burdicks."

Chapter 17
In which life would have been more satisfying if I'd actually wanted tuna.

Mom looks at me, askance, and I respond with my very best teenage put-upon expression.

"Everybody knows it, Mom," I tell her with a pained sigh, my thoughts racing.

What the hell is he thinking? No, maybe it's not really him. Maybe it's just a one of those strange things like when you're wearing a blue shirt and you suddenly notice everyone else wearing one.

"So what's he like? Your date, I mean." I say, leaning against the door frame nonchalantly.

Or at least I would have, had the door frame actually been where I thought it was. Instead, I lean into the empty space next to the door frame, lose my balance at the sudden lack of resistance, at which point my dear friend gravity kicks in and my elbow slams into the corner of the cabinet.

Have I mentioned how much I despise gravity? I mean sure, we need it, or we'd just be dust particles scattered throughout the vastness of space. But did they really have to turn it up so high?

Mom watches my performance with practiced nonchalance.

Sure, she gets the nonchalance and I get a bruised elbow.

She squeezes past me as I cradle my elbow, and relights the stove, which of course has gone out again. She looks down at the pot of water. A bubble breaks free from the bottom and lethargically floats to the surface, releasing its trapped air with a slight sigh on its arrival. Another bubble seems to be thinking about following its compatriot which makes this about as rolling of a boil as we get.

She starts to reach for a wooden spoon, but I beat her to it. "I got this," I tell her.

"Suit yourself."

I stick the spoon into the water and swirl it around as I add the pasta so it doesn't all stick together, then squeeze by Mom to the cabinets. I start rummaging through the Sharpie labeled cans with my head turned away from her so I can safely avoid her reading my all too readable expressions. "So, you were about to tell me about this guy," I say, my voice echoing in the cabinet.

"It can wait until we sit down and we can talk face-to-face. Call me odd, but I like being able to see the person I'm having a conversation with."

Great. So much for that brilliant plan.

I mumble something mostly incoherent—well, even more incoherent than normal—and bang the cans around inside the cabinet as I struggle to decipher their hand-written labels. I have terrible handwriting to begin with and my labeling system takes, well, a certain amount of concentration to use. Even for me.

You should remember that when we first moved in, we very quickly discovered that along with death and taxes, we could also rely upon the inevitability of our resident rodentia consuming any and all paper labels on our canned goods, otherwise known as armored food. In any case, for reasons I have yet to fathom, Mom decreed that the task of labeling them in Sharpie would fall upon my already weary shoulders.

I reasonably pointed out that since neither of us can read my handwriting on the best of days, I might not be the best candidate for the job, and she reasonably responded that this should serve as encouragement to change that. She furthermore made me promise that I would do my best to make all my labels legible. She neglected, however, to make me promise that they would be comprehensible which is why, just then, I pull out a can labeled as neatly as I could manage, ptwomno ghoti.

Which, of course, is the phonetic spelling of tuna fish. More or less.

In what world is that phonetic, I can hear you cry... which is itself pretty amazing given that as author and reader we might as well exist in parallel dimensions, separated by both time and space, our only commonality the information on the paper you hold in your hands. Or iPad or Kindle if you're one of those...

But back to your "in what world is that phonetic?" question. The answer, oddly enough, is this one. Here's how it breaks down. Pt is pronounced **t** as in pterodactyl. Wo is of course "**oo**" as in two. *Mn* has the silent "**m**" of mnemonic, and *o* is "**ah**" as in golf. *Gh* is "**f**" as in laugh, *o* is "**ih**" as in women, and *ti* is, of course, "**sh**" as in fiction.

The upside to my brilliant (yet admittedly not wholly original) spelling is that Mom can only decipher these labels with great effort, but the (probably predictable) downside is that it did not get me fired from this job as planned. I, of course, sweetly offered to Mom that if she'd prefer they be labeled in a different manner, I could relinquish the much coveted task into her tender cares.

Her equally sweet reply of "Nice try, thanks for playing," not only foiled my plan, but left me with a quandary. At this point I could either (a) give in and resort to actually labeling them with whatever passes for standard English spellings (yes, Colonel, I'm talking to you!); or (b) I could maintain my dignity and continue with my phonetics knowing that by doing so I'll end up not only responsible for labeling and shelving the cans, but also for identifying and deshelving them again later, when their contents are desired.

Given that I'm nothing if not stubborn, you can guess what choice I made. Not to mention the can labeled ptwomno ghoti is pretty much a dead give-away. And in case you were wondering, I got out the ptwomneh ghoti because I couldn't find any ptauxmneigptow psalps[3].

Mom sets the table while I discover the last of a bottle of capers in the freezer. As you might well imagine, it's not exactly a typical staple around here but I think she brought them home along with some bagels as left-overs after the last signing at the book store. Not that it really matters. We have them, and assuming the can opener decides to actually work as designed, leaving me with both an open can of tuna and all my blood still merrily pumping through my veins, then I think I'll throw them into the mix.

Much to my surprise, both can opener and can decide to behave themselves and after I drain the pasta (also without incident!) toss in the tuna—sorry, ptwomno—olive oil and all, add the capers and declare it dinner. And yes, I'll be taking pre-orders for my next cookbook, <u>Dangerous Dinners</u>, which will come with bonus band aids and a packet of burn ointment.

After checking for about the sixth time that the burner is now actually off and is not silently planning on suffocating us later, I bring the bowl of pasta out to the table.

"That smells great," Mom says.

---

[3] **pt** (pterodactyl), **aux** (faux), **mn** (damn), **eigh** (sleigh), **pt**, **ow** (slow) **ps** (psychopath), **al** (walk), **ps**.

"It smells like tuna."

"Fortunately, those two statements aren't mutually exclusive."

I stifle my immediate, instinctive response as she's right. I do like tuna, and it does smell pretty good. I just wish we were eating it because we had *wanted* tuna, not merely because we didn't have anything else.

"So..." I say casually as we sit down to our meal.

"So."

"You were about to tell me all about your hot date."

"I was? Oh." She takes a large mouthful of tuna pasta and I have to watch patiently as she chews.

Watching patiently isn't one of my better skills.

"So, is he tall?" I ask, already knowing the answer but praying I'm wrong.

She swallows. "I wouldn't say so, though of course all height is relative."

She takes another bite before I can ask my next question, and I'm sure she's doing it deliberately, dragging it out to torture me just like I'd probably do in her place.

"Is he dark? Handsome? Have anything in particular to recommend him?"

"No. Not classically. And, of course, or I wouldn't bother."

She's lost me, and from her satisfied expression, I know she knows it as well.

"Me, not bothering," she says smugly. "If there was nothing to recommend him."

Crap, the student has surpassed the master.

Sigh. Everything she's said is still consistent with him being Not Dad, but it's also probably consistent with him being a quarter of the men in greater Bostburbia, and I need to know for sure how bad the situation really is: merely awful or potentially catastrophic.

Well, for me at least.

For Mom it might be great... or he could be an axe murderer, I suppose. Which would be even more catastrophic than I'd been previously thinking about.[4]

Mom's staring at me, which means I've probably wandered off into my head and gotten lost in there somewhere. Mom calls it my fugue state. Since I didn't know what the heck a fugue was, and of course I couldn't admit that to her, I looked it up on the Internet once. Merriam Webster's defined it as "a musical composition in which one or two themes are repeated or imitated by successively entering voices and contrapuntally developed in a continuous interweaving of the voice parts" which of course clarified it completely... well, at least the successive voice parts as I do seem to end up arguing with myself all the time.

Yeah, that pretty much sums up my thought processes. Basically incomprehensible.

"Earth to Gwen..."

I blink at her as my focus returns back to the room.

"Where do you go when you do that?" Mom asks, not for the first time.

"I don't know. My contrapuntally developed inner world of continuously interweaving voice parts, I guess."

You know, when I say it aloud, that almost sounds like it actually makes sense. Which, of course, is even funnier as none of that had anything to do with the actual meaning of fugue she'd been talking about, which is something else entirely.

I mentally give myself a kick in the pants. Focus: Date. Not Dad. Imminent Panic Attack.

My stomach, of course, ignores me and I realize that despite my anxiety I'm actually pretty hungry. Since there's coincidentally a big plate of pasta in front of me, I start shoveling it in.

"What's his name?" I ask her between bites.

"Fitz."

---

[4] Speaking of which, what is it about axes and murderers? I mean no one goes around saying, he could be a *gun murderer*, or a *knife murderer*, both of which are probably far more likely than someone specifically being an axe-wielding maniac. I mean, who wields anything nowadays anyway?

Wait a minute! Fitz? That wasn't Not Dad's name; he was David Harry or Don Henry or something like that. I'm feeling giddy with relief. This guy's not Not Dad after all! Or at least not the Not Dad I was worried about. I mean, unless by some strange coincidence he actually happens to really be Dad, he'll have to be some flavor of Not Dad after all, but that I can deal with. At least until I meet my real Dad and we move into his castle.

"So, is he German? No, wait a minute, that would be Fritz... What is that, Dutch?"

"No, he's completely American. He told me it's just a nickname he got as a kid because there were way too many Davids in his neighborhood growing up, and it just kind of stuck."

"How do you get Fitz from David?"

As I ask, a feeling of dread starts creeping up my spine.

"You don't. It's from his last name."

One of the many contrapuntal voices in my head chimes up and says it with her. "Fitzgerald." David Henry Fitzgerald.

How could he do this to me?!!!

I somehow manage to get through dinner and then make some excuse about having to help Peter with a project and flee the apartment. I mean it's true, I do have to help Peter with a project... it just happens to be my project involving Dad, a small rectangle of cardboard, and more hopes and dreams than any sane person would normally entrust to the US Postal Service. But what choice to do I have?

The one bit of good news—well, comparatively good news—about Mom and Not Dad's date is that it isn't until next Saturday. Which means that I have somewhat over a whole week to figure out what to do about it. Not to mention an equal length of time to obsess over every possible catastrophic eventuality. But how bad could it really be if he spills the beans on everything? I mean, I'm already sixteen, the most she could legally ground me for is only slightly under two years, right?

Peter's sitting on the floor just outside his apartment. He starts to get up as he sees me approach, but I wave him back down and plop down on the floor next to him.

"What are you doing out here?" I ask. "Do you need me to climb up your fire escape again and break into your apartment?"

He shakes his head, and I can swear he's almost blushing. "No. Mom and Mitch were uh... well, kind of occupied when I got back. So I thought I'd wait out here until it stopped being so um, Nature Channel in there."

I start giggling hysterically.

I mean, I know it's not that funny, but I can't help myself. I've gotten myself so wound up and when he said that it was like my watch spring suddenly just went SPROING and broke free... and now it's whizzing me around like an unattended garden hose on full blast, spraying water everywhere. Mixed metaphor and all.

At first Peter looks shocked, and I try to reassure him that I'm not laughing at him, but I can't get out more than a word or two before cracking up again, and pretty soon he's lost it too. We are finally coming down from it and I'm catching my breath as the door I'm leaning against suddenly opens and I spill backwards half-into Peter's apartment. Mitch is standing there in a paisley bathrobe looking down at us.

"What's so funny?"

Peter and I share a glance, trying to keep a straight face.

"The Nature Channel," I finally choke out and it sets us off again.

Mitch looks from me to Peter and back again.

"Whatever you guys are smoking, I want some," he says then turns and pads back into the apartment, leaving the door open with me lying half in the apartment, and half out, laughing so hard I almost can't breathe.

The uncontrollable hilarity finally burns itself out, and I lie there catching my breath, staring up at Peter mindlessly. My cheek is resting on the cool linoleum, my normally racing brain content for the moment with the blissful simplicity of a test tone. There's a strange shadow on Peter's cheek and I reach up and touch it without thinking what I'm doing. His cheek is rough under my fingers, though as I let my fingertips slide back down, the roughness suddenly goes away.

It's so strange that I brush my fingers back upwards along his jawbone, feeling the roughness like a fine-grained sandpaper springing to life, resisting the direction of my fingers. But when I slide my hand away, it smooths back down so it's barely noticeable, leaving only the warmth of his cheek on my palm.

His cheek. On my palm.

He's not moving, his eyes closed, and I have a sudden urge to kiss him that's so strong that it almost frightens me.

So, of course I pull my hand away from his cheek like it's a red-hot coal—which it might as well be, the way I can still feel the heat of it on my tingling palm—and manage to only barely miss slamming my elbow into the still half-open door.

"I'm sorry," I stammer out. "I just, I don't know, I saw this shadow and I..."

"It's okay, Gwen."

"I wasn't thinking. I didn't mean to..."

I'm about to start seriously babbling when he takes my wildly gesticulating hands in his and holds them steady between us, the touch of his skin burning so hot against mine that I half expect to see smoke rising between us.

"Gwen, stop. It's okay. Really. It felt nice."

My heart's beating so hard it seems like the floor should be shaking with the force of it, and I suddenly wonder what his cheek would feel like next to mine, that rough smoothness brushing against me. Oh my god, I can barely think with the touch of his hands in mine and his breath so close I can almost taste it.

So I do what any normally psychotic person would do and yank my hands away from him and scramble to my feet. I can almost swear I see a flash of hurt on his face as I pull away, but the next instant he's the same, imperturbable Peter we all know and love.

Oh.

Oh!

"Do you... do you shave?" I hear myself asking him inanely.

"Yeah, sometimes." He looks at me like he's not sure if I'm making fun of him or not.

"Huh."

I wince inwardly at my scintillating wit, and I struggle to come up with something else to say that doesn't sound quite so brain damaged. "I just never thought of you that way... shaving, I mean."

He shrugs, looking a little embarrassed.

"Not every day. But if I don't do it for a while... well, you know."

I stare at him blankly. "I know what?"

"That I start looking like there's a bad fungus on my face."

"Oh. Well, at least your hair doesn't make you look like you've been eaten by a mop."

"I like your hair."

"You also like those hairless sphynx cats, so I think your credibility's kind of shot on the subject."

Oh god, which came out kind of mean and from his studiously blank expression I'm afraid he thinks so too. What the hell am I doing?!

"Uh, can you forget I just said that? I think it's sweet you defending my hair's honor and all. And maybe it is so ugly that it's actually cute... I don't know. I'm just way out of sorts right now. Mom's going on a date."

"Wow."

"With Not Dad."

"Oh. Double-wow."

I realize I'm hugging myself, my hands pressed against a stomach that has suddenly decided to take up gymnastics.

"So, what has he told her?"

"I have no idea," I say miserably.

"Well, then," Peter replies, "it's a good thing we're stopping by his office after school tomorrow so he can explain what the hell kind of game he's playing."

"We are?"

Peter looks at me fiercely. "Damn right, we are."

I look at him and nod. He's swearing for me again...

"Alright then," I say with as much forcefulness as I can muster, and with that, the awkward tension is suddenly gone. He's just Peter, and I'm just Gwen again, two lone rebels against the world. I smile at him. We can do this; I mean who does Not Dad think he is to mess with my life like this?

Peter nods back at me, approving of my change of attitude.

"Now, that's my Gwen," he says.

Oh, if only he knew.

"Hey, I got a birthday gift for you," Peter tells me as he turns and heads off into the apartment, leaving me to trail after him and finally close the door that's been open all this time.

"You do know it's nowhere near my birthday, right?"

He looks at me over his shoulder as he picks up a small, flat brown paper bag from what passes for their dining room table. As he returns with the bag, I reach for it, but he pulls it away.

"This is a birthday present," he tells me seriously, "to ensure that you get your next one."

"My next what? My next birthday present?"

"No. To ensure you get your next birthday."

He holds the bag out to me gravely, and though I take it, he doesn't let go.

"Are you sure you have it?" he asks.

"Yes, I'm sure."

"I'm going to let go now, so remember to keep your hand firmly closed."

"I'm ready. I've really got it."

"Okay, on the count of three..."

"Oh, just give it to me already."

I pull it away from him, and of course the bag rips, spilling its contents into the air between us.

As it falls, I see that it's the frame that had held the Las Vegas film strip, now repaired with a new piece of glass in it, the film strip restored to its rightful place. And it's plummeting to the floor. Again.

For once, my über-feline reflexes do something other than make me violently flinch into whatever the hardest object around me happens to be, and I reach down and snatch it out of the air.

My fingers are just closing around it when I realize that Peter's going for it as well. And then the world pretty much explodes as our foreheads come together with a massive crack. I remember thinking, "I guess I did manage to hit the hardest object around me after all..." and then it gets kind of fuzzy for a while.

The next thing I know, Mitch is standing over me and there's something really cold on my forehead. There's a strange smell that I can't place, and I can feel a thick trickle of blood running down my cheek. I reach up to wipe it away and my hand comes away sticky.

"Shhh. Don't move," Mitch tells me. "Everything's under control."

The room's still spinning around me, and my hand feels like it's just dripping with blood. Oh god, I'm really bleeding. I tell myself not to look, but as you've probably gathered by now, I'm not terribly good at following instructions, even my own. Maybe especially my own.

In any case, I can't help myself. I know my hand's just covered with... what the heck is that?!

I've seen far more than my share of my own blood, and even in my dazed state, I'm pretty confident that the thick, pale yellow liquid dripping from my hand isn't it.

I suddenly realize what the scent I couldn't place is. It's vanilla.

"You put ice cream on me?"

"Not just any ice cream," Mitch tells me. "The last of the French vanilla. So, whatever you don't end up needing, put in the bowl next to you, okay? Waste not, want not, and all that jazz."

He squeezes my shoulder then straightens and wanders off.

As soon as he's gone from my field of view, I reach up and gingerly pick up the big, cold glob of ice cream that's sitting on my forehead and drop it into the bowl Mitch had indicated, then sit up, feeling yet more melted ice cream dripping down my face.

Peter kneels down next to me with a bunch of wet paper towels and hands me a wad, then starts to use the remaining ones to dab at my forehead.

"I can do that," I tell him irritably.

"I've got it," he says, not stopping. "You won't be able to see what you're doing anyway."

I feel like crying. He somehow, miraculously, fixed my Dad's picture frame, and what do I do? I act like the world's biggest super-klutz and break it all over again.

"Ow!"

"Sorry."

I start scrubbing at my hand desultorily, feeling like a complete loser. I flinch again as he rubs the spot where we had our explosive little tête-à-tête.

"Sorry, your hair's just kind of matted there. From the ice cream," he hastily adds.

I don't respond, just blotting my sticky hand with the damp paper towel, not really even looking at what I'm doing.

"Aren't you even a little curious why you have ice cream in your hair?"

I shrug. "You probably didn't have any ice packs."

I still can't believe he did this incredibly sweet thing and the second he gives it to me, I break it all over again. I am such a loser. If I'd had even the smallest chance of... well, I don't know... something more between us, it's gone now. So completely gone.

He raises my chin to dab under my jawbone and I let him listlessly.

"You do know you caught it, right?"

"Yeah, just before I went smack into your adamantium skull."

"That was completely my fault..."

"Only if you blame yourself for hanging around with an Olympic-class spaz."

"No, I shouldn't have been joking around about you dropping it before. If I'd just given it to you instead of teasing about holding on so tightly."

"It doesn't matter. I probably would have tripped walking out the door and broken it anyway."

"But you caught it."

"I know, just before we proved once again that two objects can't occupy the same space at the same time."

"Are you objectifying me?"

Tears start gathering at the corners of my eyes. "At least Dr. Martin'd be proud of me," I say, trying to hold them back. "He's always going on about experiments not being valid unless they're reproducible. And at least now we can categorically say that force times acceleration plus klutziness equals... equals..."

I trail off as I realize I'm staring right at the wooden frame, lying on the floor next to Peter. And Dad and Mom are staring out at me with their big goofy grins. Through the unbroken glass in the frame.

Peter turns to look at where I'm looking.

"What?" he asks.

"But I thought... I was sure that I broke it again."

"What do you mean? You said you knew you caught it."

"Yeah, but when we went *wham*, I assumed it went flying."

"No. You went flying. But you held on. And it's fine, see?"

He picks it up and tries to hand it to me. "Happy Birthday? Uh, take II?"

"No, you hold onto it for a while. I don't trust myself."

He gently wraps my hands around it. "I do."

I look down at it, and although there are some small scratch marks around the nails where they hold on the back of the frame, it looks quite nearly fully restored.

"How did you do this? Where on earth did you get a piece of glass that fit it?"

"Uh, you know Dr. Ohlsen's car...?"

I look at him steadily. "Uh-huh."

"Yeah, I was just wondering. It's a nice color, isn't it?"

I don't bite. "Glass. Origin, thereof."

"I can't answer that question."

"Immoral, illegal or embarrassing?"

"Non-existent."

"So, you're claiming this glass has no origin? It just sprang into being like two atoms colliding and emitting a washing machine?"

"No. And even if that had been my contention, it would have been more like two atoms colliding and emitting a sheet of glass. Which has not, as far I know, actually happened. And it's not," he added, "my contention because something which is not, cannot begin."

I go over the conversation in my head again. It doesn't make any more sense the second time around.

"And we became Buddhists exactly when?" I ask him. "I think I missed the memo."

"Buddhists?"

"What is the sound of one hand clapping, and all that…"

"Ah. Exactly," he says, pleased.

Something which is not, cannot begin. Non-existent glass…

Oh. I tap my finger on the glass and it makes a kind of dull click rather than the sharp ring I'd expect from real glass. I sigh. "So, it wouldn't have mattered if I hadn't caught it after all."

"Possibly not. But it still could have cracked."

"So where did the Plexi® come from then?"

"My cousin from the copy shop had it. He has a little workshop in the back with tons of scrap stuff and he was able to cut it down to size."

"He didn't happen to have any scrap phones, did he?"

"No, but he was able to do this."

He pulls the Atlantic City postcard out of the half-ripped bag where it had apparently remained when we were banging our heads together trying to catch the frame. He turns it around slowly to reveal the back of the film strip neatly reproduced directly on the postcard, with the top picture of Mom and Dad from the other side of the film strip printed right next to it, faded color and all.

"That's so cool!"

"Yeah, he just scanned it in and ran the post card directly through his printer."

I give Peter a quick hug. "You're the absolute best!"

"I know," he replies in his best deadpan Han Solo impression. I smile despite myself, though I try unsuccessfully to repress it.

He does a better job at maintaining his expression, though I can still see the corners of his mouth trying to curve upwards. This of course, encourages me to stop suppressing my own smile so I can make him break the expression he's trying so hard to maintain. His eyes seem to glitter as he realizes what I'm doing, and he fights to keep from returning my smile.

Something which is not, cannot begin.

My smile fades as the words bounce around in my head. Oh crap. He was talking about us.

Get it together, or you're going to start weirding him out completely. "I should really go," I tell him as I bend down to pick up the repaired picture frame, the action conveniently hiding my eyes from his.

"Let me guess, you need to wash your hair, or something."

"You know us girls so well. Stick ice cream on our foreheads..."

"French Vanilla."

"Stick French Vanilla on our foreheads," I concede as I stand, holding the picture frame tight against my chest so I can't possibly drop it, "and the best lame excuse we can come up with is that we need to go wash our hair."

"You girls are just all so transparent."

"Like a sheet of glass. Or Plexi®..."

"That's all I'm saying."

"Okay, you caught me. I really need to go so I can report to my superiors that there's a strategic scrap reserve at the local copy shop."

"Well, alright then. That I can believe."

I know this brilliant repartee can go on all night, so I head for the door and open it.

"I'll see you tomorrow," I tell him.

"Don't forget. We're going to your Not Dad's office after school."

I nod in agreement, then turn and head out into the hallway.

"Enjoy your shower," he calls after me, putting the word "shower" in exaggerated air quotes, his knit shirt pulling tight across his chest as he does so. I try not to look, but his abs are about a mile wide and I still can feel them against me in the quick hug we shared only moments before.

He shuts the door, leaving me standing alone in the hallway.

Oh yeah, I need a shower alright. And an icy cold one at that.

Chapter 18
In which you have to choose whether to finally trust me. Or not.

As the cool water sprays down on me—and yes, we can't even manage to do icy here—I finally let it all out, thick hot tears dripping down my face. I'm not even sure exactly what I'm crying about; it's just an outpouring of raw, unbottled emotion. Probably half-Peter, half-Dad, part Yale, part Not Dad and a whole lot of self-pity.

When the water pressure starts to fail and the volume of my tears begins to approach a one-to-one ratio with the shower's output, I shake myself and tell myself to pull it together. Of course I don't listen. Which is why a moment later I hear Mom softly knocking on the door.

"Is everything okay?"

"Would you believe me," I say, sniffling loudly, "if I said yes?"

"Probably not. Can I come in?"

I shut off the water, not that it makes a huge difference at this point, and grab my favorite towel, the only one that actually has any real fluffiness left in it. I'm wrapping it around me when Mom pokes her head in.

"If you nodded," she says, "I couldn't exactly hear it through the closed door."

I can feel the muscles of my mouth pulling down into a massive woe-is-me frown.

"Do you want to talk about it?"

I shake my head mutely, feeling wretched. I thought crying was supposed to make you feel better and right now, all I feel is more acutely aware of how bad I feel.

"That's a relief," Mom says as she comes in and sits on the edge of the toilet. "I never know what to say, anyway. And there's all that pressure; one wrong word and *bam!* I send you into therapy for years."

I know she's trying to lighten the mood, but I can't even muster a small smile.

"Now, my mother... you know, Grandma," she adds helpfully. "She always used to know exactly what to say. No matter what had happened, she was always ready with a bucketful of helpful advice. Drove me nuts. Absolutely nuts."

"So," she continues, "I guess what I'm saying is that you should consider yourself lucky I'm so bad at this whole parenting thing."

Buddha squeezes in through the half-opened door, just then, his bulk forcing it the rest of the way open probably in the same way that glaciers push aside mountains. He looks around the bathroom as if trying to figure out where the party is, then pads over to my feet where I stand, still dripping on the thin, foam-rubber backed bathmat. The bathmat squishes under his weight and he stops and shakes the damp paw, looking at the bathmat balefully.

"Well, what did you expect?" I ask, admittedly rather pointlessly as his comprehension of English is probably only three or four words greater than the bathmat's.

Knowing this, what do otherwise intelligent people (sadly, myself included) do with this rather self-evident piece of information? Ignore it completely, of course. It's considered absolutely normal to have complex, one-sided "conversations" with animals of all kinds, but say the same things to some inanimate object, like a bathmat, as a random example, and you're headed straight for the loony bin.

God, we humans are stupid.

Back in the bathroom, both Buddha and the bathmat ignore me. The bathmat for obvious reasons, and Buddha because he's completely focused on his new, bathmat-shaped nemesis which apparently needs to be punished for its impertinence.

He stares at it and crouches, revving his hind legs like a bull about to charge, then launches himself at the damp mat. Well, launches might be a bit of an exaggeration as he doesn't actually achieve any air time, but regardless his front paws come smack down on the offending bathmat, his twenty-five or so pounds following.

I can actually see the two small pools of water that start to form around his paws as the foam-rubber compresses, then he leaps backwards, clearly willing to defy all laws of physics and momentum in his rush to escape the hated liquid. He slides across the slick tiles and crashes into Mom's legs, then, of course, has to try and make it look like it was his plan all along.

When he finally finishes his obligatory cover-up grooming, he stalks regally out the door, tail held high and proud.

"I sometimes really wonder what goes on in that cat's head," Mom says, amused.

Why do I have the feeling that Peter says the exact same thing about me?

The next day at school, I am firmly convinced that the building must be accelerating close to the speed of light because the normal six and half hour day stretches out to about three or four weeks of subjective time. Mrs. Beecham spends most of her class warning us of everything we shouldn't do for our father/relationship writing assignment, which is, as I see it, the teaching equivalent of explaining that to carve a block of granite into the shape of an elephant simply remove everything that doesn't look like an elephant.

And given that my father is the metaphorical elephant in this scenario, I am still at an utter loss as to what I'm actually going to write in this paper, the rough draft of which is due in two days.

I also really suck at rough drafts. First drafts I can handle, but only as long as I can polish each word like a fine gem before setting it into the mosaic of my prose. Intellectually, I know it's a bad habit as it makes the whole process take way too long, but I think it's the curse of loving to read. When I write sentences that lie there like wounded animals, I can't just walk away and leave them bleeding metaphors and similes. I can't forge ahead as they dangle from craggy participles, nor leave them sundered into fragments of thought by wayward periods.

If only I liked more than a fraction of what I typically ended up with, the whole process might be worth it. Regardless, I've discovered that I really don't have any choice in the matter. It's just the way my brain works. Or perhaps I should say functions, as works implies a level of correct operation that I kind of doubt anyone sane would use to describe my thought processes.

As evidenced by this complete tangent, of course.

Following Mrs. Beecham, Peter, and I both have French. Together.

As I walk in, I tell myself for the fifty or sixtieth time that he's just Peter and nothing has changed. Yeah, I don't believe it either, but I figure if I repeat it often enough, it will go away, just like global warming.

Or polar bears if you happen to believe in Science.

He leans over to me as I sit down next to him. "Are you ready for..."

Madame Lignedos claps her hands sharply. "Français, Monsieur."

Peter sighs. Although class isn't starting for another eight minutes, once you step foot into the room, nothing but French is supposed to be spoken, and Madame Lignedos has hearing like a bat. That in itself wouldn't be so odd but coupled with the fact that she's tall and reed thin with sharp, bony hands, a rather pale complexion, and a predilection for wearing black... well, it all makes me rather suspicious.

Peter says I'm paranoid and sure, she'd claimed that was a red wine stain the day Michelle had gone home feeling faint, but personally I'm convinced she's some strange kind of vampire who's turned her classroom into her native soil so she can comfortably rest within it, and to whom English is as deadly as sunlight is for her more pedestrian undead compatriots. Which is why I always bring a thesaurus to class, just in case I need multiple English synonyms for "stake."

"Ey too pray por le byuroh de Papapa aprey leycoal?"

I turn to Peter blankly. He's getting a better grade than me in the class, but even I can tell that his accent borders somewhere between awful and downright painful. The problem, although Peter's loathe to admit it, is that he was actually born somewhere in the South, though Mitch and his Mom have never been able to agree exactly where.

Still, the basic story is that when his Mom was pregnant with him, she and Mitch were hanging out on some pueblo in the middle of nowhere. One which coincidentally was reputed to have the finest peyote in North America and where it was even actually legally allowed for religious purposes.

As you can imagine, there were plenty of "cultural exchanges," and Mitch and Peter's mom apparently almost never missed "church."

In any case, about a week after Peter's third birthday, Mitch and his mom were, shall we say, having a religious experience, when Mitch's spirit animal came to him and said that it was time for them to leave and that he'd guide them to San Francisco. So, they all piled into their ancient VW Beetle and drove west until they hit the ocean.

Well, an ocean.

See, it turns out that Spirit Sloths who wear paisley smoking jackets apparently aren't very good at directions. Which is how they all ended up in greater Bostburbia. The aforementioned Spirit Sloth was also apparently part cat as he then proceeded to tell Mitch he'd meant to do that in the first place, and so they stayed. The relevance of all this is that Peter's mom once told me that when Peter started talking a couple of months later, he'd had just the cutest little Southern drawl. I'd never heard any hint of it in his speech... that is, until we started taking French.

"Ey too pray por le byuroh de Papapa aprey leycoal?" he tries again.

I run the sounds over again in my head. Ey too pray... est too... est-tu... pray, prey, prêt. Okay, Es-tu prêt, "are you ready." Por le byuroh must be pour le bureau "for the office." "Are you ready for the office..."

"Le bureau de papa?" I ask, but he shakes his head no.

"Duh Papapa," he tells me.

"Papapa?"

He nods, which only leaves me more confused. I'm sure he must mean "papa" and I don't understand why he's insisting it's "papapa."

I can't figure out how to say, "don't you mean" in French, as in "don't you mean 'papa'?" so I just settle for "not" which is pas and ask him in French "Papapa? Pas papa?"

Oh. As I say it aloud, I realize he's not saying Papapa, he's saying Pas Papa. Not Papa.

He's asking if I'm ready to see Not Dad.

Crap. And I'd so successfully blocked that out.

Not Dad's office is just on the other side of the river from Harvard square, probably about fifteen hundred smoots beyond the end of Harvard Bridge. In case you've never heard of the smoot, it is a unit of measurement equal to one Oliver R. Smoot, circa 1958.

In October of that year, his future MIT fraternity brothers laid him end to end across the bridge, resulting in the bridge's official measurement of 364.4 smoots long (+/- 1 ear), a designation so official that upon the bridge's renovation some twenty-five years later, not only did the Cambridge police department actually ask that the smoot markings be maintained, the construction workers apparently went one better: scoring the sidewalk slabs in one smoot increments rather than the more pedestrian six feet that's usually employed.

What is so particularly brilliant about this story is that some forty-three years later, Oliver Smoot became the chairman of the American National Standards Institute (ANSI), the organization which oversees the development and adoption of all kinds of standardizations, including those of measurement. Really.

If you still don't believe me—even after everything we've been through together—you should know that Google's search engine has built-in unit conversions. For example, if you find yourself needing to convert the ancient Egyptian cubit to medieval European rods—nearly a daily occurrence in my life—simply type something what is 15 cubits in rods? into Google's search field, press enter and away you go.

It works for smoots too.

So, now you have a choice. Either you can trust me and keep reading, or you can rush to your nearest iDevice and test it out.

If I'm telling the truth—which of course I am—then you'll feel incredibly stupid for not trusting me. On the other hand, if I am making this whole thing up—and I'm rather flattered that you think I have the imagination to come up with something like this—then you'll still feel incredibly stupid for having been suckered into checking.

This is called a no-win situation, and it pretty much describes my expectations for the imminent meeting with Not Dad.

Well, go on. I know you really want to check and I'm not going anywhere.

In far more ways than one.

Chapter 19
In which I am introduced to Not Dad's 'Bowl of Balls' and another simple plan goes awry.

Not Dad's office is just as unexpected as Not Dad was, but for precisely the opposite reasons.

Given that Not Dad himself—and no, I'm not going to start calling him Papapa despite Peter's encouragement—looked exactly how I'd imagined a P.I. would look, I assumed his office would therefore follow suit. You know, the quintessential dark and musty room with a frosted glass door with his name, Not Dad, P.I., engraved on it...

It is, instead, a Jewish delicatessen.

I turn to Peter, and he pulls out Not Dad's business card and we double-check the address. Yeah, this is clearly the place. And just as clearly, Not Dad never thought we'd actually come and check it out.

"That bastard," I say, the impact of what this means only now beginning to seep in. "If he lied about who he was, then everything he told me about Dad, where he lived... a private island... God, how could I have been so stupid to believe all that crap?!"

For once, Peter looks like he's at a loss as well. "I believed it too."

"I've got to tell Mom."

Peter looks like he's about to protest, but I cut him off. "I don't have any choice. No way am I letting her go out with this creep."

He nods slowly, considering it. "Yeah, you're right."

"Which only goes to show that being right isn't all it's cracked up to be."

There's a dull pounding in my head as I keep alternating between rage and despair, my emotions jumping from one to the other between one breath and the next.

"What kind of sicko does that to someone?" I demand of Peter, not really expecting or even wanting an answer. "I mean, how seriously messed up do you have to be to get your kicks by jerking people around, playing with their emotions?"

"I don't know."

The pounding gets louder. "I'm never going to find Dad, am I?"

"We're not giving up, Gwen. Even if everything Papapa said was pure bullshit..."

"Don't say that," I snap at him.

"Don't say what? That it was all bullshit? I mean, some of it might be true but..."

"No, not that. Just don't call him... well, you know."

"Oh," Peter looks abashed. "Yeah, sorry. But forget him. We don't need uh, he who shall not be named. If your Dad's still out there, we'll find him."

"How?"

"I don't know. But we have his books, maybe we could send the postcard to him through his publisher. We'll figure it out."

The pounding in my head's so loud I'm having a hard time concentrating on what Peter's saying, and he seems distracted as well, probably by the angry misery that I imagine is written all over my face. He squeezes my shoulder in sympathetic support, his grip so tight it's almost painful, but I relish in it, physical pain to drive out the rampaging flood of mental agony.

"What is that sound?" he says, looking around.

For a moment, I don't understand what he's saying; I mean, how can he possibly hear the pounding in my head? The answer, interestingly enough, is that he can't. And I suddenly realize the pounding isn't inside my head at all.

It's inside the deli.

We turn together, and there in the booth by the window is Not Dad, pounding away on the glass to get our attention. As we make eye contact, he stops and breaks into a big smile, excitedly waving us to come in and join him.

And for the second time in five minutes, my grasp on the situation does a complete 180-degree turn, this time taking my stomach with it.

The little bell attached to the door rings cheerfully as we enter, but in my unsettled state it only makes me want to strangle someone.

I don't immediately see Not Dad as I scan the place, filled with these high-backed, red-leather booths and those hard plastic tables sporting fake woodgrain and thick metal rims that are apparently mandated by law in sandwich shops and delis everywhere.

On the other side of the room is a large glass deli case with a handwritten sign taped to it, saying Daily Deli Special: Schmaltz and Gribenes, each $5.95/pint while they last, with Schmaltz crossed off in a thick, black line.

I feel like I should be relieved they're out of schmaltz, but the continued availability of whatever Gribenes might be isn't exactly comforting. Gribe-ness? Gri-beans? Grib-en-ess? No matter how I parse it out, it still doesn't sound like something I'd like to put in my mouth.

A middle-aged woman in a waitress uniform looks up at us from halfway across the room where she's pouring some guy's coffee.

"Anywhere you like," she calls out.

"How about Yale?" I mutter to Peter under my breath.

"I think she meant to sit."

"Really? And I thought it was the first of our three wishes."

"Over here," Not Dad says, sticking his head over the high-back of the booth almost right next to us. While the rest of the booths are against the far wall, this one is perpendicular to them, butted up against the front window which is why we couldn't see him.

I take a deep breath as Peter and I walk around to join him. At this point, I'm not sure if I should be pissed at him or not, and that in itself is pissing me off. We slide into the seat opposite him along a path on the red leather where the shine's been worn away.

If I had to guess—and I appear to be constitutionally unable not to —I'd say it was probably caused by several decades of butts sliding in and out of it like we currently are, which isn't an image I want to think about too much. There's a warm spot in the middle of the booth's seat, just across from Not Dad, which I'm sure means someone just left. I have a sudden image of Mom sitting in that seat, Not Dad grinning at her the same way he's grinning at us right now.

It is not a pleasant thought.

"I see you have my card," he says, nodding at the card still in Peter's hand. I suddenly realize that under the table, Peter's other hand is in mine, and I have no memory how it got there. Oh crap. Did I take his—which would be embarrassing—or did he take mine—which would be confusing. I mean, if he had taken it, was it just to support me 'cause I'm a basket case, or might he have taken it not just to support me, but to support me and because he actually wanted to?

Well, now it's actually both confusing and embarrassing as I still have no clue how it got there. I should probably give his a quick squeeze to tell him I'm okay and then slip mine away.

I should also probably do a lot of things, but I need the support and it is kind of comforting after all. Also, I really need to get out of my head because apparently I've completely missed the whole opening part of the conversation Peter and Not Dad are having.

"...and I realized," Not Dad says, "that nobody ever wanted to meet me there anyway, because who wants to be seen going to a private eye? If you're suspicious about your spouse, about the last thing you want them to know is that you're investigating them, right?"

Peter nods, so I follow suit as I'm apparently far better at following suits than I am at following discussions when I tune in halfway through.

"So, one day I had this epiphany that I was shelling out nearly twenty-five hundred a month and I didn't need it at all."

"You didn't need twenty-five hundred dollars?" I blurt out, despite knowing that can't possibly be what he means.

Both Not Dad and Peter look at me, confused.

"No," Not Dad says slowly, as if he's trying to figure out what the heck I'm talking about.

"The office," he tells me, still apparently confused by my confusion, which I guess I'll take as a win. I mean, normally I intend to throw people off through my mastery of the art of the plausible tangent, but I'm not proud, I'll win any way I can.

Unfortunately, if I'm being honest, I'm as confused as he is, so it's probably more of a tie. I really am slipping.

"What office?" I reluctantly ask him.

"The one we're not sitting in right now," Peter explains.

Well, sort of explains.

"But who's to say we aren't?" Not Dad replies. "Sitting in one, that is. True, I'll grant you that it's a bit unorthodox—given, among other things, that they will actually put bacon and cheese on a burger if you ask for it—but from an etymological point of view it fulfills all the salient requirements. See, the first written definition we have for the word office comes from around 1560 where it was simply defined as a place for conducting business derived from the old French ofice..."

He grins at our expressions.

"I have this conversation a lot," he adds smugly. "Anyway, Moishe, who owns this place, has been a family friend for as long as I can remember, so I buy his son's little league team their uniforms and he lets me use his mailing address and conduct my business here. And I also buy a lot of matzoh ball soup. Absolute best in Boston. Bar none."

Oh. He's explaining why his business address is a Jewish deli.

"Speaking of which, are you two hungry? When I saw you outside the window, you looked so mad—I'm guessing at me..." Right, detective. "...that I'd have bet you wanted my balls on a platter."

He smiles, enjoying this way too much. "However, the best I can offer are Moishe's, in a bowl."

"How about a candlestick in the conservatory?" I offer helpfully, my mouth apparently feeling the need to babble to cover up my nervousness.

Peter ignores me—which is probably all for the best at the moment—and instead keeps his nonplussed, unblinking gaze fixed straight on Not Dad's eyes. Normally, this kind of deadpan stare really unnerves people, especially when coming from someone the size of Peter, but Not Dad doesn't seem fazed at all.

"What are you doing?" Peter asks Not Dad quietly.

"Offering to buy my two newest client's lunch."

I shake my head no. "We're fine."

Peter looks at me, and gives me a small, sharp tilt of his head towards Not-Dad, silently urging me to do what we came here for in the first place: to lay down the law concerning him and my mom. Unfortunately, however, it seems my stomach's ears had pricked up at the word "lunch" and it wasn't so happy with my refusal. So, it took that moment to growl.

Loudly.

"I think you've been overruled," Not Dad says.

Before I can respond, he calls out to the waitress, who's now seated across the room doing a crossword puzzle. "Hey, Ruth, two bowls of balls for my friends."

She slowly looks up from the folded newspaper, sighs heavily, then sticks her pen behind her ear and walks unhurriedly over to our table.

"You know, you could just wave your hand or try to catch my eye like a normal person."

"Normal's overrated. Nothing interesting was ever accomplished by normal people."

"If you're right, then I'm sure you'll go far. Hopefully soon."

I like her already.

She turns to us, pointedly ignoring Not Dad. "And what can I get you two?"

"Nothing, we're fine," Peter tells her, but my stomach growls again, apparently having its mind set on the matzoh ball soup, even though neither I nor it know exactly what that is. Sure, you'd think it was probably safe to assume it's a soup of some kind, but I know for a fact that a "New York Egg Cream" has neither egg nor cream in it, so I'm not laying money on it.

"You going deaf in your old age, Ruthie?" Not Dad says, waving away Peter's refusal with his hand. "Or should I shout it again?"

"Oh, by all means, shout it out again. If Moishe gets enough complaints from the regulars he might come to his senses and remember that this is a deli, not a half-way house for office-less flat feet."

I turn to Peter and mouth flat-feet?

He leans over to me and whispers "Flatfoot. It's slang for a PI. Even though it's not really."

His breath's hot on my cheek, which goes a long way to mitigate the lack of information he's sharing. Still, at this point, I'd normally glare at him, even though I know that whatever carefully crafted look I'd come up with would just crash against him like the metaphorical wave against a cliff, with about as little impact. But Ruth is standing there, looking at us with an eyebrow raised, still clearly waiting for us to agree to Not Dad's exhortations that we need those bowls of balls, a description that does little to inspire me about the meal.

My stomach threatens to complain again if I don't give her the go ahead, and it's not worth fighting it. So, I catch Ruth's eye and give her a small nod. She returns it and nods, tucking her pen behind her ear as she turns and walks off towards the kitchen.

"You two are really lucky you caught me here," Not Dad says. "I only came in, because I had a two o'clock, and I was getting ready to leave when I saw you two outside. And I see that you've come to the same conclusion that I have, that the best way to contact your father is probably through the good old United States Postal Service."

"How could you possibly know that?" I blurt out, then immediately turn to Peter. He was the one who suggested going to Not Dad's office, he must have told him.

"Not me," Peter protests vehemently.

Not Dad laughs. "He didn't tell me a thing."

"Then how?"

"Well, I know you came looking for me, because you had my business card out. That's pretty much a gimme. However, I can also see the outline of a novel-sized book in the outside of Gwen's backpack. While this could be school reading, all the rest of your books seem much larger—textbooks, most likely—and I'd bet that any novel you'd be reading in school would be so old it would certainly be out in paperback. So I'm guessing it must be one of your father's books."

I must admit it, I'm kind of impressed. Well, I must admit it to myself... to anyone else, forget it; I'm not copping to anything.

"Now, I did my own homework," he continues, "and couldn't find a phone number of him, only an address. And if I couldn't find one, then you kids couldn't either."

"Egotistic much?" I ask, bristling about being called a kid.

"Being realistic. Finding information is my job, and I know I'm damn good at it. Which is why I also know you probably have a major problem with the whole writing to him plan."

Under the table, I clench Peter's hand in shock, nearly biting my tongue to stop it from blurting out yet another 'how the hell could you know that' interjection. Peter meets Not Dad's eyes coolly, giving my hand a small squeeze of support, though now that I think of it, I have absolutely no clue when we started holding hands again.

"Go on," he tells Not Dad.

"Now, I don't know anything about your home life," Not Dad says to him, "but I do know that Gwen can't put her return address on any letter because her mom might see any response before she does. I also know that Gwen doesn't have a cell phone so she also can't give him a safe number to call."

"Oh, come on, there's no way you can know all this!"

So much for the whole tongue-biting thing.

Not Dad smiles in satisfaction but before he can go on, the waitress arrives with two large bowls of soup and places them down in front of me and Peter. I try to ignore them, but the bowl in front of me is only slightly smaller than my head, and it's steaming, issuing the most amazing, mouth-watering aroma.

I glance down and there's a large, pale, dumpling-like ball roughly the size of a small grapefruit, staring back up at me. It's half-submerged in the broth, a pale golden soup with small slivers of carrots like tiny koi, but this pale globe dominates the bowl like the sun dominates the sky.

Yeah, I guess I am pretty hungry, after all.

But I tear my eyes away from my seductively steaming bowl and meet Not Dad's gaze as I have a terrible thought. "My mom doesn't know all this does she? She didn't tell you..."

I trail off as Not-Dad shakes his head no, a smug grin on his face. But I can't let it go. "So, she doesn't know?"

"Not as far as I'm aware. But all this can wait," he says, waving at the soup. "Go ahead, enjoy."

I shake my head, and neither Peter nor I reach for the spoons that are calling out to us like that little bottle with the "drink me" label in Alice in Wonderland.

Not Dad looks from me to Peter, then back again, then shakes his head and smiles.

"Actually, you can figure out how I know all this, if you put your minds to it. You guys start and I'll walk you through it, capiche?"

I nod slowly, my normal inclination to be stubborn being sapped by the glorious aroma wafting up to me. I pick up my spoon and Peter follows suit.

"Okay," Not Dad says as we each take our first sips. Wow. All I'm going to say that the flavor fully lives up to the aroma's promise. Beyond that, you're going to have to get your own bowl.

"So," he continues. "I have several givens."

He holds up a finger. "One. When you called me, you were trying to be surreptitious; you didn't want your mother to know."

I nod, okay so far.

"Two. When I did a reverse look-up on the number, it came up as a home phone. So, what conclusions can you draw?"

Other than matzoh ball soup is extremely distracting? Hmmm.

"Okay," I say, reluctantly putting my spoon aside for the moment. "Well, I guess if I'd had the option of a cell phone, then why would I have used the shared home phone rather than my own, private one…"

"Bingo."

When you think about it that way, it seems obvious. Whatever else you can say about Not Dad, he does seem pretty good at his job. Oh, and he also apparently knows all the best places to eat around here.

"Now, I don't have as much evidence," he continues, looking at Peter. "But I'd guess you don't have a cell phone either because if you did, you're clearly good enough friends that she would have borrowed it from you."

Peter doesn't seem to react but either Not Dad saw something I didn't, or he took Peter's silence for agreement, but either way he continues on as if his supposition has been corroborated.

"Which leads me to conclude," Not Dad says as he starts rummaging through his shoulder bag on the seat next to him. "That you could probably use…" he trails off as he pushes stuff around inside the bag. "I know I have one in here somewhere," he mutters to himself. "Aha."

He straightens and places something on the table. "That you could probably use one of these."

He removes his hand, revealing a small, old-style flip phone.

I turn to Peter. "You put him up to this, didn't you?"

"No, really. I haven't talked to him."

I turn back to Not Dad. "And you want me to believe that you just happen to carry around spare cell phones. Just in case."

"Actually yes. Look, remember that most of my clients don't want anyone to know they've hired a private detective, right? So if they use their normal cell phone then whoever I'm checking out for them might see this strange number or some odd texts and get suspicious. So I give them what Hollywood likes to call burner phones, pre-paid cell phones that we can use to contact one another."

"And nobody ever gets suspicious that someone suddenly has two cell phones?"

"Of course, but the simple explanation is 'Jim or Margaret, or whoever you like, left it in my car or office and I have to return it to him... or her.' In fact, if the person I give it to thinks it's at all likely that whoever I'm investigating will find the phone, I suggest they preemptively show it, tell the story and make fun about how anyone is still using a flip phone."

"And you're just going to give it to me."

"Well, lend it to you. But sure."

I stare down at the phone as if it might bite me. And given that it's one of those flip phones with the hinge in the middle so it closes like a crocodile's mouth, it's not actually completely outside the realm of possibility.

"What have you told my Mom?" I demand, still not reaching for the phone. "And what are you doing, asking her out on a date?"

"Well, I don't remember exactly, but I think I told her she has a really beautiful smile, and I really liked her laugh."

"That's not what I meant, and you know it."

"You mean, what have I told her about you? Nothing."

"And why should I believe you?"

"Why shouldn't you?"

"Really? Are you kidding?"

"No. Come on, Gwen, what have I told you that isn't true?"

I think about it reluctantly, but he's right, I can't come up with anything. I look at Peter, but he only gives the smallest of shrugs, apparently he can't either.

"I don't care, I still don't want you seeing her."

Not Dad shrugs. "That's a pity, because we have a date next Saturday."

"Cancel it."

He shakes his head, no. "Believe it or not, but this has nothing to do with you and your search for your dad."

"Yeah, right."

"Well, aside from the fact that I noticed her because of our, um, business together, I asked her out because I actually like her. She's straightforward, smart, funny, and, you may not realize it, but she's also pretty damn hot."

"Don't talk about her like that!"

"Why not? You don't think she'd like guys to find her attractive?"

"Not like that!"

"Okay," he says, smiling smugly. "If you say so, kiddo."

"Stop messing with her," Peter says quietly.

"I'm not," Not Dad says, holding up his hands in surrender. "Well, not much, at least.

"Look, Gwen," he says gently. "I think your Mom's pretty able to take care of herself. That's one of the things I really like about her."

"You don't get to like her. You just don't."

"That's not your decision."

I shake my head vehemently. "Cancel it or I'll tell her all about you and let the cards fall where they may."

"The phrase is actually 'let the chips fall where they may.'"

"I don't care!"

The room seems rather quiet all of a sudden, and I have the feeling I said that a lot louder than I'd intended to. But I really don't care about that either.

"Gwen, you can, of course, tell her anything you like. But you'll be telling her more about you than about me."

"What do you mean?"

"She already knows what I do. And I've already told her I first came into her diner while I was doing research on a case. I just didn't say which one."

"And how do you see this playing out?" Peter asks him. "No matter what happens, whether Gwen tells her now or later, Gwen's mom is eventually going to find out, and I imagine she'll feel rather betrayed by you when she does."

"True," Not Dad says, looking thoughtful. "So you're suggesting I tell her everything now to get ahead of the story?"

"Don't!" I choke out, suddenly panicked at the thought.

Peter takes my hand under the table and gives it a squeeze. I know he did it this time, but I can't think about it now; all I feel is panic at having the opportunity to finally meet my dad being snatched away from me.

"Just don't," I whisper. "Please."

"I'll tell you what," Not Dad says, pushing the cell phone toward me. "You take this, and you contact your dad and I promise I won't do anything until Saturday."

I nod, suddenly grateful, even though a small voice in the back of my mind protests that this was probably what he wanted all along.

Not Dad takes out a pen and clicks it, then pulls a clean napkin from the table's dispenser. He writes down four numbers followed by a phone number in a surprisingly neat handwriting, then holds it out to me.

"This is the phone's unlock code," he explains says, "so you can make phone calls and read texts and such. And this is the phone number. It has unlimited texts and probably about a half-hour of talk time left on it."

I nod, not willing to trust my voice.

"Alright then," he says sliding out of the booth then lifting the strap of his shoulder bag over his head. He calls out to the waitress as he stands up, ready to leave. "Hey Ruth, could you put this on my tab? And give yourself a good tip as well."

"I always do."

With a jaunty wave in our direction, he leaves, the annoyingly cheerful bell above the door playing him out. Speaking of playing, I know he's just played me like a cheap violin, but all I feel is a grudging admiration.

Man, if I didn't hate him so much, I might even like him.

We borrow a pen from the waitress Ruth, and I pull out the postcard to Dad then carefully write "Call me" followed by the phone number of the cell phone now burning a hole in my pocket.

Ruth offers to give us to-go containers for the rest of the matzoh ball soup but as we can't figure out how we'd explain to our parental units where it came from, we decide to just buckle down and do as much damage to them as we can.

I'm defeated long before Peter is, but he's a lot bigger than me and it's not a contest anyway, so I give him the rest of mine and he finishes that as well.

I feel kind of weird just walking out without paying or anything but Ruth seems cool with it and it's not like I have any money on me anyway. Well, other than my emergency ten-dollar bill and that's for, you guessed it, emergencies. This isn't, and won't be one, unless she runs after us yelling for someone to stop us for skipping out on the bill.

So we leave, and are just a couple of yards away from the deli when I hear that painfully cheerful bell ring followed by Ruth's voice calling out, "Hey, you two. Stop!"

At the sound of her voice, not only do my feet stop, but my heart and lungs do as well, along with probably half the molecules in my spine, based on the ice-cold chill that runs up it.

I have a lump in my throat only slightly smaller than the matzoh ball was as I turn. All I can think of is, I'm dead. How am I ever going to explain this to Mom?

But as Ruth approaches, she doesn't look angry, if anything she looks relieved to see us.

"I think you forgot this," she says, holding something out to us.

It's the postcard to Dad.

Chapter 20
In which time passes.
Excruciatingly slowly.

The tiny rectangle of cardboard bearing the entirety of my hopes of contacting my dad has gone into the dark maw of the post box we spent nearly an hour finding.

It was pretty pathetic actually, the whole dropping it off thing.

For starters, I couldn't put it into the first mailbox we found because it was the wrong shape: a smooth blue cylindrical tower with a single letter slot at the top. I knew at the time it was crazy, but I just couldn't do it. We were going old school with the post office; we had to use one of those traditional ones with that pull-down, one-way entry airlock thing.

Peter went along with it gamely enough, and when we finally found one in front of a used record store (not that there are really any other kind these days), the postcard made the most barely audible *dink* when I dropped it in. Yeah, a *dink*. It's bearing the entire weight of my future, and that's all I get: *dink*.

Typical.

It's getting chilly as we trek back over Harvard Bridge towards the Central Square T Station, which is neither particularly central, nor is it located in or near anything anyone would identify as a square. However, last I checked; it was still stationary so I give it a one out of three.

I make us stop at the 182.2 smoot/half-way-to-hell mark (yes, this exists, and no, I did not paint it there) despite the unseasonable chill, and we watch as the Harvard women's sculling team pass beneath us on their shell, a long, thin toothpick of a boat that seems to sit more on the water than in it.

If you don't know what sculling is, it's a competitive sport where you sit on a "shell" that's little more than a long, flat surfboard for nine with oar locks, foot pads and sliding seats, and you try to become one with your boat so as to row in perfect synchronicity with your fellow crew as fast as you possibly can.

A Novel of Mystery, Love, and of Chocolate that Defies Description

Heady stuff, I know.

The voice of the coxswain[5] drifts up as they pass under the bridge.

"Hammer those knees! Make 'em cry!"

Normally I can't fathom why anyone would want to be on a sculling team, but right now I'd love to be down there with them, making my knees cry so my face wouldn't have to. They all seem so intense, so focused and I'm suddenly jealous. They all know exactly what they're supposed to do, and where they're going. Okay, maybe not the where-they're-going part as all the rowers are facing backwards and it's only the coxswain yelling non-sequiturs about crying knees who's facing the right direction.

But still. They have purpose, and since we dropped Dad's postcard into an apparently otherwise empty mailbox a couple of blocks back, I've felt utterly rudderless, my fate adrift in the hands of the United States Postal Service. I hate feeling like I'm not in control of my life but right now I'm completely powerless to do anything but wait as the fuse of my own personal time bomb burns away with every second that ticks towards Saturday and the Date of Doom.

Not to mention the even more imminent deadline of Wednesday.

Ugh. I have even less of a clue how to handle than I do about what to say to my father if and when he actually does call. I mean, in that case, I figure I'll say "hi" and wing it from there. Which, sad as it sounds, is a lot more of a plan than I have for anything else right now.

I can hear the abacus-like clicking sounds from here as you rack your brains, trying to remember what the heck is happening on Wednesday.

Now if I were feeling less sorry for myself, I'd probably say something snarky about paying attention and make you search for the answer yourself, but frankly I don't have the energy. Suffice it to say that Wednesday is the end of the beginning, the conclusion of the inciting incident, the call to adventure that set me on the path that's brought me to where I am today...

---

[5] For those of you who think coxswain is some kind of Shakespearean insult—thou fetid, timorous coxswain—I must sadly inform you that it's actually a cross between a horse jockey and a drummer on a slave ship who keeps the beat for the rowing slaves.

In other words, the due date of the first draft of that damn father/relationship assignment.

"You're shivering."

I tear my gaze away from the water where it's apparently been stuck for who knows how long. Peter's looking at me concerned, and he's right, I'm shivering quite dramatically. Why the heck am I so cold? It's June for god's sakes!

"Come on, let's get you off this bridge," Peter tells me. "Between the wind and the water it's always about ten degrees colder out here."

Oh good, at least my thought bubble seems to be working again.

When I don't immediately move, Peter takes my hand and pulls me into a run. We dash the remaining 182.2 smoots to the far end of Harvard Bridge, where we have to stop at the light to avoid being run over by the traffic on Memorial Drive, a street so brilliantly named that no one I've ever talked to has the slightest idea what it's memorializing... other than driving like a lunatic, I suppose.

It is a lot warmer here, or it could be that my blood is flowing again from our little run. Or, as Peter still hasn't let go of my hand as we wait for the light to change, it's also possible that the heat from our conjoined palms could be the source of the warmth that's spreading outwards from my chest. I'm afraid to move for fear that he'll realize he's forgotten to let go and will pull away awkwardly, but nothing happens; we just go on holding hands as if it were something we did all the time.

"Why are you holding your breath?"

I flinch away guiltily, in the process jerking my hand from his in exactly the way I'd feared he'd do to me.

"Uh, the exhaust was getting to me," I mumble, and true to my words, a large truck drives by just then and the wind contrives to bathe us with a cloud of its carbon monoxide. I don't even have to fake a cough, lifting my now bereft hand to my mouth. "Yeah, that," I add as my lungs search for more than one oxygen molecule to process at a time.

From his expression, I can tell he doesn't completely believe me but I'm good with that. Plausible deniability is all I need.

The light turns and parts the traffic like Moses and the Red Sea, so I start across Memorial Drive before he can question me more.

Unfortunately, as I do so, a guy in a red Miata with the top down starts to turn onto the bridge I'm leaving, having apparently decided both that red means slow down (slightly), and the "no turn on red" sign is more of a suggestion than a directive.

He slams on his brakes and Peter yanks me back onto the curb pretty much simultaneously, the semi-near-death experience leaving me with my heart thudding like I've been running again.

"Are you okay?" Peter asks me.

I nod, but before I even finish, he turns to the driver.

"Can't you read?" he demands, slapping the sign saying "no turn on red" so hard the pole actually vibrates. From the poor guy in the Miata's expression, I think he's half-afraid Peter's going to turn into the Hulk or something. Or already has.

"Do you know how close you came to hitting her?!" Peter demands of the guy, stalking over to the driver's side of the car. As the guy sees Peter coming, he reaches over and quickly locks his door which is kind of pathetic given that the top's down and Peter wouldn't actually need to open the door to reach him, if he were so inclined.

"I didn't see..." the guy starts to say.

"Yeah, that was pretty obvious."

I'm actually beginning to feel sorry for the guy, who's visibly cringing back into his bucket seat. Peter can be pretty intimidating and right now he's about as mad as I've ever seen him.

"Peter, I'm okay." I tell him, crossing to him and putting my hand on his arm. "You're going to give the guy a heart attack."

"Look, I'm sorry," the guy stammers out.

"Damn right you are. A sorry little..."

"Taxidermist," I interject quickly.

They both turn to look at me. Peter turns his glance into a long, unblinking look, and while he doesn't change expression, I can still see the adrenaline slowly losing its grip on him.

"I was going to go with something a bit... more forceful," he finally tells me.

"Yeah, but taxidermists... they stuff dead animals. What kind of sicko does that?"

"Fair enough."

He turns back to the poor guy in his car. "What she said."

I can't suppress a giggle, and Peter's not looking quite so fierce now that he's having to try and keep a straight face. He gives up and gives me a rueful grin.

"Come on, the light's going to turn soon. And if we're still standing here then, we'll probably have to go through this all over again."

"Yeah, with some other addlepated coxswain of a taxidermist, no doubt."

"No doubt." We start across the road, and he gives me a sidelong glance. "You do know that doesn't actually mean..."

"Yes."

"Okay. Just checking."

In the subway car, we examine the cell phone Not Dad had given me, trying to figure out how to use it. You know, basic things like answering, turning it to vibrate, reading texts and the like. Despite the fact that it's a little beaten up and is so ancient it might actually be retro, this is new territory for us.

I see a pair of college guys giving us sidelong glances from across the subway car, probably about how excited we are when we actually figure out how to set up ring tones. They laugh at something... and from the way they keep looking in our direction, I'm pretty sure it's us.

Well, two can play that game. Or even four in this case.

"Grew up... New Guinea," I say to them loudly in my best broken English, holding up the phone to show them. "Not seen one still live before."

"Yes," Peter adds seriously in an equally thick accent. "Always dead. Kaput. Like antelope."

People in the subway car begin to swivel their heads in our direction, and, as expected, the college guys don't look that happy to be part of our little side show, so they pretend they don't realize we're talking to them.

"In our land, never have Jews." Peter tells them loudly and earnestly as he gets up and crosses the car towards them, looking right at them, refusing to let them ignore us. He gets half-way across when they finally cave and turn to him.

"Sorry, what?" The taller of the two college guys says reluctantly, clearly regretting having ever looked at us.

"No Jews," Peter explains patiently.

"Never Jews," I chime in, shaking my head emphatically, though I have as little idea what he's talking about as the pair of college guys do.

"Sorry, we're not Jewish," the guy says, trying to turn away again.

"No, not Jews. No Jews." Peter insists. "Wait."

He scrunches up his forehead, pretending to search for the right word. Out of the corner of my eye, I can see several of the people sitting closest to us—those who clearly had heard us talking normally earlier—suppressing grins. Always nice to have an appreciative audience.

"No jweesee." Peter announces, happily.

Ah, I see where he's going. "Jooze," I offer.

He nods excitedly. "Yes, no jooze. Have no juice." He points to the phone enthusiastically as we pull into a station. "This one has juice. Much jooze, make strong."

"Uh, okay then," the college guy says, clearly wanting to disengage. "That's great."

"Oh yes," I say matching Peter's enthusiasm. "Is much greatness."

I can see that everyone within earshot in the car is listening to us now, though most are trying to pretend otherwise. The college guys apparently notice it as well, because the one who just spoke to us catches his friend's eye and jerks his head meaningfully towards the open doors. There's a momentary flash of confusion on his friend's face, then he looks back at us and they hurry off the train just as the doors begin to close, barely making it out before the train lurches into motion again.

I turn to Peter. "I bet that wasn't even their stop."

And with that, we dissolve into laughter, several of the riders closest to us grinning broadly as well. Peter takes a small bow to a smattering of applause, then we are swept away into the darkness under the city towards home.

The phone's ringing as I come into our apartment—no, not the Not Dad phone or I wouldn't be so blasé about it—and I rush to pick it up before the answering machine does. It's either Mom or a telemarketer, and I'm hoping for the latter because they're so much fun to mess with.

I don't recognize the caller ID, so I think I'm in luck.

"Hello?" I say. If it were Mom, I probably would have answered it as "Ray's Pizza" or "Sophia's drive-through Taxidermy," but with the telemarketers you've got to start in easy, and then play it out as long as humanly possible. My record is 27 minutes and I know I could have gone longer but Mom made me hang up because she needed to make a call. That woman just has no sense of priorities.

"Hello," a woman's voice responds. "Could I please speak to Karen Pendergrass?"

That, of course, would be Mom.

"May I ask who's calling?"

"Mrs. van der Diem, from the Yale admissions office."

Oh crap. I look around frantically, as if something in the tiny apartment would suddenly come to life and give me some cosmic sign, telling me what to do. Not all that surprisingly, nothing does. Though in the process I do manage to pull the phone off the table, sending it crashing to the floor in a jangle of bells. Yes, it's one of those phones, with those black spiral cords and real bells inside. It came with the apartment, and no, I have no idea how old it is.

"Hello? Is everything okay?" Mrs. van der Whoever says.

"Uh, yes. Sorry, but the... uh, cat knocked over the phone."

Buddha glares at me balefully, but as that's one of his several default states, I'm fairly sure it doesn't have anything to do with me just throwing him under the metaphorical bus.

"Is Ms. Pendergrass there?"

"Sorry. Yes, this is she. Uh... her. No, 'she,' sorry..." Crap, I'm babbling. "Speaking," I tell Mrs. van der Whoever with as much confidence in my voice as I can muster.

There is a long pause, then she finally clears her throat.

"So," she finally says, sounding doubtful but determined to press forwards. "As we have yet to hear from you, I am calling to follow up as to whether you are intending to accept our offer of admission with its attached stipend. You did get our offer letter, did you not?"

"Oh, yes. Indeed. Thank you."

Another long pause. "And may I inquire as to what your intentions are? We have quite a long waiting list and we cannot hold your slot indefinitely."

"Did you not get my response letter?" I ask innocently, despite the fact that it is both (a) a question to which I already know the answer (having intercepted Mom's actual letter, of course), and (b) it's the sort of ridiculous question whose answer is painfully self-evident. In this case, because we wouldn't be having this conversation otherwise.

"No, we have no record of it. Hence this phone call."

"Hmm, that's odd, I know it was put in the mail nearly a week ago."

All true, of course. I also know it was taken out of the mail shortly thereafter, as I was the one who did it, but the statement is factual, nonetheless.

"Well, it has yet to arrive. And time is flitting by, Ms. Pendergrass."

"So it is," I say, just as I hear Mom's keys rattling in the lock.

"You're right," I tell her hurriedly. "I had no idea how late it is. I've really got to run. If it doesn't show up in a week or so, give me a call, alright?"

"I'm sorry, but Ms. Pendergrass, I..."

"So, I'll talk to you then," I say forcefully over her as Mom opens the door. "Thanks."

And I hang up, my heart beating wildly. I feel like I have this huge sign hanging over me, flashing guilty in Vegas style lights, but I try to act nonchalantly as I put the phone back on the counter. I deliberately leave it a little off the hook just in case Mrs. van Snooty-Hoosen tries to call back.

"Who was that?" Mom asks as she drops her keys into this small Tibetan prayer bowl we keep by the door for just that purpose. They're called singing bowls and whenever they're struck, their tone always goes on far longer than it seems like it should. Kind of like my tangents, I guess.

"Um, Peter. From school."

Mom raises an eyebrow at me. "From school? Since when is Peter 'from school?'"

"Not that Peter," I say defensively. "Peter Feldbar. From math class. He wanted to know if I knew the homework assignment."

"So how'd he get your number?"

"I don't know, Mom. Maybe information? How many Pendergrasses could there be in Roxbury?"

"So, you didn't give it to him."

"Mom, he takes Instagrams of his lunch. Not exactly my type."

"I see," she says, taking off her coat and hanging it up on the perfectly good coat rack Peter and I rescued from the same vacant lot we'd gotten my book safe.

"What do you see?"

"I see my beautiful teenage daughter, who has no clue the boys are all falling over themselves to be with her."

I snort. "Yeah, right."

Parents can be so clueless sometimes. And even if she were right—which she isn't—I don't care about all the boys, anyway. Just one.

And he's not falling over anything. That, apparently, is all my job.

Chapter 21
In which I am reminded, once again, that Oprah is not Greek.

I plead homework and open my netbook, in good part to avoid the rest of the conversation. As Mom starts dinner, I embark again on the eternal search to find that sweet spot where I have at least a semi-workable connection to the Internet using the café across the street's unsecured wireless network. Why this sweet spot moves around at all is one of those unanswerable questions like why congress has an 8% approval rating and a 92% incumbency rate. But both facts are sadly true, and every time I want to go online, I have to go dowsing for a signal.

Today, I end up having to perch the netbook on the very edge of one arm of my futon sofa/bed-from-hell which makes typing without sending the netbook crashing to the floor a challenge to say the least. Furthermore, now that I've finally got the connection, I'm not actually sure why I need it. Habit I guess, as what I really need to do is stop procrastinating and actually start working on my wretched father/relationship writing assignment. My earliest recollection of me and my dad doing something together.

Yeah, right. Kind of hard to write about an event that hasn't happened. Okay, I suppose that's actually the definition of fiction, but fictionalizing a real person seems like it would make him feel less real in my real life. Like when people don't want to talk about how well things are going because it might jinx it.

Except backwards. And slightly convoluted. Okay, very convoluted.

Out of the corner of my eye, I watch Mom as she slaves away over a hot salad bowl. And yes, she's actually neither slaving nor is the bowl hot, but I know she's exhausted and I'm trying to make a point. It's just not fair that she has to work so hard for so little. She's given up so much for me and all she gets from it is me sneaking around behind her back and lying to her.

I feel a nearly overpowering urge to lay it all out right then and there just to get it off my chest, but it's the near that stops me. By definition. I mean, had it been an overpowering urge, I wouldn't have been able to resist it, given its overpowering-ness and all.

But it was only nearly, so I clamp my lips tight and tell myself yet again that I'm doing this for her.

I don't think I'm lying to myself, but I'm sure all self-deluding people think this way, so that train of thought isn't really all that comforting.

A tear slips out of the corner of my eye and I wipe it away before Mom can see it. I don't even know what the tear's for, which is a kind of sad statement in and of itself. Nor do I have any idea how it got to the outside corner of my eye to leak out of, given that my tear ducts are in the corner near my nose, and for it to exit where it did seems to require it to defy gravity by going up to the far corner. My tears, however, are impervious to logic, and another one follows the first, probably just to rub in the fact that it could.

Sigh.

I force myself to open my word processor and then spend the next five minutes staring at the cursor going blink.

Blink.

Blink...

I keep telling myself to write something, anything, but my mind's a blank on the whole father / memory subject and I end up instead trying to synchronize my own blinks so that when the cursor's visible my eyes are closed, and when it's invisible I'm looking at the screen. If I could time it just right the cursor should disappear entirely, but it's remarkably hard, despite the regularity of the cursor's blink cycle.

"Are you okay?"

Yeah, that probably looked pretty weird.

"Just having a massive case of Writer's Block," I tell Mom.

"Well, you're in luck. Dinner's pretty much ready."

Relieved more than I'd like to admit, I put my netbook aside, then get up and clear the table, a process which consists mostly of combining the myriad stacks of mail and school work that perpetually live there into one tall, precarious stack at the far end that towers over us like our own little leaning tower of Pisa. But without the tourists, of course.

Mom's chopping a broiled chicken breast into small, bite sized pieces as I grab a pair of plates and some forks. Ah. She's making Salade César de poulet à la poisson. It's one of my comfort foods, which of course makes me uncomfortable because I can't think of any specific reason why I'd need a comfort food right now. Well, at least anyone that she should know about.

Great, another shoe about to drop. At this rate, I'll have more than Imelda Marcos. Shoes, that is.

And no, I'm not going to explain who Imelda Marcos was, nor why she will forever be associated with shoes; that's what they invented Wikipedia for. Or, for that which they invented Wikipedia, if you're one of those people. And you know who you are.

By the way, in case you aren't fully versed in French Cordon Bleu cuisine, Salade César de poulet à la poisson is our name for Caesar Salad with Chicken. And goldfish instead of croutons. When I was a kid, this was my absolute favorite dinner and it was always the go-to choice for birthdays. In addition to it being rather tasty, its other great appeal is that it's always my job to scatter a school of goldfish over the salads and cry "Oprah!"

Yes, I've since learned that it probably was supposed to be "Opa!" like they said in that old movie <u>My Big Fat Greek Wedding</u>, but what do you want? I was about four and knew a lot more about Oprah than I did about untranslatable Greek exclamations. And Mom has copped to thinking it was so funny she just went with it.

In any case, she puts down the salad bowl, serves us both large portions and hands me the bag of goldfish. She's managed to get the Parmesan ones for tonight, which is a particular treat as we often can't find them at our local store. I grab a big handful and we cry "Oprah!" together as I scatter them across our salads. Several of them miss and go whizzing across the table onto the floor but that's part of the tradition as well. At our cry, Buddha goes chasing after them, batting them across the slick linoleum.

You wouldn't think a cat would be interested in crackers, even if they are fish shaped, but Buddha's in heaven with them. Food that he gets to toy with, and pounce on, and which go crunch... what more could any feline want?

Other than opposable thumbs, of course.

"So, what's the occasion?" I ask warily, deciding for once to take the bull by the horns.

"Why do we need an occasion?"

I give Mom the really-do-we-have-to-play-this-game look that I'm far more often on the receiving end of, and she grins guiltily.

"I'm that transparent, am I?"

"Well, I wouldn't want you standing between me and a television, but yeah, basically."

"I don't know, you've just seemed edgy lately. I thought you could use a pick-me-up."

I shrug noncommittally and slather on way too much Caesar dressing, but hey, that's kind of traditional as well. I take a big bite to avoid responding as I know better than to talk with my mouth full. At least when it suits me.

"It feels like we never talk anymore," Mom tells me.

I swallow. "We're talking now."

"So, what's happening at school?"

"You know, stuff."

"Uh, could you be more vague?"

"Sure. Stuffy-stuff."

She doesn't respond for a moment, just staring at me as if hoping I'll cave in and actually say something with some content. But I simply eat, despite the guilt clenching my stomach. Finally, she sighs.

"You know, just because we're facing each other and vibrations are coming out of our throats in a semi-give and take fashion does not mean we're actually talking."

"Yeah, I know," I say in a small voice.

"So, what's going on with you?"

"I don't know."

"Try."

I shovel another big bite into my mouth and chew slowly, which is something you're apparently supposed to do anyway. One guy back in the 1800s insisted you should chew each bite one hundred times, apparently so you could turn even the most delightful thing into a mess of hot mush in your mouth. Yeah, really good plan.

I swallow and realize that another good plan would have been to use all that excellent delaying time thinking about what I should say rather than analyzing the delaying tactic of chewing slowly. I really need to think things through more.

I decide I should tell the truth. Astonishing, I know.

"For one thing," I say, "it's the whole stupid father writing assignment thing; knowing he's out there somewhere... all that."

Well, I never said I'd tell the whole truth.

"And I keep on thinking about this Yale thing... there's got to be some way we can..."

"Gwen, we can't. I told them to give it to someone else, you know that."

She's right, I do. But somehow hearing her say it aloud sends a wave of panic crashing over me. Which is particularly stupid as (a) I already knew that was her plan, which is why I intercepted the letter in the first place; and (b) I literally just got off the phone with Ms. Van der Hoozen who clearly hasn't yet given the opening away.

My body, however, reacts like this is some new horrible news, rather than the old, messed up, horrible news it really is. Great going body, thanks for paying attention.

"Do you want me to talk to your teacher?" Mom asks.

"What? About Yale?"

"No," she says patiently, "about giving you some leeway on the writing assignment."

I shake my head. "That will just make things worse."

"Thanks for the vote of confidence."

"Trust me, as much as she hates us kids, she hates parents telling her what to do only slightly less than she does being told what to do by the school board."

"And you know this how?"

"She rants, Mom. She rants."

"Lovely."

She looks thoughtful for a moment.

"You know," she tells me, "while I'm not particularly a fan of lying, you could just write about your earliest memory of doing something with me and say it was your dad."

I raise one eyebrow quizzically.

Admittedly, my other eyebrow goes up along with it but that wasn't my choice, and I refuse to be held responsible for miscreant eyebrows.

"Given the situation," Mom continues, "I think your sanity—and thus indirectly mine—is worth more than meeting the exact terms of a ridiculous assignment given by a rather ridiculous teacher. And remember, you did call me Dad for nearly a whole month when you were about four and you decided you wanted a dad like all the other kids."

"God, I was so cute."

"Yeah, what happened?"

I roll my eyes because I know it's expected of me and I do so little of that, I figured I might as well give it a try.

Well, it didn't kill me. I'll give it that.

Which is good as it still leaves Mom the chance to do it later when this whole tangled mess blows up in my face, as I know it inevitably will. And I owe her at least that, right?

Chapter 22
In which I discover religion.

As I said, I couldn't really argue with Mom's logic vis-à-vis the whole sanity versus assignment conundrum... and you know it's a cold day in heck when I can't argue with something, much less admit to the fact. And yes, I could have just as well said hell—I'm not seven and I do know how to swear, at least in the crude Anglo-Saxon way we do it now—but Mom once commented to me how swearing in television and books and movies is often just lazy writing.

I didn't understand at the time so she showed me this brilliant scene in the play Cyrano de Bergerac, where a noble tries to insult Cyrano by telling him he has a big nose, which he does, of epic proportions, in fact. But rather than being insulted, Cyrano critiques the insult and makes a mockery of the man by proceeding to offer several dozen far more colorful and witty insults the man could have made.

No one teaches kids how to swear creatively anymore. It used to be a real art form whose *o' so lofty heights / turn our "fucks" to lowly slights*. I mean, really, what are they teaching kids nowadays?

Oh right, they're having them write stories about their non-existent memories of functionally non-existent fathers. Or they would be, if I could ever start the thrice-cursed, hag-ridden thing.

As I stare at the blank page I tell myself in my most reasonable thought-voice that Mom's suggestion of just taking a memory of her and casting it onto some fictitious father is the simplest way to approach the problem. And if you've learned anything about me at all, you know that rule bending is one of my fortés and I'm not above casual lying if the cause is just.

But somehow, I just can't do it.

Dad... the image of my Dad... has been this pristine thing in my life. A blank slate of a mystery; one of the few constants I've ever had. And I just can't bring myself to start sullying the purity of my non-memories of him... especially not just to satisfy the unreasonable, borderline-sadistic demands of Mrs. Beecham.

And then I have a religious epiphany. Literally.

Our father, who art in heaven...

Our father who art in heaven.

And I know what I'm going to do. I'm going to write a "memory" of the first time I heard the voice of God, our father, talk to me. It's perfect, and just about as true as anything else I'd write for this stupid assignment.

It all comes to me in a flood, his voice telling me to do things, warning me of the demons running the Texaco Gas Stations. You know, all the standard stuff.

Not that you should need the Voice of God to tell you about the demon situation at Texaco. I mean, hasn't anyone looked at their logo recently?

Um, pentagram anyone?

Hello, people! They walk among us.

You know, this is going to be fun, something I never thought I'd say about any of Beecham's little pointless tasks she periodically sets us to do, much less this one.

And hey, if I end up having to go in for psych evals, that'll just be gravy.

I watch Peter's face as he reads my opus on the T as we ride it to school the next day.

Anyone who didn't know him would think he was completely expressionless, but I know better. He is the definition of deadpan—and no, don't make me go correct Wikipedia again—but there's this thing people do called *micro-expressions* where just the corner of their mouth twitches into a smile or a frown or something, but they do it so briefly that you pretty much need a high speed camera to see it.

Or me, of course. At least in Peter's case.

And from his M.E.'s, I know I've found my audience.

He flips over the last page and carefully straightens the sheets like it was some precious ancient manuscript, you know, the kind you have to wear pristine white cotton gloves to touch so the oils in your skin won't damage the pages?

Wrong! There aren't any books or manuscripts which you should wear white cotton gloves, or gloves of any kind, to handle. Well, perhaps the <u>Twilight</u> series, but that's for different reasons entirely. See, the whole white-glove thing is a modern myth (probably started by the vast, shadowy forces of the cotton conglomerates) and basically the gloves do nothing that a good hand washing won't do... well, other than deadening your sense of touch to near leper-like levels, which in turn makes it actually harder for you to handle books gently and makes you more likely to cause physical damage.

Don't believe me? Try going to the medieval manuscript room at the British Library wearing a pair of white cotton gloves and see if you don't get tackled by a burly librarian. Or just look it up on their website, your choice.

But if you do choose the whole London/library thing, (a) I hate you because I would kill to go to London, and (b) have a friend bring a video camera so the rest of the world can enjoy watching you get manhandled by medieval librarians.

"You do know you're completely unhinged."

I nod happily as he glovelessly hands me back my paper.

"Still, what's she going to do," I say. "It's not like she can challenge me on it, or I'll claim religious persecution and have my lawyer insist the trial gets moved to Salem."

"Last I knew, high school grades weren't a trial by jury kind of thing."

"Peter, Peter, Peter. Have some faith in the system."

"You mean the same one which I give a fifty-fifty chance of locking you up in a windowless room somewhere? You know, in a shirt with those really long sleeves."

"Fifty-fifty?"

"Uh-huh. It'll either happen or it won't. That's fifty-fifty."

"Yeah, that's exactly how statistics works."

"Statistics are overrated anyway. You do know that nearly 63% of them are just made up on the spot, right?"

"100% if recent company is any indication."

"True, but it had to be said."

"Some things do. I'm not sure that was one of them, but I'll let it slide."

"You're too kind."

"Don't I know it."

I put away my unexpectedly not god-forsaken father essay, and we sit in companionable silence, which is another thing Peter does extremely well. He's not one of those people who has to fill every second with talk... and much as you might expect me to be, I'm not either. Now, I can't turn off my mind, so the whole stillness of being thing that Peter seems to achieve is not exactly on the agenda, but I'm okay being with my own thoughts. It's not like I don't have enough of them to pass the time.

True, eventually my stream-of-consciousness does pretty much becomes a river-of-consciousness, and after that it's generally not long before it overflow its banks and I have to reduce the pressure by verbalizing some of it. But I can go for a good ten minutes or so and I like just being with Peter.

His leg is pressed up to mine and with the jostling of the subway car I've fallen a little against him. The heat of his body is making my heart beat faster. I consider maybe letting my hand fall against his the next time the subway car gets a good rattle on, but in the meantime, I just close my eyes and sink up his heat.

The next thing I know, I'm jumping out of my seat, in the process slamming the back of my hand against one of the support poles next to us. "Ow!!!!"

Everyone turns to look at me.

"Sorry... I'm okay," I say cradling my throbbing hand. "I just... no, never mind. Sorry if I startled anyone, but really, I'm okay..."

They all go back to their iPhones, a few of them looking like they don't quite believe me. And I can't blame them because I'm not sure I believe me either, because I have absolutely no idea what set off my über-cat-like reflexes from hell.

Peter, of course, was the one person in the car unperturbed by my sudden imitation of an ejection seat. Like Mom, Peter's learned that unless there's blood or I'm screaming for more than a couple of minutes it's probably just business as usual for me.

And sadly, more often than not, it is.

"I have no idea why I just did that," I tell him in an intense whisper as I sit back down.

"Because you're the Gwen we know and love," he tells me patiently. "Is your hand okay?"

I look down at it and there's a big red welt across the back but otherwise everything seems to be in working order. I feel a little annoyed that he doesn't seem to care why I probably just took a week off the lives of everyone else in the subway car with my sudden seat catapulting.

"You know," I tell him, "I don't just normally spaz out for no…"

This time I manage to tense up and keep myself from another wild spasm of flailing limbs but it's a close call and I manage to bite my tongue in the process. Ow!!!

Peter actually begins to look concerned.

"It was like an electrical shock…" I tell him. "Right in the middle of my chest."

I have a horrible thought. "I'm too young to have a heart-attack, aren't I? I mean, I've been really stressed…"

He ignores my question and takes my hands and looks me in the eyes.

"Where does it hurt?" he asks me, his voice calm though I can see that his eyes aren't quite as confident as his vocal cords.

"It doesn't really hurt… more like an electrical shock. And it's about… here…"

I pull my right hand from his and tap the lower part of my sternum, right under my breasts.

My fingernail clicks metallically against my shirt.

And then I very nearly do have a heart attack.

Chapter 23
In which I discover the downside of yet another brilliant plan.

I can't breathe.

I yank my other hand away from Peter and put them both where I'd just touched.

I wait a second, then it happens again and I can feel my whole body vibrating.

"Oh my god," I whisper, my voice hushed in awe. "It's Him. He's calling me."

Peter sighs. "Nice. Good act for your "God is my father" paper..."

"No, you idiot. Not Him..." I say, pointing at the ceiling. "HIM."

Crap. Why did I have to wear one of those pull-over, button-in-the-back shirts today?

I start frantically pulling the bottom of my shirt out of my jeans, ignoring the people around me. Peter clearly thinks I'm really losing it and tries to grab my hands again to calm me down but I yank them away.

"Back off!" I tell him, lifting my shirt to get to the bottom of my sports bra. It's one of those ones with a really thick lower band and I dig out the phone Not Dad gave me. It's warm from the heat of my body and as I pull it out, it vibrates again.

For once in my life, I don't freeze, staring at it transfixed like a deer-in-the-headlights, or a teenager at an iPhone. Yeah, I know, go me.

Nope, this time I actually manage to conquer my fears because I know if I don't, he'll hang up and that might be the end of it. So I flip open the phone still vibrating in a silent ring, my whole body buzzing along with it.

"Hello?" I say, with only the very smallest edge of a quaver to my voice.

There's a moment of pregnant silence, then I hear a click and a man's voice at the other end.

"Hey Gwen, is Peter there?"

For a moment they're just sounds in the air. I know they should be communicating something, but I can't assemble any meaning out of them. When they do finally coalesce, it's like a supersaturated solution where you drop in one small seed crystal and the whole thing just crystallizes at once. What the hell? Why does Dad want to talk to Peter? Doesn't he want to talk to ME?

"Gwen?" the voice in the phone says again, though it sounds like it's coming from the bottom of a really long tunnel. Or that could be due to the fact that the world seems to be going somewhat black around the edges.

"Oh Christ," the voice continues. "You didn't think I was your father, did you? Didn't you see my name on the caller ID?"

I don't even look at the phone, I just hold it out for Peter who's looking at me with an intensity that pretty much exactly mirrors the numbness which has wrapped itself around me.

"It's for you," I tell him. Or at least someone tells him, and I assume it's me because my hand seems to be the one still holding the phone.

He doesn't move to take it. "What?"

"It's Not Dad. And he wants to talk to you."

He takes it from me and that's pretty much last thing I really remember, as my consciousness collapses into the black hole of my misery.

We spend the rest of the day riding from one end of the T then back to the other one, my mind about as devoid of thought as I think it's ever been. In the back of my head, a small part of me realizes that Peter's still sitting quietly next to me and that we've ditched school, but I can't muster up enough feeling to care either way. I think Peter tries to talk to me, now and again, but I don't respond.

At one point an MBTA guy comes over to us and Peter talks to him quietly for a while and then he goes away. But it's like everything is in my peripheral vision; none of it impinges on me, people come, people go, the doors opening and closing like slow gills on some giant fish.

I must have fallen asleep at some point because the next thing I know, Peter's shaking me gently. "Our stop's coming up," he tells me. "And it's nearly six, your Mom's going to be worried if we don't get you home."

For a second, I don't know where I am, then it all comes crashing back and I pull away from Peter, even though I know I'm being completely ridiculous. But I can't look at him right now. I know he's not to blame for the phone call, but I can't help but feeling like he's betrayed me, that he's somehow stolen what should have been mine.

"Okay," I tell him, getting up and heading for the door on the other side of the still moving car.

Only problem is, you know how we've just spent the whole day sitting in the T? Well, even if you've forgotten, my legs haven't, and they remind me of that fact by nearly collapsing under me with that wonderful shooting pins and needles sensation you get when they're completely and utterly asleep. I grab the pole next to the door, and fortunately there's no one sitting right there so I'm able to more or less gracefully collapse into the seat. Graceful being a relative term, like hills and mountains and time.

Peter doesn't say anything as I grimace, massage and stamp the worst of the sleep out of both of my legs. By the time the doors actually open at our stop, I'm able to limp/shuffle my way out of there though I feel like the Little Mermaid with the grace of a zombie. And not the Disney® mermaid mind you, the real Hans Christian Anderson one with the walking on knives and all that.

Fortunately, Peter grabs my backpack or it would have been gone. I don't even want to think about what that would have meant for me. I have enough emotional baggage that I can't dwell on nearly losing the one piece of physical baggage I have to lug around. Not to mention, of course, that Dad's books are in there.

We reach the foot of the stairs heading up to the street and Peter asks if I want to take a break but I just grimly head on up them. I feel like I caught him with some other girl, which I know is patently unfair in so many ways, not least of which is that he isn't my boyfriend. But my slowly churning emotions aren't exactly listening to logic, which I guess makes sense as that's pretty much the definition of emotions anyway.

As we approach the apartment building, Peter stops me and holds out the treacherous Not Dad phone.

"I didn't think you'd exactly want me to put it back."

I'm not sure that I want to put it back, but it really is the best place to always keep it close by without Mom finding out, so I grunt noncommittally and take it from him.

"Gwen, I'm really sorry that he..."

"I don't want to hear about it."

"I know, but..."

"Just drop it, okay?"

He does, though he looks about as miserable as I've ever seen him. I put the phone away and tuck in my shirt then hold out my hand for my backpack which he's apparently carried all the way up from the T. He reluctantly hands it over but doesn't let go immediately.

"Are we okay?" he asks.

"Well, since I'm not very okay right now, I don't see how we could be. By definition."

He looks crushed but lets go of the backpack and takes a step back. I know I'm being a bitch, but I can't stop myself. My heart feels like it's inside some kind of industrial press, steel plates squeezing it tighter and tighter until it can't even beat. I want to hit him, I want to scream at him, I want to kiss him, I want him to hold me as tightly as that press is holding my heart...

So, of course I do none of those, but instead turn and flee into our building as if I could somehow outrun everything that's going on. God, I am such an idiotic coward sometimes.

Mom's not home when I get in, and there's a note on the table reminding me that she's taking her friend Sheila's shift at Katie's Kitch'n, so I'm on my own for the night. As I don't remember her ever telling me about it, I'm not sure I can really credit it as a reminder per se but those were her words, not mine, so you'll have to take it up with her if you care that much about it. Me, I really couldn't care less.

Not about her not being here—though now that I'm thinking about it, it's probably all for the best, right now—no, I mean I couldn't care less about reminders which aren't, which probably says a lot about my frame of mind. In fact, you could probably even say "I could care less" to me right now and I still couldn't care that you just said the exact opposite of what you think you said.

The note goes on to tell me about some left-overs in the fridge, but the very thought of food makes my stomach go all queasy.

Buddha apparently doesn't share that feeling as he comes out of nowhere and rubs up against my legs, meowing plaintively. He still hasn't figured out that Mom and I are able to communicate, at least as well as any teenager and mother can, and she's warned me in the note not to believe him if he insists he hasn't been fed. I point this out to him and even show him the note, but he's predictably unimpressed.

I shrug at him, lifting my empty hands to show I have nothing to give him, and he gives one last plaintive meow and then swipes halfheartedly at me and stomps away.

None of it means anything; it's just the same dance we've done a million times before and I realize I'm just running on auto-pilot, playing my part of this ritual paw-de-deux with as little awareness of my actions as he probably has. It just feels all so pointless: this, my life, everything.

There's a loud creak as Buddha manages to pull a good six inches of my futon-from-hell down off its frame onto the floor, nearly crushing himself as he does so. He's fallen onto his back, half under the edge, his claws stuck in the ragged cotton batting. Yes, once again, he's muffed the staggering high six inch leap onto the futon, but this time he's managed to get a good enough grip to pull it down with him.

He untangles himself and twists out from under it before I reach him, then gives me a disdainful glance, the one that says "why are you watching me? I meant to do that all along," then daintily climbs up onto the slumped futon, every step sounding like Velcro being ripped open as his claws dig into the already well frayed cotton covering. He settles down smack dab in the middle of the trench but seems perfectly happy to be sinking into that vile cleft, a fate I generally wouldn't wish on anyone. What cats find comfortable is often rather at odds from what you'd expect.

I realize I'm frowning, the corners of my lips apparently being pulled down by a mysterious excess of gravity so strong my face muscles are actually beginning to hurt. I can't fight its downwards pull and I sink down along with it, slumping across the sprawled futon.

And then the floodgates open, sobs wrenching from me.

I don't know how long I cry for, my tears soaking the futon, but when I eventually stop, there's a huge wet spot under my cheek and my eyes are burning from the effort.

You know how everyone tells you how much better you'll feel after crying? Yeah, well I feel like I literally have the weight of the world on my shoulders, pressing me helplessly down into the sodden cloth.

"Buddha, get off me!"

I squirm and he leisurely stands up, which of course just transfers all of his weight onto the few square inches of paw digging into my back. I can feel him standing there, stretching, in no hurry to go anywhere despite the increasing volume of my groans. Finally, I manage to knock him off balance and push him the rest of the way off. He gives me a baleful glare then stalks off, his tail held regally upright.

Now that I can breathe again, I guess I do feel a little better. I also realize that sometime in the middle of that crying jag, I've come to a decision. All of this lying, this skulking about... the lying... it's driving me crazy, and for what?

Dad'll probably never respond—if he's even out there—and Mom'll never go to Yale, and I'm just digging myself deeper and deeper into a hole that I already don't know how to get out of. I should have just left it all alone. I've made a mess of everything, and the longer I let it go on, the worse I know it's going to get.

I've probably ruined any chance I ever had with Peter, not that there ever really was one in the first place. But what's worse is that I may have managed to lose him as a friend in the process.

Yay, me.

Still, in a weird way, deciding to give it all up and come clean with Mom has lifted a huge weight from my shoulders, one heavy enough to give Buddha a run for his money, metaphorical or not. And for the first time in days, my stomach doesn't feel like it's being used by a troop of boy scouts trying to get their knot-tying badge.

I know Mom's going to be furious and I'm probably going to be grounded until I'm about thirty, but I also know it's going to be a lot better if I tell her rather than her finding out on her own. I'm still sick at heart about what's happened with Peter, but for the rest of it, I know I'm making the right decision.

I'm ready to make it right with Mom.

And then the cell phone rings.

Chapter 24
In which I discover that I'm not missing any organs after all.

Really?!

Of course, rings is a relative term as the phone's actually set on vibrate. And yes, I know this is called having it on silent, but since we both know that sounds are nothing more than vibrations in a range we happen to hear, and this phone is vibrating right now at a frequency that I'm hearing with my entire body, soul and being, just go with it, okay?

I glance at the front door, sure that Mom is about to walk in right as I'm getting the phone out, mostly because it's a worst case scenario, but also because I'm becoming fairly convinced that the universe has the same dark, mischievous streak as the Belgium government.

I'll explain that later, assuming I survive the next couple of minutes, what with my heart beating so hard that it's interfering with my breathing. Or the other way around; it's hard to know when you're panicked. But either way I expect my heart's going to explode, my lungs implode, or my mother will beat me to death with a large, heavy, blunt instrument.

As none of those instantly happen, I retrieve the phone with slightly shaking hands, because this could be *it*. Or it could be *Not-it* and I could be working myself up for nothing. And almost immediately the phone stops vibrating.

Are you kidding me?!

I frantically flip it open as if I could somehow chase after the call, like you do when you go running after someone because they've forgotten their keys on the table, or the nuclear launch codes, or something.

But there's absolutely nothing. Not even a mocking dial-tone, just no connection at all.

I stare at the phone like it's somehow its fault. I have to stifle an urge to throw it against the wall or into the fireplace, though given that the latter is just a bunch of fake plastic logs in front of a glorified space heater, I know I'd be more likely to crack the logs than the phone.

Certainly not the explosion into a million pieces of circuitry and glass that I have in my mind's eye.

I tell myself to calm down. Logically, it couldn't have been Dad. I mean, he wouldn't hang up after just two rings, would he?

Three rings, max.

Unless I was in that fugue state Mom complains about. Then, God knows how many rings I missed. Panic: 1. Logic: 0.

Wait a minute. Not Dad said I should have known it was him when he'd called earlier because of his caller ID. So, it's got to store those things, doesn't it? Then, if it was Dad this time, maybe I can call him back and explain that I'm mentally deficient and had been interrupted by my contrapuntal voices in continuously interweaving parts. Or I could lie and tell him I was using the bathroom... no, wait, shower.

I mean it's probably not the best image to start with, me on a toilet. Though me being naked might not be all that much better for a first father-daughter introduction.

Cooking. That's safe.

It's productive, self-reliant. Yeah, cooking.

True, the centerpiece of my culinary skills is boiling water, but he doesn't have to know that. Unless he asks what I'm making.

All of this angst, of course, is predicated on his Caller ID being stored somewhere in this wretched thing. Oh, and that caller IDs have phone numbers stored with them rather than just being names.

Now I'm sure you're thinking I'm a complete idiot, not knowing any of this cell phone stuff. But I've never had one, and I'm sure you'd do just as well on your first day trying to drive a starship. Maybe not quite the same thing, but to me, it feels like the same order of magnitude. I mean, I do have a general idea how Caller ID works, just as I have a general idea what quarks are, but there's a big difference between a general idea and practical knowledge. Not to mention that for the longest time I thought it was actually Collar ID and you used it to identify who was a Catholic priest and who wasn't.

I flip open the phone and stare at the small screen. It's about an inch square and it's showing the date and time, though I'm fairly sure it's off by at least a half-hour. Around that are a bunch of icons, most of which I have no idea what they mean.

I poke around through the menus and finally come across one that says Missed Calls. I hold my breath as I click the select button. A new screen comes up and it looks like there should be a list, but it's completely empty. I stare at it, willing it to continue refreshing but it stubbornly refuses to do so. It's blank and it's sticking with it.

I let out the breath I was still holding, feeling deflated in all possible meanings of the word.

How could he not be in the list of missed calls? As I'm pondering this, I hear footsteps approach the door and I frantically stuff the phone away, just as they pass by and fade away down the hall.

I know someone called.

Would it maybe not show up on the list if they hung up before I picked it up?

Wait a minute, that doesn't make any sense. I mean that's kind of the definition of a missed call, isn't it? Because if they hadn't hung up before I picked it up, then it would be an answered call which is kind of not the problem here.

Maybe if they left me a voice-mail it's not considered a missed call... but does this thing even have voice-mail? And how the heck would I access it if it does?

The footsteps are long gone so I cautiously pull out the phone and start poking through menus again. I manage to drill down to another sub-menu somewhere, which has nine icons in three rows across it. One of the icons is a little voice bubble that seems inordinately pleased with itself. As I watch, it grows to about double its size and flashes 5M5 before spinning once and then shrinking back to its original size.

I have no idea how I got to this particular sub-menu, but that spinning icon is calling out to me about as subtly as a bottle with a *drink me* sign on it. I take yet another deep breath and decisively stab the icon, a text message comes up almost immediately.

My heart is beating so loudly I almost don't hear the rattle of keys in the door.

Oh, come on, now!

As Mom unlocks the deadbolt, I scan the text furiously, but only get as far as...

It's a real pity you didn't send the postcard earlier.

...before I have to hide the phone again, stuffing it into my backpack.

Mom's clearly exhausted, but just as clearly, she's not ready to go to bed. I try to act calm but it's taking all of my will not to keep checking the backpack to see if it's about to burst into flames, or be crushed by a spontaneously appearing micro-black hole, or somehow otherwise be destroyed, severing the one slim thread of connection I have with my father. My father.

Luke, I am your father.

I have no idea what Mom and I are talking about, but I keep nodding appreciatively and grunting noncommittally now and then. I've actually gotten really good at that, giving the appearance of listening without actually doing it. This comes in particularly useful at school, but also on those nights when Mom wants to complain, once again, about all the dysfunction at her various jobs.

Really, the way she tells it, they'd all be better off run by one of those kids from that TV show, Are you Smarter than a Fifth Grader?, than they are by their current management. But, as the people in her stories don't actually change, and she always has basically the same gripes about them, I often go on full auto-pilot.

If I were Peter, of course, I would actually be listening and making appropriate comments... but as she never seems to notice the difference between his real attention and my feigned one, I figure I'll take the SparkNotes route out.

I realize Mom has stopped talking and is looking at me.

"Are you really sure?" she asks.

Her expression is strange enough that I mentally rewind our last couple of interchanges and realize I've just agreed to let her sell my right spleen on the black market.

"I'm just trying to help out any way I can," I say innocently.

"Uh-huh. By selling an organ you don't even have."

"What? You sold mine once already?! Why don't I remember this?"

"Yes, that's just what I did. Sold my child's organs off while she was too young to know what was going on."

"I knew it!"

"No, you only get one spleen to begin with. And it's on your left side just a bit below your arm pit."

"That's good to know. I mean, it might be on the SATs."

I've decided that's my new mantra for every tiny bit of random information I pick up between now and when I have to take them. Because, who knows, they all might be.

She sighs, which is something I seem to bring out in a lot of people. "So where is your head today?" she asks.

I run through all the plausible excuses. Peter. True. Father/relationship paper. Not so much, but she doesn't know that. Then there are all the real reasons: Dad, Not Dad, Not Dad and Mom's date, Yale, the inevitable implosion of my life... but I can't talk about any of them without telling her about all of them.

I know that just a couple of moments ago I'd just decided to lay it all out and get the inevitable over with, but that was before Dad, my Real Dad, texted me.

Crap. I'm really tired of lying to my Mom, so I do the only thing I can.

"Um, I'd rather not talk about it."

"Should I be worried?"

I think, perhaps a bit longer than I should. "Well... no more than usual."

"I'm not sure if that means I'm not normally worried enough, or if that's supposed to be reassuring."

"Me neither," I concede.

"You aren't feeling suicidal or anything, are y..."

"Mom!"

"I didn't think so. But you keep things so bottled up sometimes. Do you at least have someone you talk to? A teacher at school, Peter...?"

At her mention of Peter, I get this thick lump in my throat, and I can feel tears threatening.

It must have shown on my face—or the floating billboard above it— because she suddenly looks very sympathetically concerned. "Is everything okay with you and Peter?"

I'm not going to answer. I'm not, because if I do, that might make it real and then I don't know what I'll do.

My mouth doesn't get the memo.

"I don't know!" I blurt out, at which point the tears decide to join the party as well.

Mom comes over and I bury myself in her arms and sob.

She holds me, not talking, not asking questions or telling me everything's going to be okay. She just hugs me with one arm and strokes my hair with the other.

She starts singing so softly it's almost a sub-vocalization. With my head pressed against her, I feel the rumble in her chest almost more than I can actually hear the sound of the song. I remember her holding me like this and singing to me when I was younger and had banged my head, or skinned a knee, or slammed my hand in a drawer. Or face-planted, blackened my eye, jammed a thumb... you name it, I did it.

And she always did this.

I feel a little guilty, as if I'm using these tears and Peter like misdirection for all those other things. But the tears are real, as is the anguish which drives them, so I just let myself sink against her and cry.

All good things must come to an end, as do bad things, though they do seem to last a lot longer. But in any case, eventually my tears dry up and I just lie there with my eyes closed, listening to her song, feeling its rumble against my cheek. I'm feeling almost at peace, safe in her arms, the vibrations of her song rocking me like a lullaby, like a long, slow cell phone buzzing against me.

And the moment's broken.

Thanks brain. Thanks for the truly great simile.

Chapter 25
In which I am reminded to eat, for reasons best left to the imagination.

One of the many great things about Mom is that she's always there for me.

I mean *always*. And tonight is no exception.

Which presents a problem as I can feel the cell phone pulling at me like we've been quantum-entangled. Entanglement is, of course, when two particles are always in matching states regardless as to where they are in the universe. Give one particle ice cream, for example, and they'll both get brain freeze simultaneously, regardless of their distance, the speed of light or any of those other pesky little "rules."

Einstein called this effect Spooky Action at a Distance which only goes to show that he was a lot more than just a guy with crazy hair.

Now that I think if it, though, that's actually nothing like what I'm feeling with the cell phone.

Yeah, forget all that. It's more like a mental black-hole, sucking in my attention and thoughts no matter how hard I try to focus on Mom. It's also apparently sucking in my ability to form coherent similes, resulting in that whole quantum-entanglement debacle.

It's a real pity you didn't send the postcard earlier.

You're telling me! I mean, I would have loved growing up with a father, even if he and Mom weren't together. I mean, I could have spent weekends on his private island. We could have done all kinds of things together: scouring the beaches for cool stuff washed in after a storm; I could have made him pasta while he read me his books. We could have gone on bike rides together, or stabbed palm trees with forks. It wouldn't have mattered what it was. It would have been with my Dad.

I feel tears beginning to well up at the loss of all that, but I force them back because I know if I start crying again, Mom will never leave.

Just to be clear, I'm not mad at her for missing all that.

Sure, I would have loved having it, but I know she was doing her best and she honestly thought that nothing good could come out of contacting Dad. And god knows I've made one or two poor decisions in my life, so even though she's Mom, I know she's a person too, and has the right to be wrong. In fact, I normally enjoy it when she is, and I just can't hold this against her, much as it seems like I want to.

"You know," she says, looking at me appraisingly. "It seems like a pretty poor design that when we cry, we get all red and puffy and drip stuff all over the place."

"Thanks, Mom."

"I mean, what is the biological advantage to blood-shot eyes and vast mucus production if you're trying to attract someone to give you sympathy. Unless, of course, you're crying because you're about to be eaten by a saber tooth cat or something like that. Then I guess looking about as disgusting as you possibly can might be a good defense mechanism. Because really, who'd want to eat something with snot dripping down its face?"

I start to roll my eyes when I remember something, and instead look directly at her.

"Uh, Mom? Why are you here?"

"That's a question philosophers have been trying to answer throughout the ages."

"Yeah... but what about the whole 'I'm taking Sheila's shift tonight, you're on your own thing' thing?"

"Oh, that thing thing. It was all just a ploy to see if you'd have some wild, crazy party when you thought I was gone."

"That might have been a more effective scheme if I'd actually thought you weren't coming home tonight."

"What do you mean? I'm sure I told you yesterday at dinner."

"I have no memory of that."

"Which, of course, doesn't necessarily mean I didn't tell you."

"The absence of proof is not, in and of itself, proof. Besides which, one day of warning is nowhere near enough time to arrange a truly epic party."

"True. Next time I'll try to give you more rope to hang yourself with."

"That's all I'm saying. And behind door number 2?" I prompt.

"Well, Monte," she says, gesturing to an imaginary door and putting on her spokesmodel's voice. "Behind door #2 we have a lovely evening at Katie's Kitch'n, perfect but for a lack in what we in the restaurant biz like to call 'customers.'"

"So, you got sent home."

"I volunteered to go home. You know, like when you volunteer to give up your seat when they overbook airlines."

"I might, if I'd ever been in an airplane."

"You've been in an airplane. I flew back home when I was first pregnant with you."

"I don't think that really counts."

"I guess not," she concedes, getting up from my futon-from-hell and heading towards what passes for our kitchen.

"Did you have dinner yet?" she asks as she vanishes through its doorway.

"Um, not really. My stomach's not feeling great."

As I hear her moving around in the kitchen, I sneak a furtive look at the backpack, wondering if I have time to pull out the phone and finish reading the text. But just as I decide it might be safe, Mom sticks her head out of the kitchen and looks at me.

"You've got to eat something, Sweetheart. It just wouldn't be fair to all the other passengers of the crashed plane if you were just skin and bone, you know that."

Yeah, most parents try to get their kids to eat by guilting them about all the starving kids in China; mine guilts me about otherwise civilized people who might starve if I'm undernourished when they're forced into cannibalism.

And yes, I'm sure that explains a lot about the way I am.

The rest of the night goes pretty much just like that. I try to act normal and pay attention to Mom when all I really want to do is knock her unconscious, dive over the dining room table, and rip the cell phone out of my backpack through whatever side is closest to me.

Unsurprisingly, I don't do any of that. No backpack ripping, no bludgeoning of parental units, and probably not much normalcy from me, for that matter. Then again, I'm not very good at normal even in the most, well, normal of situations, and this was far from it.

I also fail woefully at paying attention to her, and she has to repeat herself several times because my brain (such as it is) is currently located in a large canvas backpack about six feet to my right.

So really, I'm not out of my mind. It left me.

She doesn't comment on any of it, just makes some kind of chicken fried rice which actually smells really good. Unfortunately, after about four bites of it, my stomach clenches its mouth shut and warns me that if I try giving it any more, it'll return all it's gotten, and I've learned from hard experience not to argue with it.

Mom does most of the talking and I try to respond as best I can, which is rather difficult when her words seem to have a half-life of only about 8 seconds, which is coincidentally exactly the length of time a bull rider has to stay on a wildly bucking bull for the ride to count. Except substitute the maddening knowledge that there is a text message from my father on a cell phone mere feet from where I am for the bull, and my current attention span for the rider.

Just as I get a coherent thought going, the knowledge hits me again, bucking me between wild heights of excitement that I've actually made contact, and chest-tightening anxiety that for some reason he's already annoyed at me, blaming me for waiting so long to contact him.

We're cleaning the dishes when a telemarketer calls, but I'm too tense to mess with him and we let it go to voice-mail. This, of course, is a major strategic error as I see Mom glance at me appraisingly. It's just one more sign that something is very off with me, and Mom's response to that is to be there for me, for as long as it takes.

It takes until about 10:30 that night.

Tomorrow is a school day, and she has an early shift, so she finally announces that she has to go to bed. She helps me reconstruct my futon/trench combo then gives me a long hug.

"You do know," she says, whispering, the heat of her breath warming the back of my neck. "You can always talk to me. And I won't even make any suggestions if you don't want me to."

"I know," I say in a small voice.

"I know you know," she says, pulling back to look at me. "But sometimes these things have to be said."

I nod. "I love you, Mom."

"I know," she replies smugly.

"Yeah, well, if you wake up encased in carbonite, you have only yourself to blame.[6]"

She smiles and gives me a big kiss on the cheek and finally, *finally* leaves. And I am alone. With the phone. And a heart beating so fast it's beginning to sound like a lawn mower.

I grab my backpack and pull it over to me, but a noise from Mom's room makes me freeze. She's probably just getting on her PJs but as she has been known to return to get a glass of water or something, I sit there with the backpack in my lap, frozen, staring at the thin line of light visible under her bedroom door, willing it to go dark.

Either the Force is strong in me, or she finally turns off the light, but I'll take it either way.

I give it another hour or two to make sure she's really settled in for the night and isn't going to spring out with a pointed finger and yell "J'accuse!"

Okay, according to the clock it's only about five minutes but since time is relative, I'm going with the two hours. I think it has to do with thinking about one thing so hard that it becomes a mental singularity, distorting your own perceived space-time with its inexorable pull.

In any case, I finally pull open the backpack, glancing furtively at her door every three or four microseconds or so. It takes me a moment to find the phone. Probably no more than 30 seconds, but long enough for me to feel a stab of panic that it is somehow, impossibly gone, fallen through a crack in our reality into some weird alternate universe where I'm not obsessed with trying to explain everything using my own distorted version of physics.

Then my hand closes on it, and I shakily pull it out. This time I know for a fact that this is IT, but I don't allow myself to freeze, dwelling on the IT-ness of it all.

I flip open the phone, my breath tight in my chest.

---

[6] For those of you insufficiently educated in the classics upon which our cultural identity is based, being encased in carbonite is what happens to you after someone says, "I love you," and you reply "I know." Well, at least if Han Solo's experience in <u>Star Wars</u> is anything to go on.

Crap, it went back to the main screen... and I still have no clue how I got to the messages menu.

The floor creaks and I throw myself over the phone and into a pose of such forced casualness that I might as well have worn a blinking sign saying, "she's up to something."

But it's just Buddha and he pads across the room, ignoring me.

Okay, take III.

I sit up and retrieve the phone again and start stabbing through the menus, trying once again to find that little voice bubble that was so pleased with itself. After a bunch of false starts, I finally manage to dig down to whatever arcane part of the menu structure it's buried.

I take a deep breath and stab the icon.

> **You have used 80% of this month's data.**

What?! Wait a minute, where's Dad's message?

I scan the rest of this text and finally realize it's from the phone company. When I get to the bottom there is another icon labeled prep and I stab that one as well.

> It's a real pity you didn't send the postcard earlier.

My heart sinks back down from inside my throat, where it had apparently climbed when I thought I might have lost the message. It's still going like crazy—my heart, that is—but at least it's back where it belongs.

> The situation is complicated. Too complicated to explain by text.

Complicated? What does that mean?

I suddenly have a flash about how this whole thing must be like for him. Those three days in Vegas are probably a dim memory, or maybe he does remember them and its even one of those stories he pulls out now and then, reminiscing about his youth or what might have been. But either way, he's moved on and now this girl he'd met over a decade and a half ago suddenly drops him a postcard and presumably wants back in his life.

He's probably married, maybe even has his own kids, and he has no idea what this blast-from-his-past wants. Yeah, it's probably pretty damn complicated now that he mentions it.

Especially because, while Mom had given him a fake phone number, he had given her his real one... and she'd completely blown him off. That must have hurt like hell. You think you've made this great connection with someone you really like, and you're all excited about the future, but as soon as you get home and try to reach out to them, you find they've lied to you, given you a bogus number and basically written you out of their lives.

God, if some guy did that to me, I'd be a wreck. I'd probably try to convince myself that I'd just written his number down wrong, and I know for weeks that every time the phone'd ring I'd hope it was him, calling me.

Mom, you really screwed up this one. You should have come clean with him. I don't know, maybe you could have not told him about being pregnant, but you shouldn't have left him wondering if this great connection he thought he had with you was all in his head. You shouldn't have just left him not knowing.

The more I think about it, the more wretched I feel, a wonderful mélange of heartsick guilt and the pain of abandonment, as if I were both the person who did this to him, and also him experiencing the aftermath of it all. Yeah, ain't empathy great sometimes?

A quarter box of tissues later, I pull myself together enough to go back to the text and re-read it, trying to squeeze every iota of meaning out of the words. On about the fifth time, I realize there is this thin scroll bar thing to the very left of the text of the message. I hadn't recognized it as anything because it's on the wrong side; I mean scroll bars are always on the right, aren't they?

Who designed this phone's interface anyway? The Marquis de Sade?

I press the down arrow and the text indeed does scroll downwards.

> It's probably best that we meet. Tell me when and where and I can send a car around.

OhMyGodOhMyGodOhMyGodOhMyGodOhMyGod.

I'm actually going to meet Dad.

Chapter 26
In which bovine end products feature prominently.
(Though you'll have to wait to find out which end)

I hit the reply button and am instantly faced with the worst case of writers block I can imagine. I mean, what do I even call him?! He thinks he's talking to Mom, he doesn't know I even exist, and the whole situation's complicated. Oh, man, he doesn't know the half of it.

Frankly, right now I can't think of a single part of my life that *isn't* complicated.

After staring at the blank reply screen for several hours—and this time the clock actually agrees with me—and rereading his text nineteen or thirty times, I realize he doesn't use any names, salutations, or sincerely's, so maybe that's the text etiquette. Peter would know these things but it's already after midnight, not to mention that I still have no clue how things are standing with us, so I couldn't go over there even if it weren't so late.

One crisis at a time. (Yeah, I know. Wishful thinking.)

Still, I need to go to sleep, because tomorrow's a school day, but I also know it will never happen if I don't get this text out.

So, I spend the next half-hour writing and erasing apologies, explanations and other gibberish and finally decide that less is more. I remember that we have Friday off for teacher self-affirmation day or something like that. Presumably where they all stare into mirrors and tell themselves their lives have meaning after all. Or maybe they all sit in a circle and go around and tell the person to their left how worthwhile they are. Or it could be the person on the right; I don't know how these things work.

All I really care about is that we're off from school, and I could presumably meet with Dad without Mom being any the wiser. So after nearly three hours, I finally settle on the oh-so-elegant "How would this Friday be?"

I stab the send button before I can change my mind. The phone makes a brief whooshing sound like my text message is being sent down one of those old fashioned pneumatic tube systems.

Then I start second-guessing myself. I should have thanked him for getting back to me. I should have told him how glad I was that we can meet. I should have told him who I was. I should have...

The phone vibrates in my hands and I almost drop it in surprise.

Oh crap, it must have bounced, like emails do. No way would he still be up now, it's nearly two am! But if it bounced, I have no way to contact him.

I frantically flip open the phone and start stabbing through menus trying to find the one for texts. For once the universe takes pity on me —and yes, I will gladly take its pity; I'm not proud—and I find it almost immediately. I hold my breath, dreading what I might see, but force myself to push the button to open the message.

Where should I send the car?

I stare at the text, reading it over and over, unable to believe it's really there and that it says what I think it says. Finally, my lungs start complaining and I realize that I've never stopped holding my breath, so I take in a deep, ragged one.

Why is he still up? I didn't wake him, did I? That'd be just like me. Long-lost dad and in our first interaction in 16 years I wake him up in the middle of the night. And suddenly I can't stop giggling. I mean he missed out on all my middle of the night wakings when I was a baby, so it's about time... I know it's not that funny, but I can't stop myself.

I don't want to wake Mom, so I grab a pillow and stuff my face into it. I hold it there until the lack of oxygen finally overcomes the slightly hysterical giggles.

Where should I send the car?

That's a darn good question. I mean, it can't be here for obvious reasons. And it can't be any place that Mom might show up at. I rack my brains but the only place that I can come up with is under the turret at the main Cambridge Library. It's not perfect, but it's small enough and there's only one turret so I guess it's as good a place as any. Not to mention, it has the added benefit that I can tell Mom I'm going there and actually be telling the truth. Well, at least part of it, and that's got to count for something, right?

With this brilliant rationalization ringing in my mind, I compose a text to send back to him. This time I do apologize if I woke him, and then offer my suggestion of the front entrance of the library. The phone whooshes away my text and I don't even bother closing it this time, just staring at the screen, willing it to refresh with his response.

Even though I'm expecting it, when the phone vibrates again I jerk, startled by the sensation. I do manage to keep a tight grip on the phone, though, which is a good thing as throwing it across the room would probably have done bad things to the phone, Mom's sleep, my already fragile mental state, and any hopes of a connection with Dad. On the other hand, tightly gripping the very thing you're flinching away from is kind of a no-win situation. Either you didn't need to get away from it, which made the whole flinch thing utterly pointless, or you did need to get away from it but you've just brought it along with you, which makes the whole flinch thing thoroughly ineffective.

Still, I'll gladly take pointless and ineffective over plain bad, though now that I mention it, at some point in my life I would actually like some better options. In any case, I gather my frazzled nerves, loosen my death-grip on the phone and open his text.

No worries, you didn't.

I didn't what?! I have no idea what he's talking about and I start trying to compose a response that doesn't make me sound completely dense when another text comes in from him.

I'm almost always up this late.

Oh, I didn't wake him. Duh. But his text goes on:

So I'll have my man pick you up on Friday at noon under the turret at the Cambridge library. He'll have a sign.

With Mom's fake name, no doubt. I wonder if I should give him a heads up that I'm not her, but I can't figure out any simple way of breaking the news, and he might not want to meet me if he knew. He's right. It's complicated, and it's probably best done in person. So I just tell him that I'm looking forward to it and send the text off into the ether.

I wait for a response, but after about fifteen minutes, I give up. But it's okay, it's not like I particularly need a response; we have a plan. Not to mention, if he had responded, then I would have responded back to him, and then he would have responded back to me, and the only way it ever would have ended was when one of our phones ran out of batteries.

I am reluctant to let go of the phone, but Mom still doesn't know I have it and I want to keep it that way. So I carefully slip it into the waistband of the sweat pants I'm currently using as my PJ's, even though I know there's no way I'm going to fall asleep after all that.

My brain is just racing around, imagining our first meeting. "His man" will probably pick me up in a stretch limo and then drive me across some secret bridge to his private island, then up a long, winding driveway to his Downton Abbey-like mansion, gravel crunching under the tires. As we pull up, he'll be standing in the doorway, beaming at me, looking exactly like he'd just stepped straight out of the Vegas photo strip.

He'll be a little surprised when I get out of the car, but once I explain who I am he'll take me in his arms and give me a big welcoming hug.

Then he'll take a long look at me and say, "Come on, Gwen! Get up, get up, get up...!"

And Mom's shaking my shoulder. "You're going to be late for school!"

I dash down the four flights of stairs from our apartment to the street, taking them two at a time. I'm at least a half-hour late, and I have to get far enough from home that I can safely check and see if Dad sent me any more texts without the chance of Mom seeing me.

I'm hoping Peter will be waiting for me at the T-Stop, but he's nowhere to be seen and my heart sinks. I know I'm overreacting. I mean, we don't ride to school together every day—I mean, some days I have mental breakdowns and we never actually make it to school—but even discounting those, we do wait for each other more often than not. Still, I remind myself that I am about a half-hour late, and try to convince myself that his not being here doesn't mean anything beyond that.

All I can say is that it's a good thing I'm not in debate club, because my powers of persuasion don't work that well even on me.

While I'm anxiously waiting for the next train to arrive, I surreptitiously dig out the phone, and flip it open. There's nothing new. Still, just seeing those words "I'll have my man pick you up on Friday" sends a shiver down my spine. I'd been half-fearing I'd dreamed the whole thing, but there it is staring up at me with about as much solidity as pixels can manage.

But without Peter here, there's no one to share the news with, which frankly sucks. A part of me feels like I should be shouting and dancing, and screaming the news from the rooftops... but without anyone to cheer me, and pull me back off the edge if necessary, it just feels like shouting into the void. Of course, another part of me feels like it wants to push that first part off straight into that void because it's just feeling too lonely without Peter, and all that yelling and dancing is getting annoying.

For a moment, I consider calling Not Dad just to tell *someone*, but it's his fault I might have messed everything up with Peter, so that's pretty much a non-starter. Well, maybe not his fault per se; but he certainly was the inciting incident. And that's the beauty of blame, there's always more than enough to go around.

I somehow manage to make up most of the lost time getting to school through a perfect storm of train connections. Sadly, however, most is not all and when I arrive I'm still more than ten minutes late which makes me officially tardy. A designation I thoroughly despise, because it sounds like something a kindergarten teacher would say to a five year old.

"You're tardy, Missy. Did you have problems making your wee-wee?"

Gah! Like the proverbial white rabbit, I'm late, I'm late, I'm late! Why can't we just leave it at that? But no, late is off the table; we have to be tardy.

My theory is that they know we've all taken Sex Ed, and we girls are old enough to become "late" in its more euphemistic biological meaning (that is, if we have the common sense of the aforementioned rabbit and its uncontrollable mating urges). So, they are afraid to call us late because some other young, impressionable child might overhear and jump to the wrong conclusion.

But frankly, that's a chance I'm willing to take.

I am late. I'm a dilatory, belated, punctuality-challenged laggard, and proud of it.

Which isn't to say that I intend to sign in at the office as such.

Remember, I didn't show up at all yesterday, and if I sign in late today, I know I'll have to deal with Mr. Clavell, our vice-principal, who has the unenviable job of trying to discipline today's youth.

Now we aren't one of those inner city schools with metal detectors and a cop permanently stationed there, but there's still enough vandalism, weed, pornography, alcohol, bullying, sexting, plagiarism, cheating, class disruption, smoking, vaping, impudence, vampirism, and of course, the worst of the bunch, tardiness, to give him complete job security.

Admittedly, the vampirism has yet to be actually proven, but some of these goth kids are so pale and listless during daylight hours that I personally have serious concerns as to who or what is sucking the life out of them.

But back to Mr. Clavell. Unlike all those bald, bull-headed vice principals you see in movies and television shows who always seem to get infinite glee from catching anyone in even the smallest infraction, Mr. Clavell actually cares, which I'm sure makes his job way more difficult than it could be. This whole "caring" flaw in his character could be due to the fact that he has a very nice, full head of dark brown hair and his neck has a circumference significantly smaller than his head. However, as my sample set consists of television vice-principals and Mr. Clavell, I'll need some serious funding to get to the root of this possible hair-to-care ratio.

The bottom line, however, is that Mr. Clavell doesn't actually seem to like doling out punishment, which you'd think would have been part of the job description. *Vice-Principal needed. No experience needed, sadism a plus.*

"Okay, so I see you're here for the vice-principal job."

"Yes, that's right."

"Your resumé says that you spent the last five years as a Navy Seal, and you know how to kill people in sixty-seven different ways."

"And thirty-eight of those don't even leave a discernible mark."

"Excellent. If you do run into an irredeemable youth here, a studentae hooliganous—and God knows we've got quite an infestation of them—those thirty-eight would be the way to go."

"Noted, sir."

"And your skill at smelling guilt?"

"Certified at thirty yards. Fifty, if the wind is in my favor."

"That's certainly more than satisfactory. Last question, then. On the scale of Mother Theresa to Vlad the Impaler, where would you rate your enjoyment of meting out punishment? All justified and appropriate, of course."

"Of course, sir. I'm not a savage. But overall, I think I'd have to say Attila the Hun."

"Just what I wanted to hear. Congratulations, you have the job."

Mr. Clavell, on the other hand, actually seems to believe in redemption, which, along with care, is almost certainly not in the vocabulary of the kids who repeatedly darken his doorway, even though the latter technically is a four-letter word. To be frank, I have no idea why he's doing this job, unless he's under the same misapprehension that I was, which is that he'll become principal upon old Dr. Schneider's demise.

I mentioned this once to Peter who explained to me that vice-principal isn't like vice-president. No, the vice in vice-principal is more like the opposite of virtue.

In any case, I'm trying to avoid signing in and talking with him not because of any latent guilt or anything. No, Mr. Clavell often seems so stressed out that I just want to save him all the extra work of dealing with me. Really, that's all there is to it.

A couple of school lunch ladies are coming in just as I arrive, so I surreptitiously join their group and calmly walk past the front office and into the school proper. Well, calmly enough, as no one calls out to stop me.

And I'm in.

Now, I could describe the fog of my day, the teachers drowned out by this little voice in my head saying "my man will pick you up on Friday" over and over and over.

And over.

And over.

I could tell you about the anxious, gnawing feeling in my stomach, as the day dragged on without any sight of Peter. Again, not all that unusual as the only class I share with him is French and today that's second to last period. But the desire to see him, coupled with the fear of how he'll react might as well have been the creepy, anxiety-inducing soundtrack of a Hitchcock thriller for all the good it did my state of mind.

At some point I ate lunch, though I have no idea what it was. This also isn't that unusual, given that their specialties seem to be mystery meat and road kill, with a side of vaguely tubular green or orange objects which probably once had happy, fulfilling lives as green beans and carrots respectively. At least I hope so.

The lunch room's too small for the whole school to eat in at once, and this semester Peter's in the second shift and I'm in the first, so I just sat down in a corner and mechanically stuffed whatever they'd put on my tray into my mouth. Today, however, I didn't even taste it, for which I can only be grateful.

The first time the school day actually impinges on my consciousness is when I find myself walking into Mrs. Beecham's classroom. Good thing my schedule's so hard-wired into me that I'll apparently be able to keep it even after the zombie apocalypse claims me as its first victim. A state which one might reasonably argue has already happened.

As I slide into my assigned seat/desk combo, I realize that today is Wednesday, the day the first draft of the father/relationship paper's due. I slip my copy out of my backpack as Mrs. Beecham starts writing on the board, her chalk squeaking perilously close to that dreaded fingernails on blackboard sound. None of my other teachers' chalk is so painful to listen to, so she either does it on purpose, or her blackboard is possessed.

Even today, the sound cuts through the endless litany that's been looping since this morning, and I look up to see that she's written *Our Founding Fathers* on the board. Huh? What does that have to do with English?

I look around me, but no one else has their father/relationship papers out. Mrs. Beecham is still scratching away at the board so I lean over to Jill Evans, a girl I've kind of known all my life, but with whom I've probably only shared a dozen or so words over all that time. See, the fundamental stumbling block in our "relationship" is that we barely share the same space-time continuum, her being one of the popular kids while I'm down here in the murk scrabbling around for the scraps of meat her kind generously toss us now and then.

At least I think that's how she'd describe it.

Still, I need information, and she's the only one within whispering distance. So, I softly call out to her. "Jill..."

She doesn't react, so I try a little louder. "Hey, Jill...

She turns her head a couple of degrees towards me, just enough to get me more fully into her peripheral vision, but not far enough that anyone might think she was actually looking at me. Despite the oblique angle, I can make out her expression, an annoyed puzzlement, as she's clearly wondering why I suddenly think I can talk to her.

"Today's Wednesday, isn't it?"

She does a micro-change of expression, the barest hint of an eye roll, as if I weren't worth the effort of a full one. But she nods curtly, a yes—apparently unwilling to up our total word count—then turns away.

But I persist. "So why isn't Beecham collecting our papers?"

See, you have to understand that Mrs. Beecham believes that all assignments are due the moment the bell rings to start class. If something is due that day, even before the vibrations of the bell fully die away, she'll randomly start down one row, collecting whatever the assignment is from your desk. And if it's not there when she passes, it's late and you're docked points, even if you're in the process of digging it out of your binder.

Teaching us reliability, she calls it. I call it teaching us abuse of power.

Jill pretends she can't hear me, but as there's no one to my left and I'm in the front row, I really don't have a lot of options.

"What's going on?" I whisper insistently at her.

She studiously ignores me.

Mrs. Beecham doesn't.

"Do you have something to share with the class, Ms. Pendergrass?"

Now everyone's looking at me. Including Jill, who's finally turned in my direction, and who's smiling at me superciliously, despite probably not even knowing the word.

"Actually, yes," I reply. "I was trying to find out why you weren't picking up our father/relationship papers. I worked really hard on mine."

"I'm sure." she says dryly, clearly not meaning it. "Do you not read your emails?"

I can hear some snickers from behind me but I ignore both them and the vague feeling of panic that something is terribly wrong with the world. I mean, even more wrong than usual.

"When I can," I say defensively.

"When you can."

"I'm sorry, but we don't always have the best signal at my place."

"And you also just show up 'when you can?' No, never mind, don't answer that. You've already wasted enough of what little time they give me to get through their oh-so-daring syllabus. The assignment was canceled. If you'd read your email, you would have known that."

"You can't do that! You can't just give us an assignment and then cancel it as the last second."

"Please. Like any of you lot ever do anything except at the last second."

There's a smatter of nervous laughter from around me, because, for the most part, she's absolutely right.

"Now, Ms. Pendergrass," she goes on smugly, "the new father-related assignment, as I was about to tell you all, is to write a three page paper on one of the founding fathers. Someone other than Jefferson, Washington, or Hancock." She looks around the classroom. "And no Wikipedia, or ChatGPT."

She's looking at us all imperiously as I grab my essay from the desk and stand up, slinging my backpack over my shoulder.

"Where do you think you're going?"

"To the office."

"Not until I say you are."

"You will," I reply angrily. "Because this is bullshit."

I guess I am seeing Clavell today, after all.

Chapter 27
In which I make a grown man cry.
And make him love it.

I've never actually been in Mr. Clavell's office before, but I know where it is, down a short hallway immediately next to the main office. To enter it, you have to pass his prune-faced assistant whose sole job—as far as I can tell—is to look disapprovingly at the stream of wrong-doers who file by her desk on their way to judgment.

She looks like she'd be a lot happier if she had a three-headed dog and a burning sign above the door saying "Abandon hope, all who enter here." But what with school budgets as they are, all she got were a pair of uncomfortable looking wooden benches for us troublemakers to wait on.

His office door is shut, so I drop my backpack on the floor then drop myself down onto the bench next to it. The bench turns out not to be as uncomfortable as it looked like it would be, which I'm sure was a big disappointment for Assistant Prune Face.

Normally I'd be feeling anxious about this meeting, but right now I'm mad enough that I've singed to ashes whatever butterflies would have otherwise been fluttering around in my stomach. After all that stress trying to figure out how to do this stupid assignment—not to mention Mrs. Beecham's flat-out refusal to make any concessions to my utter lack of father-daughter memories—I can't believe she thinks she can cancel it on the day right before it's due.

It's just not fair. And yes, I know that life isn't fair, but as the great philosopher Calvin said: *when is it going to start being unfair in my favor?* By the way, that's not the Calvin who invented Calvinism, it's the one who hangs with Hobbes. As in, Calvin and...[7]

It must be a slow day for evil, as I'm the only one sitting here. I briefly consider getting out the cell phone to check if I've missed any new calls or texts, even though I know that's pretty impossible given the way I react to even its smallest vibration. Not to mention, there's also a large,

---

[7] In case *your* mother doesn't keep comic-strip books from the 90's, Calvin and Hobbes were the adventures of a young boy, Calvin, and his stuffed tiger named Hobbes, as they fight monsters, eat tuna fish sandwiches, and discuss life's great mysteries.

hand-written "No Cell Phones" sign on the wall behind Clavell's assistant, just above a clear plastic box containing a dozen or so (presumably confiscated) phones.

Yeah, not a good idea; I can't afford to have my lifeline to Dad added to her collection. Especially not with the inevitable signed letter from a parent that would be required to get it back.

On the wall opposite me are optimism-mandated motivational posters spouting such pithy bits of wisdom like "A river cuts through the rock, not because of its strength, but because of its perseverance" over a picture of the grand canyon, and "Dream Big: your attitude, not your aptitude, will determine your altitude" over a picture of some guy hang gliding.

Oh yeah, I'm sure those turned some kid's lives around...

I sigh, which earns me a glare from the Keeper of the Room and Confiscator of Cell Phones.

"Are you sure he knows I'm out here?" I ask reasonably, redirecting her eye contact for my own purposes, which I'm sure is against some rule. Thou shalt not turn thy neighbor's glare into a conversation, or something like that.

"Oh, he knows." she says in a tone that implies I should be afraid of what he knows and how it might be used against me. But I'm not convinced. Now that I think of it, I never saw her intercom him, knock on his door, or in any way actually let him know I was here. Unless they've upgraded to telepathic intercoms, I'm pretty sure this is part of her punishment game, the outermost circle of the nine rings of hell she's trying to create here.

I smile at her guilelessly, which of course absolutely no one does without a good helping of guile as otherwise they'd just, well, smile. "Could you remind him again, please? Just in case he's forgotten."

"No."

"So you're saying you have no way of contacting him?"

She glares at me again, clearly annoyed that I'm not taking the message to sit down and shut up, and baffled by my apparent non sequitur. "Excuse me?"

"I asked if you could remind him, and you said no. So if you can't remind him, who should I talk to who could?"

"Zip it, Missy. He'll see you when he'll see you, and not a moment sooner."

That sentence just makes my head hurt. My anger has been slowly draining away into a feeling of frustrated disgust, but she's just fanning the embers. And after what's just happened in English class I'm not exactly in a mood to just roll over and take it.

"Could you at least tell me how he was informed about my arrival? The method, I mean. I don't need to know the actual content."

Her prune-like face gets even tighter. "I said, zip it." she spits out. "I've had about as much of your sass as I'm going to take."

"I'm really not sure how asking reasonable questions, in a reasonable tone, could reasonably be called sass."

"Don't get smart with me, young lady!"

"Or what?" I ask, maintaining my maddeningly reasonable tone. "You'll send me to Mr. Clavell?"

"Enough!"

"Well, normally I'd agree with you, but your poster over there on perseverance really inspired me..."

She slaps her hand down on her desk angrily, "I said that's ENOUGH."

And it apparently is, because just then Mr. Clavell sticks his head out of his office.

"Is everything okay, out here?" he asks.

After Prune Face sputters out her complaints against me, and I helpfully add "color," he calms her down and sends her off for a coffee break and ushers me into his office.

"Have you been here before?" he asks as he shuts the door behind us.

"Nope, I'm a newbie at this whole miscreant thing."

"Somehow, I doubt that. You did quite a job pushing Ms. Nightingale's buttons."

"Oh, I'm very good at buttons. I've never met an elevator I couldn't master just like that."

I snap my fingers for emphasis and he snorts despite himself as he sits down in an old leather-backed chair that looks like it might have been really nice once.

"Is her name really Ms. Nightingale?" I ask.

"Yes, Sharon Nightingale, why?"

"Charon Nightingale? Like the Greek ferryman who takes people across the river Styx?"

"Sharon, with a shh."

"Oh, that makes a lot of sense too. She certainly does seem to like her Shhh."

He's trying not to smile, but not doing a very good job at it. I'm beginning to like him already.

"So, Gwen. Why are you here?"

I start into my whole "that's a question philosopher's have been asking for centuries" spiel, but he holds up a hand to stop me as soon as I hit philosophers. Okay, one point, Mr. Clavell.

He looks at me expectantly.

"Okay," I say, "but before we get into all that, did you know I was waiting out there or not?"

"In fact, I did."

Hmmmm.

"Your teacher texted me when she sent you down here, not to mention I've got a mirror up in the corner that lets me see what's going on at the benches."

He points it out to me, and I cross over to join him behind his desk to take a look. Yep, it's one of those small convex mirrors that looks down through the wired glass above his door and gives a perfect, if somewhat fish-eyed, view of the benches. Double good thing I didn't get the cell phone out. From here me reaching up under my shirt like that would have looked seriously weird.

Okay. Clavell: Two, Pendergrass: Zero.

"Is that what she said," I ask as I cross back to the wooden chair on the other side of the desk. "That *she* sent *me* down here?"

He glances briefly at his cell phone, one of those ridiculously large iPhone 6s, and scrolls through something I can't see. "She said you were swearing at her," he tells me.

"Not at her. I said that what she was doing was bullshit. And I stand by the term."

He looks at me expectantly, unfazed by my vulgarity, clearly waiting for me to explain. So, I sigh and tell him the whole story, starting with the original assignment, my fruitless discussion with her about it, along with a minimally self-incriminating version of what I've been going through vis-à-vis my whole father thing.

At the end of it, it is his turn to sigh. "And you'd already finished writing the first draft?" he asks.

"Yeah. So, it's just not fair that she made me do it, then changes the assignment the night before it's due."

He looks thoughtful, then leans forwards. "Gwen, I'm going to tell you something, but it doesn't leave this room. Alright?"

I nod.

"Really, I mean it."

"Okay, I promise."

"She actually didn't have a choice."

"What? What do you mean?"

He leans closer to me, and I follow suit. "Timmy Meronni's moms threatened to sue the school district if Mrs. Beecham didn't drop the assignment."

"Wow."

"Yeah."

"Oh, man, she must have been pissed."

"She wasn't happy about it. But she also could have handled the situation with you a lot better. Now if you've actually already done the work you've said you have, I'll make sure you don't have to do the other assignment. But this is just between you and me. I'll deal with Mrs. Beecham on your behalf, but if I hear you've been talking about this, the deal's off."

Hey, maybe this whole caring thing he has going has its upsides as well.

"But, I'm curious," he tells me. "After everything you said, what did you end up writing about?"

Oh, crap. It was one thing if Mrs. Beecham was the one to see the "God is my father" essay as I knew she couldn't give me too much crap if I just acted innocent and pious and all.

But Mr. Clavell is another story all together. He could be offended or just call bullshit and then I would be back where I started, well, actually in a worse position probably.

"It's just stupid," I tell him. "It's a really rough first draft."

"I'd really like to read it."

We both know this isn't a request, so I bite the bullet, silently draw out my paper and hand it over.

I needn't have worried.

Half-way down the first page, Mr. Clavell starts laughing out loud, and by the time he gets to the end, he's wiping tears away from his eyes. He straightens the pages, a huge smile on his face. "I haven't laughed that hard," he tells me, "Since I don't know when. Texaco! And that goat!"

"It actually happened, too. Just without the celestial choir."

"Do you mind if I make a copy of this?" he asks. "My wife just lives and breathes The Onion, you know that satirical newspaper..." he pauses, thinking. "Yeah, living and breathing onions, not quite the image I had in mind. Anyway, I think she'd get a huge kick out of this. So, with your permission?"

"Um, sure," I say eloquently, my mind racing. The Onion? Oh, my god, they're brilliant. And he thinks my stuff is like theirs?

As he brings my essay over to his printer/scanner/fax box, I suddenly have an epiphany as to why they're called The Onion. Maybe I'm just dense and everyone knows this, but I'll bet you that million dollars I don't have they're called The Onion because they make you laugh until you cry...

"But I was right," he says as he feeds the essay into the scanner. "You really are a master of pushing buttons. Mrs. Beecham would have hated this."

"I know, right?" I reply happily.

He laughs. "You are an evil young lady, Ms. Pendergrass."

"Thank you. And Mr. Clavell, you aren't half-bad yourself."

I sit back in my chair with a satisfied grin.

The Vice-Principal of my school called me evil. My job here is done.

By this time, the class period is almost over, so there's no point in hurrying back just to catch the very end of English. And since the benches have remained stubbornly empty, Mr. Clavell and I just talk to kill the time until my next class. He's actually really funny in his own way, and he showed me his own private motivational poster taped to the inside of one of his drawers. It's of a storm trooper from the movie Star Wars, sitting at a table, still wearing his full white plastic storm trooper armor, helmet and all.

He's holding his head in his hands dejectedly, and where you'd normally see a happy word like SUCCESS or TEAMWORK it says FAILURE, and then underneath, where the insipid quote would normally go, it simply says *Those were the droids you were looking for*.

He tells me his wife gave it to him for their anniversary and he sounds so in love with her, I have a sudden flash of jealousy.

No, not like that. I'm not getting a crush on him, though he is kind of cute for an old guy. No, I just want what he has, that feeling of belonging and love. That feeling that was kind of growing in me towards Peter…

I consider maybe talking to Mr. Clavell about it, him being a guy and all. Maybe he'd have some insight, but I don't know, it's kind of weird talking to a grown-up about what is probably just a crush on my part. And particularly one that I've most likely thoroughly crushed anyway.

I am saved from having to make a decision by the bell ringing, signaling the end of the period.

And I have French next. With Peter.

I get to my French class with plenty of time to spare, even though I have to stop by my locker and somehow pry it open. I don't know if it's just my school or not, but about half the lockers here need something akin to a crow bar to open them, while the other half are either infested with crickets or ants or worse. The wildlife ecologies I can't really fault the locker designers for, but the impossible to open ones?

I mean, come on, this is a glorified metal box stacked two high. Are you really telling me that the country which put a man on the moon, invented dental floss, duct tape, and arguably the first steam-powered motorcycle, can't master building a box that will reliably open and close?

My heart's beating a little fast as I walk into French class, but I don't immediately see Peter, which of course means he's not there. It's not a big room, and he's not a small guy, so there's not really much of a question whether I've missed him or not.

Disheartened, I slide into my chair towards the back of the room, and pull out the textbook, which I swear must have been printed on lead sheets, based on the weight of it. Mine lives in my locker because no way am I lugging it around with me. Particularly as Madame Lignedos almost never uses it. Still, she insists we always have it in class anyway, for the rare cases where it has a picture of the Eiffel Tower or the Mona Lisa or some such thing she wants to show us, or there's a short story she wants us to read. Pardon, un histoire court.

Peter steps into the doorway just as the bell starting this period begins to ring, literally stopping Madame Lignedos from closing the door so he can squeeze through.

"Dey solay kuh je sweeze un retard," he tells her somewhat breathlessly.

Have I mentioned how terrible his accent is? A couple of kids snicker because of course it sounds like he just said he was a retard, which is annoying on so many levels, not the least of which is that I immediately knew why they were snickering. Some words I'd just like to wipe from my understanding, but it's like reading; once you've mastered the skill it's virtually impossible to look at printed text without immediately understanding its meaning. Well, unless it's something I wrote, I suppose. Then all bets are off.

Of course, what Peter was really saying was Désolé que je suis en retard, or *Sorry I'm late.*

She makes a token correction to his accent, though it's pretty clear she's given it up as a lost cause, then waves him to his chair, next to mine. His hair is still wet from a shower, which tells me he's just come from weight training, which is what he does for PE credit. He smells like soap and shampoo, with just the hint of musky sweat that curls into my nostrils and sends my heart racing.

"Hey," he whispers as he slides into his chair next to me.

Madame Lignedos claps her hands sharply, though I can't imagine how she could have possibly heard him. "Français, mes enfants. Nous sommes en France."

She's telling us, of course, that we are now in France, which she does every day at the start of class. Yet despite her repeated instance, I have never needed a passport to get into the room, and I'm fairly sure that if you gave birth here (something I am not recommending, by the way), it would not grant your child European citizenship.

All of which only goes to show that you can't trust anything adults say.

I lean over to Peter as she turns and walks to the blackboard.

"Salut," I tell him, which is as close to hey as I can manage in French, though it's really more like aloha. Hello, goodbye, how are the kids... you know, that kind of thing. Somehow not as satisfying as a good hey, but it's the best I can do.

He gives me a typical Peter micro-expression smile then turns to face Madame Lignedos, who's starting the lesson, sorry la leçon.

And that's the sum total of our interaction this period.

French class runs long, so as soon as it's done, everyone starts frantically gathering their stuff to get to their next class. And Peter and I are no exceptions. So much for having a chance to talk.

"Ride home after school?" I ask Peter with as little chalance as I can manage. I'd been going for total nonchalance, of course, but a small quaver in my voice blew it.

"Sure," he says with a small shrug—which, admittedly, is totally Peter—but in my hyper-sensitive state, it feels like a lack of enthusiasm.

"By the big tree?"

I cringe as soon as I say it because we ALWAYS meet by the big tree. It's like telling someone that it's raining outside and they reply, "So, I'll get wet if I go out there?"

Peter doesn't comment, just swinging his backpack onto his shoulder as if it weighed little more than a standard musk ox. Which for him, means easily.

I'm so frazzled, I make the mistake of putting my lead-lined French Book in with my other books in my backpack and nearly strain my shoulder trying to mimic him. He gives me another small smile and easily lifts it the rest of the way for me, settling it onto my now aching shoulder.

"Thanks."

"No worries."

"Yeah, if only."

The bottleneck of retreating French students at the door has mostly cleared and we hurry after them. Once in the hallway, I have to go left while his next class is to the right. He starts to walk off but I find myself calling out to him.

"Peter?"

He turns, cocking an eyebrow at me. And I suddenly have no idea what I was going to say.

"Uh, catch you later," I stammer out. Dumb. Dumb. Dumb.

But he just nods, expressionless as usual.

"'Course." he says, then walks off, heading for his next class while I just stand there watching him, a huge, gaudy, Las Vegas-style sign flashing over my head, spelling out a single word: **Idiot**.

Chapter 28
If it wasn't my blood, then why is my heart bleeding on the floor?

My last class of the day is physics. As you've probably gathered by now, I really like this class. Not only for all the brilliant rationalizations it supplies me with, but also because a lot of the concepts are just plain cool. It's the first science-y class I've actually gotten into, normally being firmly on the geek side of the great geek/nerd divide.

And yes, I know that to the casual observer geeks and nerds may appear to be interchangeable. But trust me, they're not. While the likelihood of members of either group going to prom is somewhere between "are you kidding me," and "when hell freezes over," the short version is that the wild geek tends to be obsessed with books and music as a way to escape, while the nerd is all about numbers and computers.

What any of this has to do with my day is also in the "are you kidding me" range, but I wanted to point it out as a way of avoiding pointing out that my last interaction with Peter threw me fully back into the distracted daze that had been filling my mind all morning.

And yeah, that brilliant trick worked about as well as most of my plans do, thanks for noticing.

In any case, like almost all of my classes today, I manage to sit through this one without any information actually penetrating my consciousness. Which leads us, of course, to the Schrödinger's Cat-like question: if a teacher lectures, but no one is paying any attention, did they actually make a sound? This, in turn, has the corollary question: if no information is conveyed, are they still a teacher? And, if not, what have they become?[8]

On the plus side, I didn't get called on by the teacher; I didn't try talking to anyone socially inappropriate; I didn't get sent back to the

---

[8] I think the simple answer is "frustrated," but I've never actually liked simple answers. As you may have gathered.

Vice-Principal; none of my vital organs exploded, imploded or otherwise stopped working.

So, all-in-all, it was a good class.

When physics is done—something I determine only by noting that all the other kids have accelerated out of their chairs, and are all simultaneously heading through the one door leading into the hall, jockeying in a rough simulation of fluid dynamics—I get up and join them, struggling to get my overladen backpack onto my shoulder.

Have I mentioned that I've long maintained we should get weight-training PE credit for lugging our twenty or thirty pounds of books around all day? It seems only reasonable, given the utterly unreasonable weight we are called upon to carry. Or maybe we should join the Sherpa's union and at least get dental coverage, under the "if you can't beat 'em, join 'em" plan.

I get into the hall and stagger down to my locker to dump the worst of my load. Having left my crowbar in my other pants, it takes me a good ten minutes and a broken nail to pry the blasted thing open. Hinges and parallelograms do not a happy couple make. That's all I have to say on the subject.

Well, unless you happen to know the bozos who designed these things, in which case I have five more words for you to pass along: *Buildings settle. Factor it in.* Oh, and you owe me a manicure. Not that I've actually ever had one, but between the pain and suffering I've had dealing with this warped bane of my high school existence, not to mention my newly broken nail, I figure someone owes me one.

Still, I rationalize that the delay is all for the best. Peter's probably been weirded out enough by my melt-down yesterday and then my Captain Obvious impersonation after French Class. If he comes out there and finds me waiting anxiously, he'll probably run for the hills.

So I fuss with my locker some more, and try forcing it back into a shape which more accurately matches its still rectangular door. Yeah, that works about as well as you'd probably imagine. Though on the plus side, I do manage to pinch my finger in the door, quite painfully in fact, which at least burns away a good bit of the fog I've been swimming in.

As I suck my finger, I shoulder the stubborn locker closed. Which painfully reminds me that I'd kind of strained that shoulder earlier, picking up the overloaded backpack. At which point I decide that if I try to kill any more time here, I may end up killing myself instead. So, still sucking my sore finger, I head out to the street and the ever-shadeless Big Tree to meet Peter.

Who isn't there.

Crap. I was sure he'd be waiting and I'd stroll out, the very picture of composure. Well, at least the picture of composure if the artist were about three and only had a box of half-broken crayons. But some picture of composure, nevertheless.

Maybe he's waiting on the other side of the trunk, I tell myself. After all, it IS the Big Tree, and though shadeless, it does have a massive enough trunk that even Peter could easily hide behind it. Unfortunately, reality rudely doesn't agree with my brilliant hypothesis and I am now faced with two possibilities.

Well, three.

The last possibility, of course, being more of a grab-bag for a bunch of ridiculous ones such as Peter simultaneously moving around the trunk as I circle it, always remaining on the other side, plus the old tried and true ones like *Alien Abduction*, *Spontaneous Human Combustion*, and *Ascension to a Being of Pure Energy*.

But back to the Big Two.

1. Peter "forgot" that we were catching the T together–either accidentally, deliberately, or subconsciously / deliberately–in which case standing here waiting for him is both a waste of time and rather pathetic, or;
2. He's even later than I am, in which case not waiting for him would be blowing him off, which would be just one more nail in the coffin that I'm making of our relationship.

My knotted stomach is insisting it's #1. Peter's incredibly reliable and often annoyingly punctual. Well, annoying in that I'm not the most organized/punctual person in the world—probably not in the top two billion, if I'm being brutally honest—and his extreme punctuality only highlights how extreme my own version of punctuality is. Just different extremes, that's all.

My mind also agrees that it's most likely #1 but refuses to accept it. Based mostly on the supposition that that if it is #1, then all my fears are completely justified and I don't know if I could bear that. So, it has to be #2 because it just has to be.

So I wait. After a while, I realize that I'm slowly walking the perimeter of the tree, unconsciously testing the theory that's he's just messing with me by staying exactly on the opposite side of the tree. I start randomly changing directions and rushing back the way I came to better catch him in the act. For a moment, I'm sure I hear him, the crack of a foot stepping on a small branch. But when I get to the other side, I can neither find him nor a good contender for the stepped-upon branch.

"What are you doing?" Peter asks from right behind me, generating the fully predictable result. He is apparently as unsurprised as I imagine you are at this point, and grabs my hand before I once again test the theory that two objects cannot occupy the same space at the same time. The objects in question being the Big Tree's trunk and my left hand. And yes, I have tested this theory many, many times before, but the key to good science is repeatability, and I figure I'm just being thorough.

Though in this case, the "thorough," has more to do with being thoroughly annoyed with Peter for messing with me than it does with completeness.

"Don't do that!" I tell him, yanking my hand free of his. Though as soon as I do so, one of my many internal voices petulantly points out that we like having him hold our hand.

I stubbornly ignore it.

"How long have you been hiding?" I demand.

"Hiding?"

"On the other side of the tree."

"Oh. So that's what you were doing. Trying to catch me."

I give him a disbelieving look. Normally I like messing with Peter and he messes with me right back. But I'm just too close to the edge. Actually, it feels like it's all edge and any way I turn I'm going to go crashing down.

"Whatever." I tell him, feeling completely pathetic even as I say it, knowing I've sunk so low that 'whatever' is the high point of my wit. "I can't do this right now."

"Do what?" he protests. "I just got here."

"Sure," I say, shrugging. "Let's go with that. Now can we go home already?"

"Sure, but I really just got here," he protests. "I'm late because Hannah Evans fell down the stairs and hit her head pretty bad."

"Is she okay?"

"She got up and kept insisting she was, but she was bleeding all over the place and she couldn't focus her eyes. I ended up having to carry her to the nurses office."

I am a terrible person.

You see, Hannah Evans is probably the most drop-dead gorgeous girl in our school, and you can just watch the line of boys tripping over themselves to do things for her. Not to mention that she's the head cheerleader, which puts her pretty much at the top of the popularity pyramid in addition to the cheerleading one.

In fact, she's so high up in the social stratosphere that she doesn't even have to be mean to everyone beneath her.

Even that's probably not being fair to her. Last year at cheerleader tryouts, one of the special need girls at our school showed up and really wanted to be a cheerleader. While the rest of the cheery crowd were mocking this girl—Nancy, I think her name is—Hannah pulled her aside and asked if she wanted a special assignment.

At first everyone thought she was pranking Nancy, but no, Hannah created a special position for her, and now Nancy always leads the cheerleaders onto the field wearing this little drum major type uniform and is the happiest girl on the planet. And Hannah apparently told the rest of the cheerleaders that if they didn't like it, there's the door.

But back to me, and why I'm so terrible. See, while Peter may have saved her life for all I know, all I can see is this beautiful girl cradled in his arms, pressed up against his chest... and it makes me a little crazy.

"Good for you," I tell him. "You're a hero, while I've just been wasting the past half hour chasing no one around a tree."

"Gwen, she was really hurt. I'm sorry I kept you waiting but what should I have done? Just left her there so I wouldn't be late?"

I know I'm losing him. I know I'm pushing him farther and farther away from me with every word I say, but I can't help myself. "If she was bleeding so badly, how come you aren't covered in blood?"

"I changed my shirt. Which is another reason I'm so late; I had to go back to the gym to wash off and get another one from my locker."

It makes no sense, but somehow the juxtaposition of him cradling her in his arms followed by him immediately taking off his shirt—maybe even in front of her—is just too much for me.

"I'm going home," I tell him, picking up my backpack and starting off in the direction of the T without waiting to see if he's going to join me.

But he does, and he easily catches up with me. "I don't get why this is such a big deal," he says, trying to make eye contact with me. But I can't turn to look at him, and I just keep on staring straight ahead.

"You're always late," he points out.

"But you aren't!"

I can tell he doesn't quite know what to make of my overly passionate response, and I'm not fully sure I even understand it myself... but it's just wrong. He isn't late. He just isn't.

"True..." he says, drawing out the word. "But I never make a big deal of it when you are."

"Well, maybe you would if I..." I trail off. It's so stupid I can't even say it.

"If you what?"

"Nothing. Forget it."

"No." He gets in my way, forcing me to stop. "What's going on?"

"Nothing."

I try to go around him, but I might as well be trying to go around a mountain, especially one that keeps stubbornly moving to get in my way.

"Peter, stop it!"

"I will when you tell me what's wrong. And if you say nothing again..."

"Please, I just want to go home."

"So, do I. But this is more important."

"Oh, now I'm more important. Pity you didn't think of that back when you were sweeping Hannah off her feet." Oh my god, I can't believe I said that. He looks about as stunned as I feel and I run past him towards the T, the tears flowing.

Even though I have a couple of moments head start and the power of pain driving me, his long legs easily make up for it and he blocks me again, this time taking me in his arms and holding me against his chest. I struggle a little, but it takes too much energy, and the tears are flowing too hard.

Damn. I'm always crying on his chest. Way to go, Gwen. Who wouldn't just love that?

I feel him stroking my hair, but I know he's just doing it to calm me down, the same way you would any child. Still, it slowly works... either that or my body's water percentage drops below 60% and it shuts off the waterworks just to avoid dehydration.

"You can let go of me now."

"But there's a whole area on my shirt that's still relatively dry."

I kind of choke out a laugh but push away from him and he lets me.

"For the record," he says, "you really have nothing to be jealous about with Hannah. Unless you've always wanted a concussion, that is. Because I think she might have a pretty good one."

I pull some Kleenex out of my backpack and blow my nose.

"Why do you even hang around with me?" I ask.

"Well, masochism mostly. Though you do have your qualities."

"Yeah. Such as?"

"Height, and depth for sure. And then there's width, and mass. Oh, and you move through time at the same pace I do. That's a big plus."

"Meaning you can't think of anything."

"Meaning that I don't think you can reduce people to a set of characteristics. People are complicated, you especially."

"You say the nicest things."

"Now that we've got that settled, I think you'd mentioned something about going home."

I nod and we start walking towards the T station. Yet again.

"I just wish..." he says, after a while. I wait, but whatever he was about to say doesn't seem to be coming.

"Yes?" I say, prompting him.

"I just wish," he says, trying again. "I wish you'd be happy; I want my old friend Gwen back."

Yeah, his friend. His old friend Gwen.

"Look," he continues. "I know you've been really stressed recently. Between your Mom, that stupid paper, and trying to find your dad..."

"He texted me," I blurt out.

"What? Who did?"

I can see his eyes light up with understanding before I can even respond.

"Your dad did?" He asks, visibly excited. "Your real dad?!"

I nod.

"What did he say?!"

"That it's complicated."

Peter bursts out laughing. "Oh man, he's your dad, alright. But what else did he say? Are you going to talk? Do you have a time scheduled, or what?"

"He said he wanted to meet in person. That he could send a car."

"Oh my god, that's incredible!"

His enthusiasm is so impossible to deny that it's getting hard to stay mad at him.

"He's going to have 'his man' pick me up on Friday," I tell him, "to take me to his island."

"This Friday?"

"Uh-huh. At noon. I was wondering, well, if you might want to come with."

"Crap. This Friday. Gwen, I'd really like to..."

"...but you can't," I finish for him, the excitement of the moment dissipating like smoke in a cold wind.

"If it were any other day. But Fitz and I..."

"Fitz?" I interrupt. Who the hell is Fitz?

"Fitz, uh, Not Dad."

I feel like Peter just punched me in the stomach. First Hannah, then Not Dad?

"Yeah," Peter goes on a little sheepishly. "He and I are..."

"I don't want to hear it. You do whatever the hell you want with him, but you just keep him away from me. I don't want that guy dating my mom; I don't want him anywhere in my life."

"You've got him all wrong, Gwen. He's taking the day off to drive me..."

"I said I don't want to hear!"

"You really do."

"I really don't."

"But I told him all about your mom, and Yale…"

"I don't care what you tell hi… no, wait a minute, I do care. Tell him to stay the hell away from my Mom. My dad's coming back into the picture, and I don't want him anywhere near her to mess things up."

Peter looks like he's about to argue but then just stops and sighs. "I'll pass the message along. But I really wish you'd let me…"

I don't.

"So, are we going home or what?" I demand.

Without waiting for a response, I pick up my backpack and sling it over my aching shoulder and head out for the orange line. I don't care if it's an ugly color, right now all I care about is getting home. And doing it as fast as possible.

I can feel Peter's presence behind him, but unlike Orpheus, I have no desire to turn around to see if he's really there.

And I don't think we say another word the entire trip home.

Chapter 29
In which the month of Thursday happens.

It feels just like Yale all over again. What was supposed to be this great thing, the scholarship, the chance for Mom... all of it turned on its head in an instant, becoming a quagmire of lies and untruths that's still sucking me down. And just as soon as I'm fully submerged, I know it's going to erupt, pouring out even more hurt and betrayal for Mom.

Yeah, feeling crappy just does wonders for my writing. But hell, if I'm hurting, why shouldn't my sentences be painful as well?

And then there's meeting Dad. I've been dreaming of this my entire life, so why is the only thing I feel a heartsick abandonment that Peter is choosing Not Dad over me.

That night, I have formless dreams of black nothingness in which I can hear voices and laughter, but no matter how hard I search, I can never find whoever's making the noise. I'm just alone, always alone. Finally, I can feel my Mom shaking me and I claw my way up out the pit of sleep, fighting its pull as if it were a physical thing, a riptide of unconsciousness that doesn't want to let me go and lose its prize.

Yeah, that felt just as refreshing as it sounds.

I have a foul taste in my mouth that no amount of brushing will remove, and my whole body just hurts. As I brush my hair, the bathroom mirror shows me dark circles under my eyes so bleak they would make a goth girl proud. I grimace at myself, but can't dredge up enough feeling to care that I look like a member of the undead. And not even a particularly well preserved one at that.

I really don't want to go to school, but I know Mom. If I don't have a fever, chills, an obvious physical injury, or some visible malady like chicken pox or scurvy, then there's no point in even asking.

When I come out of the bathroom, I see that Mom's made cinnamon toast and I dutifully sit down at the table, though I can do little more than nibble on the corner of a piece. Mom looks at me, clearly noticing my lack of appetite, but not commenting, for which I am simultaneously both grateful that I don't have to try to explain, and hurt that she doesn't care enough to find out.

Peter meets me at the T and we pretend everything's normal. He tries once again to explain why whatever he's doing with Not Dad is more important than supporting me with my real Dad, but I won't let him and he drops it.

We get to school, but when we walk inside, everyone starts clapping the way you sometimes see crowds do when soldiers in uniform walk into airplanes or bus stations. Everyone's talking about Hannah and how Peter may really have saved her life. She's still in the hospital with some brain swelling, and the way all the girls are fawning over Peter he may soon have some brain swelling himself.

I slip away from his circle of new admirers but he doesn't seem to notice.

Yeah, big surprise there.

As for the rest of the day, I don't want to talk about it.

Nothing new happens, good or bad. It just passes at what feels like a geological rate. It's like I can physically feel time passing: one second grinding into the next, slowly collecting into the shape of a monolithic minute, heavy and solid and unmoving. Then the process reverses, moments like grains of sand being slowly chipped away by the interminable tick tick tick of the second hand until the minute is finally worn to nothing under time's implacable pace. And then it begins all over again.

And again, and again, and again, until I'm about a million years older and the day finally ends.

Peter is waiting under the Big Tree, though a pair of girls are standing with him, flirting up enough of a storm that I can see it whipping the leaves above them.

The sidewalk goes right next to them so I don't have any real option but to keep walking, though I turn away and stare straight ahead. As I approach, however, Peter excuses himself and jogs over to me, matching my pace.

"Hey, I was waiting for you."

"Yeah, I could see. With your new friends."

"They came over to me. I didn't really have much of a choice."

"Whatever. You can do what you want; you don't owe me anything."

"Yes, I do. I owe you a lot."

"No, you really don't."

"Can I tell you a story?"

"Could I stop you if I tried?"

"No. Not really. Because before you moved in, the building we live in was just this stack of old bricks where I happened to sleep. I felt about as connected to it as I do to this sidewalk. But since you arrived, I don't know, it's different somehow."

He stops talking as we walk, and I can see out of my peripheral vision that he's thinking, trying to figure out what he's trying to say.

"It's like you somehow turned it into my home," he finally says. "By making it yours. Even when I don't see you all day, I know you're there with your book-safe, and your Frankenstein, and your crazy sumo-wrestler sized cat. And I don't feel so alone."

I can feel a single tear rolling down my cheek, but I make no move to wipe it away.

"So, if I've done something wrong... if you're mad at me for some reason, please tell me because I want to make it right."

I don't respond. Not because I don't want to, but because if I do, I'm afraid I'll start crying for real. And I'm really sick of doing that, particularly on him.

"Gwen, please talk to me."

I stop walking and knuckle my eyes, brushing away the wayward tear in the process and threatening my eyes with worse if they don't behave.

"It's not you," I say, my voice cracking.

"Then what is it?"

"It's everything... I'm just a mess."

He smiles. "Yeah, you are."

I nod, and I can feel my frown loosening.

"So what's going on?" he asks gently.

"You know. Everything. Mom, Yale, Dad, dating... I mean Mom dating. Not Dad." I swallow heavily. "It's like there's that sword hanging by a thread over me. You know, the one in the Greek myth?"

"Sword of Damocles."

"Yeah, that one. Except there are a whole bunch of them, all waiting to drop and no matter what I do, I only seem to add more of them."

"Yeah, I can see that," he says, looking over my head as if he really could. Then he looks down and meets my eyes. "Have you thought of maybe taking up sword swallowing?"

So I hit him, and immediately remember why this is such a bad idea. Owww.

Hey, didn't I ask you to remind me not to do that? Some help you are.

"You'll get through it, Gwen. I know you will. I mean you got through that father/relationship paper, didn't you?"

"Only by the grace of Mr. Clavell."

"What did he have to do with it?"

"It's complicated."

"With you, it always is."

"Come on, I'll tell you on the train."

We start walking again.

"So, we're good?" he asks.

"Yeah, we're good." And to my surprise, I actually mean it.

Maybe I will survive this after all.

And tomorrow, I get to meet my long-lost dad who doesn't know I even exist. I mean, what could possibly go wrong?

Now that the thick malaise of despair at losing Peter has been washed away, the butterflies are out in force. I am going to meet my dad tomorrow. And I have absolutely no idea what I'm going to say to him. And I literally mean no idea.

I can't even decide if starting with "hi" is a good plan.

I know this may seem like a no brainer, but if you think about it, "hi" and "hey" are informal, oh it's you again, type greetings. Unless you are trying to be über-cool, you wouldn't say either of them at the start of a job interview, to the Queen, or the Lord High Commander of an alien invasion force.

Wait a minute! That's what I really need. No, not the invasion, but a set of first contact protocols like the government supposedly has for when we meet our future galactic mentors, overlords, or chefs (either *of* us or *for* us) depending on their inclination and eating habits. Though I suppose, *We welcome you in peace to the planet Earth* probably wouldn't fly that well as a first sentence for meeting dad.

Moving onwards, "hello" feels too formal and telephone-y. "Greetings" sounds like you *are* the alien Lord High Commander, "Pleased to meet you" sounds like you're channeling Ms. Manners, and "What's up" is out for obvious reasons (not least of which is that the appropriate response is always *the direction against the pull of gravity*).

I could go with something like "I'm so excited to finally meet you," but as he has no idea who I am, nor what our biological relationship is, it kind of comes off like a crazed fan/stalker combo.

"You have a beautiful island," might work, although planning on that is a calculated risk. I mean, what if it isn't beautiful? Am I going to start our new relationship with an out-and-out lie? Or worse, might it come off as if I'm eyeing the island as a possible asset for a massive child-support grab?

"I'm so glad you invited me," seems somewhat disingenuous as I was the one who initiated our contact and he could feel like he was basically forced into it.

Admittedly, I could just come out with it in a kind of reverse Darth Vader: "Luke, (asthmatic breath) I am your daughter." Though I imagine calling him Luke might throw him off somewhat, but calling him Holden seems both presumptuous and too formal, and calling him Dad... yeah, that would be a guaranteed freak-out.

Maybe I should skip the whole first sentence thing and just plan on babbling incoherently. Much as I am now.

I get through dinner with Mom by being so hyper-focused on her every word that I don't have the processing power to freak out. The downside of this is that I think it freaks her out a bit. Still, she seems a heck of lot better equipped to handle it than I do, and you know, from each according to their abilities, to each according to their needs. Or something like that[9].

---

[9] Points if you know who said it. And *marks* off if you don't, *Karl*. (hint, hint)

"So, what are your plans for tomorrow?" Mom asks, though I imagine her real interest is to change the topic and get me to stop fixating on her.

"Um," I say eloquently. "I haven't really gotten too far, plan-wise. I'm going to head out to the Cambridge library, and then I guess I'll just wing it from there."

"What's at the library?"

It never occurred to me that she'd ask that question. "Uh, books?" I offer in my best teenage wise-ass voice.

"Really?" she responds, matching me ass for ass. "They've upgraded from scrolls, then? Modern wonders will never cease."

"Is there a point in here somewhere, oh mother of mine?"

"I don't know. Is there? I just asked because it seems odd to have a specific destination without a specific reason."

Crap. So much for the whole truth telling part of my plan.

"In case you haven't noticed, Mom, I like books. You wouldn't ask why Sir Walter Raleigh was going to the tobacconist, or why the Cookie Monster was going to Mrs. Fields..."

"As one has been dead for well over four hundred years, and the other is a fictional blue monster, you're right. I really can't see myself asking anyone about why either of them were doing anything."

"That's all I'm saying."

"You, however, as my daughter, are neither dead nor blue, though at times, I will admit that the monster part is sometimes up for discussion."

"I could hold my breath until I turn blue," I offer helpfully.

"You've tried," she points out. "You've never even gotten to periwinkle. So, are you meeting someone there? At the library?"

Really?! Just one time, I'd like to not be utterly transparent to everyone around me.

"From your blush," she says, "I'll take that as a yes."

"I am not blushing."

"Well, you're certainly not turning blue. So, is it Peter?"

"He's busy tomorrow."

"I see. So, who is the lucky guy... or girl? I'm good, either way."

My thoughts are racing. I can't just deny that I'm meeting someone as she'll never believe it. Also, since I've already said I don't have plans, I can't say we're studying or anything. And even if I just say we're hanging out, she'll want details and I know there's no way I'll be able to keep my story straight.

So, I do the only thing possible. I tell the truth.

"I'm meeting with the man of my dreams," I say earnestly, "who's going to pick me up in his limo and sweep me away to his private island."

"It's an amphibious limo?"

"I truly have no idea. There might be a yacht involved or a private airplane. Or, just possibly, his island might even have a bridge."

"Seems like it wouldn't be very private if anyone could drive over to it."

"There are such things as gates, you know."

"And that's your story? Dream men, limos, private islands?"

"And possibly yachts or bridges, yes. Are you happy, now?"

"Not really. But if you don't want to tell me, you don't want to tell me. If he's someone important to you, I'll get to meet him eventually, right?"

I have to stop myself from telling her that she already has, well, more than met him, so I nod to cover my near slip-up. "I promise," I tell her.

She thinks for a moment. "Just be smart, you know. Don't let yourself feel pressured into anything you don't want to."

Ew.

"Trust me, Mom. Absolutely nothing like that's going to happen. Guaranteed."

"But you have protection, right?"

"Not going to happen, Mom. It's just not going to happen."

Mom has an early shift tomorrow, so after we clean up from dinner and she slaughters me at cribbage, she decides to call it a night.

"Have fun on your private island," she tells me. "And call me if you aren't going to be home for dinner."

"I will."

She starts to leave, then turns back in the doorway.

"And remember," she tells me, "you can't legally get married until you're eighteen without parental consent, and I ain't giving it."

"Yeah, that's not on the agenda."

"I know. But whatever you think, you're a beautiful young woman..."

"Mom. I'm sixteen."

"I know that, and you know that... but to the outside world, not so much. When I look at you, you could be a college student."

"Mom, give it a rest. This thing tomorrow, trust me, it's not romantic."

"So, there IS a thing tomorrow!"

"Go to bed, Mom."

"I love you."

"I know."

Hey, why should she get to be Han Solo all time?

Okay, so Mom's off to bed and I have WAY too much nervous energy to sleep. I can't believe I'm finally going to meet my father.

My father. My father.

Gwen. I am your father.

God, suddenly the word father sounds just plain weird. Fah-ther. It's like, keep going, you're almost there. Just a little father.

Maybe "dad." After all, it is Mom, so it should probably be Dad.

That somehow sounds less threatening.

So, what are you going to do tomorrow? Nothing much. I'm just going to meet my dad.

FOR THE FIRST TIME EVER!!!!!! AAAAH.

Okay, so much for the less threatening idea.

Hmmmm... They say that when you're on stage it helps if you imagine the audience naked. I think the idea behind it is that it makes you feel like they're vulnerable as well. So, I should probably imagine what he's thinking about right now. I mean, he hasn't seen Yvette in over sixteen years, that's got to be unnerving, right? He's got to be at least a little bit nervous...

I think it's working.

He's probably wondering what he's going to say to her. How to act cool and composed as if being blown off by her didn't hurt at all. That's got to stress him out. And knowing that he's probably stressing out is somehow relieving mine. It's like there is a stress equilibrium and the more one person is stressed, the calmer the next has to be.

Sure, in my life, I'm normally the big stress case and Mom's the calm rock. But those few times when I have seen her really stressed, like when she's lost a job and we've had to move, I've turned into the calm one and I've talked her through it, one step at a time. Funny how that even works in your imagination. I just need to imagine Dad being stressed and mine seeps away.

Though I think I'll pass on the imagining him naked part. That's just too weird.

So, back to Dad lying awake—fully clothed—trying to plan tomorrow down to the very last detail. I mean, he's probably pretty used to controlling things, what with owning a private island and all. Not to mention, what is a novelist anyway, but a paper god, directing the actions of his paper creations?

Oh crap.

Oh crap, oh crap, oh crap.

Dad is a novelist. A big, successful novelist.

And I haven't yet read any of his novels.

Chapter 30
In hindsight, this was probably inevitable.

After I finish saying oh, crap to myself a couple hundred more times, I realize I can't put this off any longer. I've got to read his book, <u>A View From Midnight</u>. And I've got to do it before tomorrow.

God help me if I don't love it.

Chapter 31
Two am.

Leave me alone, I'm reading.

Chapter 32
4 am

Can't you go read another book for a while? I'm busy!

Chapter 33
Oh my god.

It's 5:17am and I feel like I've had my hand in a light socket for the past several hours. I'm shaking all over and I'm not ready for it to end... but somehow, I've slammed into the back cover like I was on an out-of-control roller coaster that just jumped its tracks and plowed into a brick wall.

Except that's part of the ride and I'm not a pancake. Instead, when the smoke clears, I'm sitting back in the roller coaster loading area, and it's time to get off and rejoin the slow-moving "normal" world. But I want more! I'm not ready for it to end.

Don't get me wrong. It's not like he trailed off in the middle of a sentence or cut to black or left any huge unfinished storylines. He just took me somewhere I didn't know even existed, and I'm not anywhere near ready to go home.

So, I go back and reread the last chapter again.

When I hit that brick-wall of a back cover again, I force myself to close the book. It's getting light outside, which even I know is a little ridiculous. I'm going to get about four and a half hours sleep on one of the most important days of my life... and I wouldn't change it for the world.

I slip Dad's book into the bottom of my pillowcase because I'm not ready to let go of it, and I'm somehow still coherent enough to remember that I can't let Mom see it.

And hugging that pillow, Dad's book pressing into my palm through the thin cloth, I fall into the most refreshing, dreamless sleep I've had in weeks.

Chapter 34
In which I realize that I might as well be in Oz.

Despite my late night—or early morning, if you prefer…, which I don't but I'm too excited to argue semantics—I wake up filled with energy.

Today's the day.

The Day.

D-Day.

Daddy-Day.

And I have no idea what I'm going to wear.

Ahhhh! I've been so obsessed with the fact that I have no idea what to say, that somehow the whole wearing clothes thing didn't even make it onto my radar. I mean, I'd always intended to wear clothes, but the fact that I have none picked out speaks both to my extremely limited options and to my utterly stellar planning skills.

Still, in some ways I suppose it's a good thing I didn't think of it until now as it does put a limit on my indecision. I have to be at the Cambridge Library at noon. It takes maybe 45 minutes to get there, and I do NOT want to be late, so let's call it an hour. Since it's about 10:30am now, and I still have to take a shower, brush my teeth, fight with my hair… that leaves me… uh, about fifteen minutes to freak out over what to wear.

While I'm in the shower, however, I realize that I can multi-task, which gives me probably a whole extra five minutes of panicked indecision as I mentally catalogue my entire wardrobe. It doesn't take me long to realize that absolutely nothing I own is appropriate for an occasion of this significance. Or really an occasion of any significance, but particularly not one I care about.

So I cut my shower short, get out and hurriedly dry off. I wrap the towel around myself and go to twist the last of the water out of my hair when I realize I've completely forgotten to rinse out the conditioner. Argh.

Rather than get back into the shower again, and have to do the whole, full-body drying off process—which is always an exercise in contortionism in this small bathroom—I decide to take a short cut. So I turn the shower back on, and adjust the water temp to an acceptable level of tepidness. I then lean into the shower while still standing outside of it, and stick my head under what passes for the shower's stream in our water-pressure challenged apartment. Or at least, I try to.

What actually happens, of course, is that in order to get the conditioner out of the back of my hair, I have to stick my head far enough into the broom-closet sized shower that the water decides to make a break for it and starts running down my back and onto the bathmat, in the process completely soaking the towel I still have wrapped around me. The one and only towel I have in the bathroom.

On the plus side, I suppose, at least I don't have to do the whole, full-body contortionist, drying off thing again, because there is no longer anything sufficiently dry to do it with.

I come out of the bathroom to discover that all the rest of our towels are in the dirty laundry basket, which Buddha is sleeping in. So faced with the choice of pushing Buddha off and using a dirty towel covered with cat hair and probably smelling of old socks, or alternatively, going to meet my father in the nude, I do the only possible thing.

I dry myself off with my blanket.

Sure, I have no idea whether it will dry out before I need to go to sleep tonight, but I live in Boston. I'm used to sleeping in 98% humidity, when the air is so super-saturated with water vapor that if you spit in the wrong place, it'll suddenly start raining.

This whole little shower mishap has cost me a precious couple of minutes, so as soon as I'm dry enough (or rather, reduced down to an acceptable level of dampness) to pull on my bra and underwear, I immediately go shopping.

In Mom's closet.

Aha! So that's where my Eeyore "The Power of Pessimism" sweatshirt has been hiding.

But there's no time for that; I'll have to steal it back later.

I skip past all her waitress clothes and start looking through her bookstore ones. Sure, they're nice enough and they're completely unstained, which is certainly more than you can say about the bulk of my wardrobe.

But they're all also kind of generically boring, which isn't that surprising when you do nearly all your shopping at second-hand stores and thrift shops. I mean, except for the odd jacket worn by L. Frank Baum, there's generally not a whole lot of interesting clothes there.

Never mind that, I'm getting stressed. I'm nearly halfway through her closet and I've found nothing.

On second thought, do mind it; babbling helps keep my panic at bay and this is actually almost relevant in that it has to do with thrift stores and not having anything to wear, with a magical dash of the universe just plain messing with people.

In other words, my life.

See, L. Frank Baum was the author of the <u>Wizard of Oz</u> books, and when they were making the movie version, the film's costumer apparently couldn't find anything good for the Wizard to wear for the carnival scene in Kansas. So, with nothing suitable in his or her own usual stock of clothing—sound familiar?—this costumer went to *our* shopping venue of choice (aka, a thrift store), and bought several racks of old coats and presented them to the actor and director, who found one that was absolutely perfect.

Um, hint, hint, Universe. I'm open to some good parallels here. Any time now...

In any case, while finding a decent jacket from a thrift store is perhaps surprising, I'll be the first to agree it's not actually miraculous. What made it so, however, was that the actor idly looked through the jacket's pockets and discovered that this completely randomly picked jacket had actually been owned by none other than L. Frank Baum, the author of the Oz books himself!

Cool right? Unfortunately, what is <u>not</u> so cool is that I'm almost through all of Mom's dresses.

Please let there be *something*... please.

I start mentally cataloging all her nicer blouses that I might try to use to pull something, *anything*, decent together, barely glancing at the drab dresses as I flip past them...

And cue the angelic choir.

This is it, no question.

Forget the droids, this *is* dress I've been looking for.

It's floral, but not so busy that it looks like wallpaper. It's got a pale blue background like a summer's day, with the kind of bright spring colors that Mom always tells me bring out my eyes. It somehow looks really familiar even though I can't remember ever seeing Mom wearing it.

I silently promise myself and Mom (in absentia), that I will take amazing care of this dress and will go the entire day without spilling anything on it. I know that's a tall order, but today, it feels like anything is possible. I slip it on over my head and I have a moment of panic when it feels like it's going to be too small, but then I realize it has a fitted waist and I didn't unbutton it all the way. I release the offending buttons and it slips down like it was tailored for me.

Unfortunately, Mom and I don't share the same shoe size, so I have to go back to my closet and dig out a pair of mostly white sandals. They don't look perfect, but they're the best I can do and I'm running out of time.

So, I hastily take off the dress and go brush my teeth. I've learned the hard way that tooth paste is actually affected by gravity, and that the bond between it and my brush is inversely as powerful as the fineness of the clothes I happen to be wearing. Or to put it another way, the chance of it falling off onto my shirt is directly correlated with how nice my shirt is.

I floss, brush my hair, floss again because I can't remember if I actually did or not, and then put on the dress and am out the door. All with a whopping minute and a half to spare.

All I can say is that it's a good thing I gave myself those extra fifteen minutes, because the T ride over to the library is excruciating. I remember that Not Dad's phone has a clock built in, so I basically spend the entire ride flipping open the phone and calculating and recalculating when I'll arrive. I tell myself I am being crazy; it's not like Dad's "man" will just turn around and leave if I'm a couple of minutes late.

But even with all my reasoned arguments, my adrenal glands decide that we are on a race against time, and every time the subway car pauses and opens its doors at yet another station, they go into overdrive, screaming silently at the driver to GO, GO, GO!

A Novel of Mystery, Love, and of Chocolate that Defies Description

I squeeze through the subway car doors at Harvard Square Station even before they are fully open, and race up the stairs despite the fact that it's only 11:40 and I have twenty minutes for what is basically a five to ten minute walk.

I burst out into the sunshine at Harvard Square and pause for a second, blinded by the bright light after the dimness of the station. My heart is racing and I'm already breathing heavily, though I haven't done anything other than run up several flights of stairs. Well, okay, I guess that does kind of explain it.

It's another hot day, and despite the fact that my feet are dying to run all the way to the library, I refuse to give in because I know that if do, I'll arrive all hot and sweaty, with my hair even more disheveled than usual. My feet don't agree with me, but for once I remember that I'm actually in charge of this whole body thing, and I set off in a brisk pace towards the library.

As I approach, I see this guy standing by the tower where we're supposed to meet with a large, elongated placard. I'd guess that it's about three and a half, to four feet long and maybe a foot and a half wide. I can't really see what's on it too well, because he's flipping it up into the air and spinning it around like he was a drum majorette spinning a baton.

There's a small crowd of people watching him and I figure he must be a street performer or something. As I approach, he flips it up over his head and spins it around like a helicopter propeller, first using both hands to get it going faster and faster, then dropping one arm down and bouncing the whirling placard up and down on a pair of extended fingers.

He's really good.

He snatches it out of the air as it begins to slow down, flips it once around his back and ends up holding it out in front of him. He's got it the long way up, and now that it's stopped moving I can finally see what's on it.

The entire placard is a huge blow-up of a set of four still frames of a couple in a photo booth. In the top two they're kissing passionately and you can't really see their faces, but in the third and fourth, they've stopped and turned to face the camera.

I've got the weirdest feeling of déjà vu, but it's coupled with the equally strong feeling that I've slipped into an alternative reality. Because I'm staring at Mom and Dad in a photo strip just like the one

I've grown up staring at. One that I know so well I can describe it with my eyes closed.

And this one is completely the same. And completely different.

I must have the strangest expression on my face because out of the corner of my eyes, I can see the people standing around looking back and forth between me and the film strip blow-up. And I suddenly realize why this dress looks so familiar.

Somewhere, L. Frank Baum must be laughing his ass off.

Chapter 35
In which I realize that knowing how to turn dead bodies into plastic might come in quite handy.

I'm staring dumbstruck at the placard when I notice the guy holding it is staring dumbstruck back at me.

"How is it that you've gotten younger?" he finally asks me, looking back and forth between me and the pictures on the placard.

"Um, it's complicated."

"I'll bet," he says, then shrugs, accepting it as if it weren't even the weirdest thing he'd seen today. He tucks the placard under his arm and walks towards me. As he does, he smiles at the people who've been watching him.

"Sorry, folks, the show's over. Enjoy the rest of your day."

Everyone disperses except an elderly woman who walks over and presses a dollar into his hand and utterly refuses to let him refuse it.

"You kids make an adorable couple," she says, leaning over to me and whispering confidentially, but doing so at a volume that makes the effort completely pointless. "Don't let this young man get away."

"No, we're not..."

But she's already turning away, and she stride off waving cheerfully at us as she goes. I stare after her as I feel the heat of an epic blush creeping over my cheeks. Great.

"Well," I say, turning to the guy. "That was awkward."

"I have no idea what you're talking about," he says, smiling innocently. "I didn't hear a thing."

He sticks out his hand. "I'm Chris."

He's got a nice smile and his handshake's warm and firm. He's also actually a little shorter than me, which is kind of weird after hanging around with Peter for so long. And where Peter is big and weight lifter strong, Chris is small and wiry, like a gymnast. He's probably in his early twenties, with short brown hair and intense blue eyes, and he's dressed casually in a black t-shirt emblazoned with Carpe Noctem written in large white letters, with Seize the Night beneath it.

"Do I pass inspection?" he asks, still smiling.

"Sorry, you're just not what I expected," I say, hastily releasing his hand.

"Thank god. I hate being predictable. He probably told you he was *sending his man*, didn't he?"

I nod, slightly embarrassed, though I'm not altogether sure why.

"He just loves saying that," Chris tells me, rolling his eyes. "Comes from watching way too much Downton Abbey, if you ask me. Anyway, come on, the car's this way."

He turns and we start walking towards the parking lot.

"So, uh, how did you learn to flip that thing around like that? It was pretty cool."

"I spent a couple of years out in California, and places like self-storage and condo buildings hire guys to stand out on the sidewalk with big cardboard signs advertising their wares."

"And they let you flip it around like that?"

"Hell, they encourage it. Gets a lot more attention than if you're just standing there holding it like a human signpost. Of course, you're supposed to stop every so often and brandish it so people can read it, but half the guys out there are just having a good time putting on a show."

"Well, you were really good."

He shakes his head. "Nah, I'm strictly middle of the pack. For some of these guys, it's almost like break-dancing. Just mind-blowing."

We reach the parking lot and he heads straight for a black Lincoln Town Car, which isn't exactly what I was hoping for. I mean, I've looked in the windows of them and they look like pretty fancy luxury cars, but they're more like limo-wannabes than a real limo.

"You want this, by the way?" Chris says, holding out the blown-up photo strip placard.

I'm so surprised by the offer that I almost blurt out "really?" which always bugs the hell out of me when people say it to me, as if they think that by asking it, I'll suddenly change whatever statement I just made. Instead, I settle on "You're sure?" which, although a cousin to "really," is at least a valid question.

"Yeah, why not? As cute as you two are to look at, I can't really see me hanging it up in my apartment."

He starts to hand it to me, then stops himself and looks at it. "You don't think that old lady thought this was me, do you?"

"I thought you didn't hear anything."

But I look back and forth between him and the picture, nevertheless. "I really don't see it."

"Yeah, me neither. Although..." he says, looking at me thoughtfully. "Before I give this to you and whisk you away, I should probably make sure you're actually the person I was sent to pick up."

"Technically speaking, I'm not."

"Excuse me? You're not Yvette?"

"Well, also technically speaking, there is no Yvette. But I am the person you were sent to pick up."

"So, how does that work?"

"Um, it's complicated. But I really owe it to Hol... to Mr. Baxter, to tell him first."

Yeah, that feels really weird. Calling my Dad Mr. Baxter. Not that Holden or Dad is really any better.

"Holden Baxter, Inc. you mean."

I have no idea what he's talking about, but I figure it's like DDS or PhD or CSI or something. Still, since I know that he has no clue what I'm talking about, it doesn't feel fair to ask him anything when I'm not ready to answer any of his questions. "Sorry, I guess so."

"Okay," he says, shrugging. "Good enough for me."

He hands me the giant-sized photo strip and I take it, though I have absolutely no idea what I'll do with it. I mean, it's not like I can exactly hang it up in our apartment... well, at least until I drop quite a number of bombshells on Mom. But I desperately want this window into my past and I can't stop staring at these almost, but not quite familiar images.

We reach the Lincoln Town Car and I tear myself away from the photos.

"So what's the etiquette," I ask. "Do I sit in the back, or can I sit up front with you?"

He laughs. "In order to sit in the back, you'd first need to build one."

Huh? I look back at the Town Car but it's this large four-door sedan...

"That's not my car."

He pulls out his keys and presses the remote. I can see the flash of headlights from the other side of the Town Car, but I still can't see what it is. I follow Chris around the Lincoln's pretentiously large hood and there is a small, sky-blue, two-seater convertible.

"So, what do you say?" Chris asks. "Ready for some wind in your hair?"

Oh man. I get to ride in a convertible. This is better than a limo any day.

We put my new, precious photo strip placard in the trunk, and he pulls the top down, flips some latches and we are open to the sky! The car is like a mini race-car with the rear of the body coming up to meet the seats' headrests in two raised bulges like the barrels of a giant double-barreled shotgun. It's a Saturn convertible, which I've never seen before, but I already want one.

As I get in, I suddenly remember that I'd asked Peter to come with me. Oh man. He could barely fit in this thing by himself; we would have had to truss him up and tie him to the back like a Christmas tree. For some reason, the image just cracks me up, and I can't stop laughing.

Chris is very confused, and in between my gasping for breath and bouts of uncontrollable laughter, I struggle to explain, but it comes out more like: "My friend... (deep breath, try to get a straight face) Peter... (uncontrollable laugh)... like a Christmas (you can hang on... no, I can't!) Tree! On the back!"

"Alright then," he says starting the engine, clearly no closer to understanding than when I'd started what we'll charitably call my explanation. "I think it may have lost something in the translation."

He puts on his seatbelt and turns to me. "Now, if you would kindly restrain yourself, we can be off."

"I'm trying!" I say between unstoppable giggles and gasping for breath.

"Actually, I meant your seatbelt."

"Oh." This sets off a whole other set of giggles, but I manage to put on my seatbelt despite them.

I can tell he's amused by my current hilarity, but I'm sure he's also wondering if I'm not a complete nutcase. A question I ask myself quite often.

He pulls out of the parking lot the way you should pull out of a parking lot in a hot car like this, with a roar and just the tiniest screech of wheels. As soon as we get even a little bit of speed, the wind picks up and start batting my hair around me like a cat playing with a ball of yarn. The feel of the wind in my face (not to mention the hair in my face) both calms and energizes me simultaneously.

I close my eyes and lift my face to the sky, feeling the sun on my face and the air whipping my hair round me. I've always loved the wind in my face, and somehow being buffeted around also knocks me out of my head, something you'll probably only understand if you've ever wished your brain had an "off" switch. Right now, with my eyes closed, I imagine I'm soaring through the air, rather than just driving through it.

Or passenging through it, as Chris is the one doing the actual driving; a fact which is probably all for the best as I don't have a license, have no idea how to drive, and have no clue where we're going. But I want this car more than ever.

It's pretty hard to talk with the top down, but I do manage to apologize for being so giddy, shouting to him that I'm both really nervous and severely sleep-deprived. Or at least that's what I say. For all I know, he hears me telling him I'm an old biddy who both loves gerbils, and is deeply depraved. But in either case, he nods pleasantly in agreement and I guess that's what mostly matters.

We're heading north up the coast to Gloucester, up Route 1A which pretty much hugs the coast up through Lynn and Swampscott, past Marblehead and Peabody and straight through the heart of Salem. They're, of course, pronounced Glaw-stah, Swamskit, Mahbl-head, Pee-b'dy and well, Lynn and Salem. The most famous residents of Glaw-stah are the Gorton's of Gloucester Fish Company, established in 1849, whose website proudly proclaims them to be a "leader in countless seafood innovations like Fresh Lock processing in the late 1950's, and the now-famous Gorton's Fish Sticks in 1952."

Yes, the innovative idea to take fresh fish and somehow turn it into a frozen, rectangular, bread-crumbed "stick" is the kind of into-the-box thinking that's helped make America what she is today.

Salem, of course, is known for its infamous witch trials in the late sixteen hundreds. The Salem Witch Museum, with its iconic "multi-media show" (that consists mostly of static scenes featuring wax figures that get dramatically lit and then doused with over-dramatic sound effects and narration), is a de rigueur elementary school field trip around here.

If you go to its website, you'll see that it proudly lays claim to the title of "Salem's Most Visited Museum" and its extensive, in-depth examination of this historic tragedy caused by fear and hysteria will take you "at least an hour" to experience.

All of which begs the questions: Are there actually any other museums in Salem? Why else would you travel up to Salem except to learn about the Salem Witch Trials? I mean, it's not like hordes of tourists are descending on Lynn, and it's only about 5½ miles away. And, lastly, a tragedy that cost twenty men and women their lives and which still reverberates in our cultural identity well over 300 years later really takes an entire hour to experience?

God, with innovation and attention to detail like that, it's amazing that the primaeval us didn't break our necks getting down out of those trees in the first place.

I open my eyes to the sound of gravel crunching under our tires.

We've turned off the main road and pass a sign warning that it's a private lane. It's pretty heavily wooded on either side and I can't really see where we're going, through from the sharp, salty smell I'm fairly sure it's towards the ocean. Which makes a lot of sense if you think about it, as that's where you'd be likely to keep your private island.

A wood-carved sign hanging from a tree branch that extends over the road says in ornate lettering **Beware the Todal**. A little while further is another one. **And the Geese.** this one says.

Okay, this is going to drive me crazy. It sounds so familiar but all I can think of is something about it gleeps and sounds like rabbits screaming. I look at Chris, but he has an expectant expression like he's waiting for me to ask. So, of course, I don't.

The car comes around a tight curve and I can see the ocean beyond, with one last sign hanging for us. This one says: **The oyster is a blob of glup, but a woman is... a woman**. As we pass under it, I see, carved into the very bottom of the sign, the name James Thurber.

Of course! I turn to Chris triumphantly.

"The Baker's Dozen of Timepieces," I tell him.

"Excuse me?"

I repeat it, enunciating each word proudly, savoring his confusion.

He pulls over in front of a small wooden building, well worn by the elements. Bleached wooden sides that look like they might have been blue once face us, split by a heavy wooden door with a torpedo shaped lobster cage buoy hanging on it, bracketed by large, tightly shuttered windows bound with rusting iron. It's in that glorious run-down state where it could be an eyesore, but instead somehow exudes history with the same dramatic air of past glory that a castle ruins might have.

I can see Chris trying to make sense of what I said, running it over again in his mind, and I can also see the moment when it all clicks.

"Nice," he says appreciatively. "The Baker's Dozen of Timepieces. I'll have to remember that."

If you have no idea what we're talking about you're (a) probably not alone, and (b) are so missing out. See, all of those signs are from The Thirteen Clocks, this half-book/half-poem/half-fable/half... *something* that James Thurber wrote back in the 1950's when he was supposed to be writing another book entirely—one that was on deadline—making it almost certainly the most worthwhile procrastination in the history of delaying tactics. And my Dad's putting it up on signs leading towards his island? How cool is that!

We get out of the car and Chris puts the top back up, the whole process taking less than a minute. Yeah, I've definitely got to get me one of these.

"I'd recommend you leave the photo blow-up here in the car," Chris tells me, "because the ride over to Glenhaeven can get a little... moist."

Glenhaeven?! That was the name of the house in A View From Midnight!

Chris pulls out what I'd imagine a skeleton key would look like and uses it to unlock the shed's heavy wooden door. "And before you ask," he says as he leads me into the dim shed. "The novel came first."

"He didn't put in all the secret passageways and strange dead ends, did he?"

"But of course. It's as close as he could make it."

In that moment, I finally understand the appeal of the question "Really?!", at least when you've been told something so fantastically amazing that you can't actually believe you heard what you know you did. Oh my god; Glenhaeven. It was almost as much a character in the book as the characters were. And we really get to go there?!

He flips on the light switch by the door, and a single bare bulb comes to life, lighting the room with a harsh yellow glow.

"Though unfortunately" he adds, "the Grey Walkway didn't get put in until late last year. And the gardens are still kind of struggling; the salt air is the current theory why."

"And the ghost?"

"Well, some say he contributed that himself."

Now that my eyes are adjusting to the harsh lighting after the dim interior, I realize that shed is filled with bright yellow rain slickers hanging on the walls, each with matching pants and hats, just like you see the Gorton's Fisherman wearing. It's kind of creepy actually, like they're the discarded skins of hazmat-suited government agents.

I suddenly realize that I know nothing about Chris, and here I am, alone in this secluded shed with him. Not to mention that nobody knows exactly where I am, not even me. He could kill me, then die my skin yellow and use whatever process they use on the people in those "Bodies" exhibits to turn me into just another one of the slickers hanging limply on the wall around me.

Maybe he's already done that to dozens of people, and they're all staring at me mutely from their shiny yellow hells.

Or, I could do all that to him and make off with the car.

Yeah, but then I wouldn't meet Dad, nor see Glenhaeven, so I should probably at least wait until after. Also, I should probably learn to drive first, and figure out how to turn dead people into plastic. Oh, and get lots of yellow dye.

Man, why does everything always get so complicated?

Chapter 36
In which I have absolutely no idea what's going on.

The less said about the ride across the bay to Glenhaeven the better. It is cold, wildly choppy, and even the Gorton's Fisherman costume Chris has me wear does little to stop the near constant icy spray of our little motorboat from soaking all of my extremities.

Chris chats merrily throughout, seemly impervious to the wet, the cold, and the nauseating choppiness. He shouts out what I imagine is tour guide type information, pointing at what I suppose are sights and sea life, but I'm not actually sure because I can't hear more than a word or two over the combined roar of the outboard motor, the wind, the sea, and my rebelling stomach.

The island finally looms up before us, sheer granite cliffs turned white by the legions of seagulls nesting and cawing and fighting there. Not to mention their generous contributions of copious amounts of their droppings as well.

You have no idea how relieved I am when the rocks abruptly give way to a tiny beach with a wooden dock sticking out into it, offering the glorious promise of dry land.

Chris guns the engine and heads directly for our salvation.

"Hold on to something!" he says, and I barely have time to grab the railing before he cuts the engine and spins the wheel, the boat following suit. He gives one last short burst from the engine and the boat comes to a dead stop right next to the dock, the bow pointing back towards the ocean.

"Stay put until I finish tying her up," Chris warns me as he steps out onto the dock, holding a rope attached to the boat's bow. Even though we're totally at rest in relationship to the dock, I still feel like I'm being tossed around by the waves and I desperately want to get off this amusement park ride from hell.

"That wasn't so bad, was it?" Chris says as he loops another line from the rear of the boat—sorry, the stern—over a large metal cleat built into the deck. "You should try it when it's not so calm."

I have no idea if he's being sarcastic or not, but if that was calm, I think drowning might be preferable to rough. He holds out his hand to help me disembark and I gratefully take it, then step on to the blessedly solidity of the dock.

Except it isn't.

Despite the fact that the dock appears to be firmly attached the ground, it feels like the whole world is still bucking up and down. I try to take a step towards the beach but my balance is completely shot. Instead of the straight line I'd intended to walk, I lurch abruptly to the side and am about to go pitching off the dock when Chris grabs my arm.

"Whoa there. Are you okay?"

"Please tell me this island isn't built on the back of a giant turtle, or something like that."

"No, nothing so pedestrian."

"Let me guess," he says, continuing to hold my arm to steady me, for which I am extremely grateful. "You're feeling like you're back in the open water, with everything going up and down."

I nod, closing my eyes, hoping that will make it better, but it actually makes it worse so I quickly open them again.

"Come on," Chris says, and with his help we slowly walk off the dock towards the sand. I feel ridiculous; I know everything's rock solid —I can see that it is—but my brain is insisting otherwise, telling me that the ground is alternatively pushing up abruptly against my feet then dropping away from under me. I can only imagine what I look like from the top of the bluff, staggering down the dock.

Not exactly the entrance I'd had in mind.

"What you're feeling is called Mal de Débarquement, or land sickness depending on its severity. Basically it has something to do with your inner ear getting acclimatized to the boat's motion and then not resetting when you get back on land."

"And you don't get it?"

"Not anymore."

We step down onto the sand, but it's no better.

"And how long does this just lovely feeling last?"

"It's typically over in a couple of months."

"Months!?"

"Usually. Sometimes longer. But I've never heard of it lasting more than ten years, at the most."

"Oh, stop torturing the poor girl!"

I look up and a young woman in her mid-twenties is coming down the path towards us. She has vibrantly red hair with that natural look that dyes never quite match. As she gets closer, I see that she's also got tons of freckles, ones that I'm sure she hates and everyone else thinks are really cute. Much like my hair, except without the "everyone else thinking it's cute" part.

"What he's talking about is real Mal de Débarquement," she says as she joins us. She's got a lilting accent that I can't place, though I'm thinking Ireland or Scotland just based on her looks. "And you only ever get that after having been on a ship for weeks or months. You've just got a touch of land sickness and you'll probably feel completely normal in less than an hour."

"Speaking of which," Chris adds. "A lot of people think ginger helps shorten the duration, so Gwen, let me introduce you to Ginger."

"Really," the red-headed girl says, turning to him. "You aren't getting tired of that?"

"Apparently not."

She rolls her eyes and turns back to me. "You must be Yvette."

I shake my head. "Gwen, actually."

"Oh. Sorry about that, I guess I'm waiting for someone else."

"No, there is no Yvette. I mean, there kind of is, but that's not actually her name. And I'm not her."

I realize I'm babbling. "Anyway, I am the one you're waiting for."

God, that sounded messianic. I am the one you're waiting for.

"I mean," I add hastily, "that I'll be playing the role of Yvette in today's meeting. As it were."

Ginger smiles at me, which is a hell of a lot better than calling for a straight jacket, which seems like equally appropriate response.

"Good enough for me. Anyway, as you've probably gathered, I'm Ginger. And yes, my parents have a really bad sense of humor. Much like Chris's."

"You're just mad I won last week's Pun-a-thon." Chris says, pointing at her, leaving me standing on my own, the moving ground threatening to send me stumbling.

"Whoa, dizzy person here."

Ginger takes my arm to steady me, and Chris grabs her other one.

"Make that dizzy people," he says, swaying and giving Ginger big puppy dog eyes. "I think I really need some of that magic ginger cure..."

Ginger rolls her eyes, but I can see that she's amused.

"Not that you deserve it..." she says as she leans over to give him a quick kiss on the cheek. But he turns to face her at the last second and she ends up kissing him on the mouth instead. After her initial surprise, she pulls back laughing.

"Bad dog," she tells him, though clearly she's still pleased. "We have guests."

"Guest, singular. Don't exaggerate. But I feel so much better, now."

Chis turns to me, grinning. "Sorry, I couldn't help myself. Ginger's Romance." he says by way of an explanation.

"Along with Lunch & Desserts," Ginger adds.

Okay. As explanations go, that one kind of sucks, because I have no clue what they meant.

"It makes perfect sense, if you think about it," Chris adds. "Given that the conventional wisdom is that the best way to a man's heart is through his stomach. Though personally, I still think it's through the rib cage. I'm Horror and Errands."

Okay, I'm now completely and officially lost. What the heck is Horror and Errands? As you know by now, I am not above messing with people, but what makes this all the weirder is that I get a really strong feeling that they think they're making sense.

"Anyway," Ginger says, as I'm debating whether I should just go with it or confess my confusion. "Mr. Ink is waiting for you up at the house, and since I got Island Gopher of the day, well, here I am."

All I really got out of that was that someone, presumably Dad, is waiting for me. So just go with it seems like the most expedient choice. "Uh, lead on?"

* * *

Chris takes my dripping yellow fisherman outfit and I'm kind of surprised to find that my dress isn't as badly soaked as I'd feared. Seems like the bright yellow rubberized suit was good for something after all. Beyond making me look like a giant rubber ducky, of course.

By the time all that's taken care of, I seem to be getting my land legs back, or have at least sufficiently adapted to the apparently moving ground that I am finally able to walk a relatively straight line all by myself. Whoo-hoo! I won't look like I'm completely drunk when I first meet Dad. Big win!

However, though my dizziness is fading, my confusion isn't. I mean, this island would be surreal enough in and of itself, what with the massive Glenhaeven estate looming down at us from the top of the bluff, almost exactly as I imagined it. But add the fact that I've barely understood a third of what Ginger and Chris have been saying, and it's like I've literally stepped into a different world.

I suddenly remember that Dad wrote a book <u>Down the Rabbit Hole</u> or something like that. You know, the one I could only find in German. Obviously, I have no idea what it was about, but as he actually built Glenhaeven... What would stop him from populating it with people, I don't know, actors from his other stories?

Yeah, I don't even know what I'm saying, which only seems appropriate given that I don't know what anyone else is saying either. As if on cue, Ginger turns to me.

"So, what are you?" she asks, her accent only adding to the otherworldliness. "No, wait. Don't tell me, let me guess."

That's fine by me as I have no idea what she's asking. Pisces? High school student? Homo Sapien? Really and truly confused?

I try to keep my bafflement off my face as she looks me up and down while we walk. I'm going for a mysterious Mona Lisa type smile though I probably just look like I have indigestion.

"Hmm. I think I'll have to put my money on Why-A..."

She trails off. I wait a moment for her to finish her thought, but she is just looking at me expectantly. Okay...

"Why a what?" I finally ask.

"I'm not sure," she says. "Could be straight... or disto... no, you're straight, aren't you?"

"Uh, that's a kind of personal question."

She looks confused for a second then laughs.

"No, I didn't mean it like that." She grins sheepishly. "Yeah, that kind of came out completely wrong, didn't it?"

"Pretty much. So, what did you mean?"

"That you didn't have a sub-flavor. You know, esseff, fancy, disto. So, am I right?"

I have literally no idea what she's talking about, though it does kind of sound like flavors of quarks... you know those subatomic particles that make up everything. Well, they come in flavors too: up, down, strange, charm, top, and bottom.

None of that, however, explains why she thinks I might or might not be disto or fancy flavored, sorry sub-flavored, and frankly it's beginning to make quantum mechanics sound positively rational, spooky action at a distance and all. Still, I figure that agreeing with the crazy person is probably the safest route, so I nod, which seems to satisfy her.

We reach the top of the path, and the wind picks up as we come out from the lee of the bluff and make our way out onto it. We've come up in the middle of the Grey Walkway next to one of the huge statues that give it its name. Intellectually I know it's only a year or so old, because Chris had said that they'd only finished the Grey Walkway last year. But my gut doesn't believe it. This massive thing in front of me feels ancient, like it would be completely at home in Stonehenge, or at least would be if they had statues there.

You know how sometimes when you wake up you aren't completely sure if something happened in the real world, or if you just dreamt it? Yeah, well take that feeling, multiply it by about a hundred and you'll start to understand how I'm feeling right now.

If you haven't read <u>A View From Midnight</u> yet, you have to understand that it kind of gives you that feeling all by itself. The characters are so real, the places so vividly drawn, they have a truth to them that transcends their fictional origin. And now, walking here, literally inside the book's world, it's giving me a whole new kind of land sickness.

But this time it's my sense of reality that's gone all topsy-turvy.

The closest statue is probably at least seven feet tall, though its plinth raises it another foot or two off the ground. It's made of some kind of gray stone, almost the color of concrete but with the barely visible striations that show it's real stone. Or at least a very cleverly wrought fake one.

Although it's clearly a tall and slender woman, it's a woman as seen through a fog, all of her features and details sand-blasted away by the winds of time. In the book, no one knew how old they were, nor where they came from. They were discovered by Burdick Glen, a local fisherman who'd sought refuge here in the tiny bay now below us, fleeing from a sudden storm. Hence the name of the mansion: Glenhaeven.

"Pretty mind-blowing, aren't they?" Ginger offers.

"God. They just *are* the Gray Sisters."

"Yeah. I saw them put in and I still can't believe they haven't been here forever."

We slowly start walking towards the building, my head still reeling with it all.

"And the book really came first?"

"Yup."

Humans have an amazing capacity for compartmentalization, where we can hold multiple conflicting ideas and values at the same time. Death is a big one. We all know we're going to die but we don't really believe it. And how could we without becoming completely paralyzed trying to protect ourselves from every possible danger? The reason I bring this up is because right now I know that everything around me was created to bring to life words on a page.

I also know it wasn't; that every word Dad wrote was simply true.

In the book, Burdick Glen said that as soon as he saw the Gray Sisters, he knew they'd led him here, though for what purpose he didn't know. We never learned exactly what else he found on the island, though apparently it was valuable enough to turn him from a subsistence fisherman into lord and owner of this island overnight, not to mention making him rich enough to afford the construction of Glenhaeven.

There are dozens of the Gray Sisters staring out over the bluff, forever gazing out to sea. Some are little more than featureless lumps while others are tantalizingly sensual, their true features and form just barely out of reach under the veil of their weathering. Burdick himself insisted they were statues of a race lost well before recorded history. This was their last stronghold, he claimed, and they'd set the Gray Sisters on the bluff as guardians awaiting their return.

Or at least all that is what Dad wrote in his book.

"It's such a pity he never got to see them installed," Ginger tells me. "I mean he saw all the artist's renderings, of course, but that's nothing compared to actually standing here and seeing them."

"Who never did?"

"Bax."

"Sorry, am I supposed to know who that is?"

She looks at me like I'd just asked her who Jesus Christ was.

"How did you get here without reading any of the fellowship material?"

"I'm not here on a fellowship."

"Oh," she says, obviously confused. "I just assumed... so, what are you doing here? If you don't mind my asking," she hastily adds.

"It's kind of personal. But I can tell you after my meeting."

"With Mr. Ink?"

That's kind of a cute nickname, considering that he inked our entire surroundings. Yeah, sure, he probably used a word processor like the rest of us, but Mr. Electron or Mr. Notebook just don't have the same caché. Hmm, I wonder if he came up with it or if one of the fellows did.

"Right, Mr. Ink."

"But now you've got me curious," Ginger says. "I can't wait to hear what this mysterious business of yours is."

"Yeah. So, what kind of fellowship do they give here?" I ask, changing the subject.

"Writing. Free room and board for up to a year. You have to help out a little with the running of the place, but otherwise you can just write."

"So that's what Chris meant when he said you were romance. And desserts."

"What did you think he meant?"

"Frankly, I didn't have a clue!"

We both laugh at the absurdity of it all.

"No wonder you were acting so weird," Ginger says, grinning, "when I asked you what you were. That's shorthand around here for your genre."

Duh. YA, Young Adult. Not Why-A.

"The last half hour is making a lot more sense now," I tell her.

"I'll bet."

"But what the heck is disto?"

"Dystopian."

Ugh. I can't believe I didn't get that. And esseff isn't esseff, it's SF... Science Fiction.

"But who's Bax?" I ask.

"Mr. Baxter, the guy who built this place."

I have to stop myself from insisting that Burdick Glen had built it. I know it's stupid, but at the moment, Dad feels more like a fictional character than his own characters do, what with so little I really know about him.

I also almost ask why Dad never got to see it, but something stops me. Oh my god, he must have gone blind. No wonder he sent Ginger down to meet me. The path up the bluff wasn't that steep, but it didn't have any railings and if you couldn't see where you were going...

My poor dad! Of all my senses, that's the last one I'd want to lose because books are my window to the world, my escape from what can frankly sometimes be a depressing reality.

No wonder he only wrote two books. He couldn't see the words to write any more.

I feel my eyes start to well up but I force the tears back. I won't finally meet my Dad with red, puffy eyes.

I won't, even if he can't see them.

Chapter 37
In which I discover a terrible truth.

Even though I want to stop and examine each of the Gray Sisters—and they are all astonishingly different from each of their companions—I need to finally meet my brilliant, blind dad, the very man from whose mind these statues sprang.

So Ginger and I walk down the Gray Walkway towards Glenhaeven, the gravel crunching under our feet. I've been waiting for this moment my entire life, and now that it's actually here, all my senses seem so alive, it's almost frightening. The tang of salt on the moisture laden breeze assaults my every breath; the crash of the ocean mingles with the calls of the sea gulls, then echo through me like I am a sounding board, vibrating to their ebb and flow.

The pounding of my heart joins the din, and even the air seems to have taken form and substance so that as I walk through it, I feel it pressing on my skin like cool water.

I am so lost in the sensations that our arrival at the main entrance to Glenhaeven comes upon me as a surprise. It's a heavy oak door bound with brass studs and, as it should be, the door handle is a sea serpent, frozen in the act of swimming through the wood, leaving it half in and half out of its oaken sea.

It's even more wonderful than I'd imagined.

Ginger opens the door, and we enter the grand hall.

I could go on describing everything but I won't. Suffice it to say that whoever designed this place is a genius, and this simply *is* Glenhaeven. If you want to know more, read Dad's book, because frankly I can't do it justice.

Ginger leads me across the hall and knocks on a half-open door, which seems rather unnecessary given the volume at which my heart is beating.

"Come in," a pleasant baritone voice says from within the room, and Gwen pushes open the door. It's a home office, which was never mentioned in the book, but I guess everyone still has to actually live and work here so I'll give them a pass.

He's seated behind his desk, and I do what any normal person would do in this kind of situation. I freeze completely.

Gwen gently pushes me into the room and out of my paralysis.

"Hey, Mr. Ink," she says, "This is Gwen, who will be playing the role of Yvette today."

She glances at me mischievously but I'm too busy staring at my dad to do more than barely register it in my peripheral vision.

He's changed a lot since the photos, particularly as he's lost all his wavy brown hair except for a small, close cropped fringe just above his ears. And that's pure silver now. But he has kind eyes and a bundled up energy that's evident even though he's still sitting.

"Thanks, Ginger," he says. "If you could close the door on your way out, I'd really appreciate it."

"Sure thing. See you later, Gwen. And don't forget to find me before Chris takes you back; I want to hear all about it."

She leaves and I'm alone with Dad, who has a kind of sad smile now as he looks me up and down.

"Well, then," he says. "You are not exactly who I was expecting."

"I know. But I was afraid that if I told you, you wouldn't want to see me."

"Hmm."

He pushes back from the desk, his chair gliding backwards. Then he spins and comes around the desk, revealing that he's in a wheel chair.

"Why don't we move over here to the sofa so you can sit down. I'm told it's quite comfortable though I haven't actually tried it myself, well, for obvious reasons."

I sit down on the sofa and start to lean back casually, but that feels so completely wrong, I stop almost immediately. I smooth down my dress and suddenly have no idea what to do with my hands. I don't know about you, but for me, what I do with my hands when I'm talking or gesturing or sitting just happens on its own, an unconscious act like blinking or breathing.

But I suddenly seem to have lost that ability.

Placing them in my lap feels like such an unnaturally demure pose that I feel like a complete impostor and dropping them limply by my sides is just so weird; it's like what you'd do if you'd lost all motor control over them. I start to cross my arms but that feels so closed off that I drop one of them, ending up holding my right upper arm with my left hand in a kind of half-crossed arms. Yeah, I know this is probably all very fascinating, but really, what the hell do people normally do with these things?!

"It's Gwen, right?"

I nod.

"So, Gwen, where exactly did you get those photos?"

"Their mine," I say, more defensively than I mean to. "Well, my mom's, really. She's the one in them. Yvette. Except that's not her real name. As you've probably guessed."

I'm babbling, in case you didn't notice.

He looks at me thoughtfully. "She doesn't know you're here, does she?"

"No." I say in a very small voice. "But I know she'll be glad I came. Eventually."

He sighs heavily. "I see."

And with a shock I suddenly realize he does. See I mean.

"You're not blind!" I blurt out.

"Why would you think I was?"

"Everyone's been saying you didn't get to see the Gray Walkway... I just assumed..."

It's suddenly icy cold in the room and it feels like it's spinning, my land sickness coming back with a vengeance. This is all so wrong that I refuse to accept it; I refuse to follow it to its logical conclusion as if my denial will somehow keep it from being real.

"No," I say, half to myself and half to the universe in general. "You're my Dad. That's you in the photo with my Mom, and you're my Dad."

"Oh, Gwen. I'm so sorry..."

"Don't be sorry! Don't. Just be my Dad. You have to be my Dad!"

"I can't. I'm not."

"But that's your nameplate on your desk!" I say pointing frantically at the brass nameplate holder sitting there as if that will somehow prove it to him and change everything. There's no question, it says

Holden Baxter. It's engraved in large bold letters, clear as day: Holden Baxter, Inc.

Oh, my god. Inc. He's not Mr. Ink; he's Mr. Inc.

For the second time today, the ground gives way under me, but this time it swallows me whole and I vanish into its darkness.

There is something cold on my forehead and I can feel a wet drip making its slow way down my temple. For a moment, I think I'm back in Peter's apartment with Mitch's French vanilla "ice pack" on my head. I try to hold onto that belief, scrunching my eyes shut, willing it to be true as if this were a Schrödinger's universe and as long as I don't observe it, everything that just happened, didn't.

"I think she's coming around."

It's Ginger's voice, the universe observing me, and my waveforms collapse into a despair so deep that it feels like it has no bottom. There's no point in keeping my eyes closed. I have been observed and there's no going back.

I open my eyes and Ginger's sitting next to me on the couch, which I'm now apparently lying on. My head hurts, both inside and out. I try to sit up, but the world starts spinning again so I let myself fall back against the couch's pillows, in the process dislodging the ice pack that had been on my forehead.

It's just a plain, pedestrian ice pack, the kind filled with blue gel, but I find myself staring at it as if it were some miraculous sea creature incongruously plopped onto dry land.

"Slowly, now" Ginger tells me. "You clocked your head pretty good on the coffee table going down."

She picks up the ice pack and hands it to me. "You should try to keep this pressed against it for as long as you can, but you're still probably going to have one hell of a bruise in the morning."

I numbly do as she tells me as Mr. Ink wheels into my field of view. And yes, I know it should be Mr. Inc., but I just can't do it. I've heard it as Mr. Ink all morning and that's how he's stuck in my head.

"Do you know where you are, Gwen?"

"Yeah."

"Could you be a little more specific?"

"I'm in Glenhaeven. I'm Gwen Pendergrass, she's Ginger, I don't know her last name, and you're... you're not Holden Baxter."

"No, I'm not. At least not in the way you mean."

"What other ways are there?"

He doesn't respond for a moment.

"It's complicated," he finally says.

A bark of laughter bursts from me, not a healthy sound, but fortunately, the pain in my head quickly ends it.

"When was the last time you ate something?" he asks me gently.

"I don't remember."

"Do you not remember because that part of the day is hazy," Ginger asks. "Or do you just not remember?"

"No, it's not hazy. I was so nervous this morning, thinking I was going to meet... I couldn't stomach anything. So, I don't know. Dinner last night, I guess."

"No wonder you keeled over!" she exclaims. "We have got to get some food in you. Do you like peanut butter?"

"Yeah, but I'm okay."

"You are not okay. You just fainted and whacked your head on a table."

"Okay, when you put it that way... But I'm not hungry."

"I don't care," Ginger says. "You are going to eat something, and you're not getting up until you do. Understand?"

I nod. It's kind of freeing to have no decisions, to just do what you're told. Ginger turns to Mr. Ink. "Don't let her try to stand."

I'm not sure how he'd stop me, being in the wheelchair and all, but the still spinning room is discouragement enough that I don't think I'll put the question to the test.

Ginger leaves, gently shutting the door behind her.

And once more I am alone in a room with yet another man who is not my father.

"So," he finally says. "How sure are you that Holden was your father?"

I sit up more to better face him, and he begins to protest but I lean back heavily onto the cushions before he has the chance. But I'm a little more upright, now. Yeah, big win.

"Completely," I say. "If the man in those pictures is Holden Baxter..."

"He is."

"Then he's my Dad. Or was," I add, curiously calmly. "He's dead, isn't he."

It isn't really a question. I know the answer already in my bones, but he tells me anyways.

"I'm afraid so."

I can feel a twitch in my cheek at the words, but that's it. No frenzied crying fit, no world shifting around me. Just a numb acknowledgment of an irreconcilable fact: I will never meet my father.

"I didn't even know he had a daughter. If I had..."

"He didn't know. Mom never told him."

"He talked about her sometimes, I think. The love of his life, who he wasn't completely sure even existed. He told me that if it weren't for that photo strip, he would have been convinced she was all just a dream."

His words are tearing at me, taking chunks of my heart with them as they go piercing through me. If ever I wanted to cry, this is the time, but my eyes remain stubbornly dry, too numbed with despair to react. Oh Mom! What have you done...?!

"I know he even hired some private detectives to find her but no one found even a whiff of a trail." He looks at me searchingly. "Why did she do it? Vanish that is. Was she already married... or in witness protection?"

I shake my head, not trusting my voice.

"Nothing so reasonable," I finally say. "It's... it's uh..."

But I trail off, unable to tell the story, the words catching in my throat.

"It's complicated," I lamely say.

"Yeah," he says, smiling wryly. "I expect it is."

"Knock, knock," Ginger calls out as she pushes the door open. She's carrying a tray overloaded with food, apparently having just picked up one of everything in the kitchen. Most of the fruit I recognize but there are some strange spiky ones, one of them a bright orange, another like an alien artichoke, reddish pink with large scaly leaves tipped in green. Next to them is a small pile of sandwiches, a carton of milk, several cans of soda and a pair of bottles of beers.

She puts it down on the coffee table in front of us and one of beers tries to take a nose dive, threatening to spill on the sandwiches, but for once my reflexes serve me well and I manage to grab it before it can do any harm.

"Nice catch," Ginger says. "That would have been pretty bad. But hand it over, alcohol on an empty stomach is a bad combination."

I relinquish the bottle. They must think I'm a lot older than I am if they think I might want it. And that actually makes a lot of sense, given that they haven't threatened to call my mother. A fact for which I am extremely grateful.

"I wasn't sure what you liked," Ginger says to me as she passes the beer to Mr. Ink.

"So, you brought everything," Mr. Ink says.

"More or less. Including a couple of the cheese puffs, I made for tonight."

"She's desserts," Mr. Ink tells me. "And the best one we've had in a long while."

"But you can't have them until after you eat something real," Ginger tells us, looking pointedly at Mr. Ink. She gives us a quick tour of the food.

"Apple, pear, orange, etc. This is a kiwano, or blowfish fruit," she says pointing at the strange orange, spiky one. "It tastes pretty much exactly like what you'd expect if a cucumber, kiwi and banana were fused together in some strange industrial accident. But without the radioactive aftertaste"

She points at the reddish-pink scaly one. "This is a dragon fruit. It's got a pretty mild flavor, think somewhere between rice and kiwis. I thought it might be good if your stomach's acting up. Sandwiches: PB&J, Turkey and a BLAT, which is a BLT plus Avocado. And drinks are self-evident."

My stomach is a pretty tight knot, but I know that Ginger's right. I really should eat something.

"I guess I'll try the dragon fruit," I say, picking it up.

But now that I have it in my hand, I'm not sure how one goes about eating it. That small fact is apparently obvious as Ginger leans over and takes it from me.

"Here, let me," she says, picking up a small knife from the tray and expertly cutting the dragon fruit in half, then handing the two halves back to me. The inside is not what I expected at all. I mean, I'm not sure what I was expecting, but a milky white flesh infused with tiny black dots—kind of like a starry sky in negative—isn't it. "Some people like to just dig in," she adds, "but personally I prefer a spoon."

"Spoon it is then."

She's right, it's pretty mild, with a texture kind of like a kiwi, especially with all the tiny crunchy seeds. It's just a little sweet and it's apparently just what my stomach ordered because with each bite, I can feel the knot in my stomach begin to ease up. I follow it up with a sandwich and one of the cartons of milk. And for a little while, none of us really talk, just giving the food in front of us our full attention.

Eventually my hunger pangs subside, only to have the pangs of my heart reassert themselves.

"I know I'm in your place and everything..." I say hesitantly. "And I don't mean to be rude, but since you're not my... um, Holden Baxter, who are you? And why, when I asked you if you were him, did you say *not in the way you mean*."

He takes a long swig of his beer, finishing it, and then carefully puts the bottle back on the tray.

"My name is David Fischer, but that's not really what you're asking. I'm a lawyer, and I am the legal embodiment of Holden Baxter, Incorporated. The non-corporeal corporation that he became upon his death."

"Excuse me?"

"Let me explain it a different way. I don't know if you follow such things, but do you remember that ridiculous Supreme Court ruling a while back that basically said that corporations are people?"

"Yeah, generally."

"Well, Bax... that's what we all called him... your father that is..." He loses his train of thought for a moment, probably trying to wrap his head around the idea that Holden, um, Bax, was a father at all, much less mine.

"Anyway," he continues. "Bax was one of the many people who thought it was just outrageous. So, half in protest, and half probably just to see if he could do it, he decided that if corporations are people, then logically people can be corporations. So together we set up Holden Baxter, Incorporated, a non-corporeal corporation as he called it. And one that literally owns itself.

"It's not that straightforward, of course, but that's basically the bottom line. I am its sole employee, with a lifetime appointment, and my job title literally is Holden Baxter."

"Oh, man, that's brilliant. That's just genius."

"It's classic Bax," he tells me. "He always loved rocking the boat. Pointing out the absurdities in the world."

"So that's where I get it from." I brush away a tear. "God, I would have loved... I would have loved so much to meet..."

Let me just say that my previous tear is no longer alone and I am sobbing in Ginger's arms.

I eventually pull myself together, because even I can't cry forever. But I feel so incredibly stupid and embarrassed. I've been here probably less than a half hour and I've already collapsed once and soaked someone I basically just met with my tears. That's a definite record, even for me.

Ginger hands me some tissues that she's produced from somewhere and I blow my nose and blot the leaking holes that are my eyes.

"I'm sorry. You both have been so nice to me, and I'm just a mess."

I stand up and am grateful to discover that I'm not dizzy any more. "I should go."

"But you just got here," Ginger protests.

"Yeah, but I don't belong. I probably never should have come."

"You didn't have a choice," Mr. Ink tells me kindly. "Sometimes a hero's journey is inevitable."

"I'm hardly a hero. What kind of hero breaks down and cries all the time?"

"Odysseus," they both say, almost in unison.

Okay, we read The Odyssey this year in English class and he does do a hell of a lot of wailing and wrenching of hair.

"That still doesn't make me a hero," I protest. "And if we're going all literary analysis on it, I'm probably not even the main character in my own story, given the whole tragic, star-crossed lover thing my parents had going on. I'm just a roadblock keeping them apart. A device."

They look at each other helplessly, because, after all, how can you respond to that except with the falsest of platitudes? Particularly if you don't really know anything about the person, other than that they can cry their body weight in tears.

"If you really want to go," Mr. Ink says. "I can call Chris up and have him take you back to the Cambridge Library, or your apartment, or wherever you like."

I can see that Ginger is about to protest, but he holds up his hand and preemptively stops her.

"However, I would rather you stay," he tells me. "At least for a while longer. Bax, I mean, your father that is... Sorry about that, this is going to take a little getting used to."

"Tell me about it."

"Anyway, he and I have known each other since elementary school, and we've gone... we went through quite a lot together. Since he never had the pleasure of getting to know you, it would be my honor if I could."

I hesitate, torn between my desire to just crawl into a hole and pull it in after me and the opportunity to learn even a little bit about my dad.

"You should know," Mr. Ink goes on, "that if you had grown up with Bax, I would have absolutely been your Uncle Steve..."

I can feel a tear roll down my cheek, but I don't do anything about it.

"You've come this far. And as your almost uncle," he says smiling, "I really think you owe it to yourself to see it to the end."

Yeah, he's right. If only Mom had rolled the dice and tried with Dad, who knows what our lives would have been like. And now, if I just run away, I haven't learned anything.

"Okay," I say, sitting back down. "I guess I can stay a little while longer."

"Excellent."

"Do you want me to go?" Ginger asks.

"No. Not unless you want to," I tell her. "Though, to be honest, I can't promise there won't be more tears."

"No worries. I go back and forth to the mainland a lot. I'm not afraid of a little salt water."

They're both being so nice, but I still feel so alone in this strange place, my emotions ricocheting in all directions. I really wish Mom were here, so she could hear and see all this, but if it's tearing me up this badly, I can't even imagine how she'd feel. No, the person I really want here is Peter, to hold my hand and get fierce and protective, even if he's just protecting me like I'm his little sister. But hey, I'll take him any way I can get him.

I hope whatever he and Not Dad are doing is going better than this.

"So," I say, swallowing heavily. "When did he die? And how?"

"Two years ago, March. Cancer. By the time they discovered it, it was too late to do anything. It was quick. Too quick. But he never was in any real pain. He just kind of faded away."

I know what he means, but my mind insists on painting the mental image of Dad getting more and more transparent until he is gone, like the Cheshire Cat. It's stupid and it's funny and it hurts like hell. Two years. I missed him by just two fucking years.

"I know this probably isn't going to help you at all right now," Mr. Ink tells me. "But perhaps it will when you've had more time to process all this. When Bax knew he had only a week or two left, he told all of us here at Glenhaeven that he didn't want us to mourn him. He felt that he was the luckiest man in the world, because he'd gotten to live his dream. And then he'd gotten to build that dream and live inside it, even if only for a little while."

Mr. Ink smiles wryly at whatever he's remembering.

"He also planned his own version of a New Orleans Style funeral," he says. "Crossed with Mardi Gras and an Irish wake or something. He had us all get into these crazy outfits. And then those of us musically inclined..."

"And `Uncle Steve'" Ginger interjects helpfully. Mr. Ink slowly turns and gives her a nonplussed look. But she only grins back unrepentantly.

He sighs and turns back to me. "As I was saying, we formed ourselves into a rough approximation of a Jazz Band and we all paraded through the Great Hall while your father sat in the Sea Throne, his face painted like a technicolor <u>Nightmare before Christmas</u> character. It was a skull, but a joyful skull, full of life. It's kind of hard to explain. Anyway, we ate, and we drank and danced, and people read poems and short stories, told funny stories, and he lorded over it all."

He pauses, clearly not wanting to go on. But after a moment, he does anyway.

"He died three days later. That day was one of the worst days of my life; he was my best friend, and I'd probably spent more time with him than I have with any other person, including my wife. But in a strange way it was also okay. I only hope I have a third of the courage he had when my time comes."

I can't find the words to say what I'm feeling, so I don't say anything at all.

"If you like," Ginger says. "I can take you out to his grave before you go. His ashes are under a very special Gray Sister we had commissioned just for him."

"I'd like that. I think."

"You don't have to do it today," Mr. Ink says. "If you don't feel up to it. You're always welcome to come back. Your mother too."

I can feel the tears threatening again but I'm clenching my right fist so hard, my fingernails are digging into my palm, the physical pain distracting from the mental one.

"Thank you," I manage to choke out. "I probably wi... we probably will. At some point."

Right now, my future planning skills are pretty much at their limit just holding back the tears and planning my next breath.

"Speaking of your mother, do you know why she decided to vanish? Why she never contacted Bax?"

I nod, then take a deep breath, gathering my voice. "The simple answer is me."

"I don't understand."

"Yeah, I didn't either until just last week."

Is that possible? Did this whole thing really start just last week? It feels like I've been walking this tightrope of lies and half-truths for months, but when I do the math, it's been only nine days since the stupid father/relationship assignment.

They're both leaning forwards, clearly dying to know more, but also just as clearly trying to act casual. "You have to understand," I tell them, "that everything my mom did, she did with the best intentions. And I guess I recently haven't acted all that differently."

Chapter 38
In which I discover I might be
the next Dalai Lama.

I have no idea how long I talked, but the story basically spun out of control. I started with what Mom had told me about the weekend of my conception—their one and only time together—and why she'd decided to go it alone. I then somehow segued into her dropping out of college to raise me, me getting her into Yale only to have her turn down the scholarship, me intercepting her letter, Not Dad and his crazy office, and even some stuff about Peter and Mitch.

The only time they interrupt is when I describe why Mom turned Yale down and they figure out that I'm still in high school. Which then brings up the father/relationship assignment that started the whole thing, or at least the renewed searching part of it, Mr. Clavell and god knows what else. When I finally wind down, they're both staring at me with something approaching awe... or it could be something receding away from awe; it's hard to tell from this angle without a clear red or blue shift.

And even if it is awe, it could very well be awe that I manage to get out of bed every morning. I don't know.

"You have got to write that down," Ginger tells me, her eyes gleaming.

Yeah, right. Like that's going to happen.

I shake my head. "My mom's the writer, not me."

"She may be the writer," Mr. Ink tells me, "but you're a born storyteller, and that was one hell of a story."

Ginger turns to Mr. Ink. "If Yale still doesn't know she's turned down the scholarship, can't you do something to help them out? It doesn't sound like they need that much, and you know Bax would want to, that's basically why he set up this place, isn't it? To help writers write?"

My heart stops beating for a moment. Could he really? With Dad dead, I guess I'd figured that any help from him was dead along with him. But Mr. Ink is Dad, at least legally. All he'd have to do is say the words.

"I'm sorry. There's nothing I can do. I wish I could..."

Okay, those weren't the words I was looking for. But it doesn't matter. I knew it was too good to be true.

"That's okay," I tell him. "I wasn't really expecting anything. I mean, I could be making all this up, for all you know."

"Are you?" Ginger demands.

"No. But it doesn't matter..."

"Yes, it does." She turns to Mr. Ink. "You could do a paternity test; with all the time Bax spent in hospitals, they've got to have something they could match it against."

"That's not the problem." He shakes his head sadly, then turns to me. "Truly, Gwen, I believe you, and if I could help you, I would."

"So why can't you?" Ginger demands. "We both know Bax was loaded when he died, and you're Holden Baxter, Inc. so what's the hitch?"

"The hitch, as you put it, is that while Bax was extremely wealthy, Holden Baxter Inc. has corporate assets of exactly two dollars and forty-seven cents."

"What?!"

"Bax and I both knew that this whole person as corporation idea could never really hold up if anyone challenged it. It was an act of protest on his part, but he also knew it was essentially a house of cards. So before he died, he transferred his entire wealth, less two dollars and forty-six cents..."

"I thought you said forty-seven cents." I know it's completely unimportant but I can't stop myself.

"I found a penny in his coat jacket. But the point is, all the real money is locked up in the Glenhaeven Trust, a non-profit we set up with Holden Baxter, Inc. as its director. But should he prove unable to serve, then I, personally, automatically take over the position. But it doesn't matter which of us is nominally in charge, the Trust has an extremely strict charter and there's no legal way I can give you any money, paternity test or not."

"There must be something you can do," Ginger protests.

Mr. Ink looks really sad as he shakes his head. "All I'm allowed to do is give writers fellowships to live on the island. You know that. It's room and board and the space and time to write. That's it."

"So, give Gwen's Mom one of those."

"I probably could. If she got into Yale, she's clearly got the skills. But what good would that do? There's no high school here and a twice daily commute for Gwen to the mainland plus shuttling back and forth to the nearest high school is neither practical, nor could I justify it within the charter."

"Ginger," I tell her, putting my hand on her arm. "I really appreciate what you're trying to do, but it's okay."

"No, it's not."

"No, it's not. But sometimes it has to be anyway."

Yeah, I know. I'm just a regular Dalai Lama.

It's nearly 5pm when I finally leave Mr. Ink at the door to Glenhaeven with the promise that I will return. He suggests that perhaps Mom and I could come for a summer, which sounds great, though I don't know how we could make that work without giving up the apartment in the process. But I don't say any of that. I just tell him that sounds great and that I'll discuss it with Mom (assuming I live long enough after coming clean with her to do so).

Ginger offers to show me Bax's grave, but I don't think I can take it right now and she doesn't push it. As we leave, Mr. Ink says he'll call Chris and have him meet us at the dock, and indeed he's filling up the small motorboat when we arrive. Ginger gives me a big hug and we swap emails. She promises to write, and I promise to respond so at least the ball is in her court.

I feel emotionally burnt out. I'm just numb, resigned to my failure in finding dad, my failure to salvage Yale, my failure to be truthful with Mom. I'm even numb to the icy spray that tries to soak me on the way back to the mainland.

I don't know if Ginger or Mr. Ink said something to him, but other than asking where I want to be dropped off, Chris doesn't try to talk on the ride back, for which I'm grateful. It's getting late and there's really no point in trying to keep anything secret anymore, so I give Chris my home address and he takes me straight to my door.

My building looks even shabbier than usual, through whether that's due to my mood or just in comparison to the majesty of Glenhaeven, I can't say. Nor do I particularly care. It is what it is, and what it is isn't great.

Chris and I say our goodbyes at the car and he says he hopes to see me again soon. My mouth says something in return, which seems to satisfy him, though I really have no idea what platitude I muttered. He roars off back to his world of the Gray Walkway, and I enter mine, the one with the Gray Wallpaper.

I climb the four flights of stairs up to our floor but find myself turning left rather than right and end up in front of Peter's apartment rather than my own. I hesitate, and am just about to turn away when Mitch opens the door.

"That board squeaks," he says by way of a greeting.

"Um, I'll try to remember that."

"You should. It's an excellent security system. Far better than a dog, because a board never sleeps you know. It never sleeps."

"I would imagine not."

"And you don't need to feed it, or take it to the vet, or send it to college or anything. It's really quite revolutionary if you think about it."

"Um, is Peter in?"

"Yes, though not here "in." He's "there" in," he says pointing down the hall towards my apartment. "Your in, not mine."

"He's in my apartment?"

"That's what I said, isn't it?"

"Do you know what he's doing there?"

"Should I?" He furrows his forehead then leans his head out into the hallway, looking down the hall towards our apartment. "No, I don't think so. I can't see anything with the door closed. My recommendation is that you go ask him yourself. That's what I always do."

I thank Mitch and head over to my apartment.

Peter probably came looking for me to find out what happened today and then got waylaid by Mom. Sometimes it's a little unnerving how well they get along, but I guess that's better than the alternative.

I fumble the key out of my backpack and unlock the door. I open it to find Peter, Mom and Not Dad all crammed into the little room. They are all staring at me and my immediate thought is that it's an intervention.

Thank God. It's about time someone stopped me.

Mom looks like she's been crying, which is probably not that surprising considering all the lying and sneaking around I've been doing. But she also looks like she can't quite decide what emotion she should be having right now. Disappointment... disbelief... shock... excitement? They all seems to be fighting for control, and I have a feeling my face is mirroring hers, but with my own set of expressions. Sadness... regret... confusion... and yes, relief. Endings, even bad ones, can be a relief in their own way.

"Hey," Peter says, seated on my futon-from-hell, currently in its couch alter-ego. Despite my Mom's turmoil he seems quietly pleased, as does Not Dad, now that I think of it.

I turn and meet my Mom's eyes. "I'm sorry."

She gets up and crosses to me and for a moment, I don't know what she's going to do, and I'm not sure she does either. But then she enfolds me in her arms and hugs me so hard I can barely breathe. The numbness that had been wrapped around me melts away at her touch and all my disappointment and regret just floods out in a hot salty stream. At this rate, I'll have grooves down my cheeks, worn away by my tears just like the Grand Canyon was.

"I just wanted to make things better," I choke out.

Mom's nearly crying herself, now. "You did."

"He's dead, Mom. Dad's dead."

"What?" Peter exclaims. "No!"

"He's gone," I tell him, somehow lifting my head to look at him despite the several gravities of pull dragging every muscle in my face down into a frown.

Mom pulls away to look at me. "What's this about your dad?"

"He died," I tell her, gratefully taking the box of tissues Not Dad silently holds out to me. "Two years ago. Cancer."

"Damn it!" Peter says as he launches himself from his chair, looking like he's about to punch the wall. "Gwen, if I had known..."

"You couldn't have." I'm still in Mom's arms but I reach out my hand to Peter and he takes it. He nearly crushes it, of course, but realizes immediately and relaxes his grip to merely vice-like firmness.

"Well, *I* should have," Not Dad says.

"Wait a minute," Mom says. "What do you have to do with this? No, hold that thought."

"It's just not fair," Peters tells me, ignoring the other conversation going on. "I know life isn't, but sometimes... sometimes it just really isn't."

Mom's looking back and forth between us. "What's going on? Gwen, how do you know your father's dead?"

"I found him, Mom. From the phone number on the back of the photos. I just came back from his house."

"His house?"

"His island, really."

Mom's speechless.

"It's my fault, Mrs. Pendergrass," Peter tells her. "I helped her track him down."

"I guess I did too," Not Dad confesses.

"What?!"

"But I should have looked into it deeper," Not Dad continues, turning to me. "Gwen, once I saw that Holden Baxter was chairman of the Glenhaeven Trust, I just stopped and handed it over to you. God, I feel like shit, giving you false hope like that."

"No, you didn't. And I never would have known what happened without you."

"Could someone please tell me what's going on?"

Mom's beginning to look a little white eyed around the edges.

"Yeah," I tell her. "But it's going to take awhile. It's... complicated. You should probably sit down."

She sinks back into the kitchen chair she was sitting in when I came in.

"Remember that stupid Father/Relationship Assignment?" I ask her.

She nods.

"Well, it got me thinking really hard about Dad."

So, I tell her the whole story, not holding anything back. From dropping the photo frame to calling Not-Dad, to finding Dad's books and sending the postcard. Peter and Not Dad chime in periodically, filling in details while Mom just sits, taking it all in.

Peter and Not Dad join her in silence as I recount the rest of my day, telling them about Mr. Ink and Ginger and Dad's farewell party. Tears are dripping down Mom's cheeks, but she's making no move to wipe them away.

I feel wrung out when I finally finish, and both Peter and Not Dad look a little moist about the eyes as well. No one says anything for a long time, just letting it all sink in.

"I shouldn't have lied to you, Mom," I finally tell her. "And gone behind your back."

"I didn't leave you much of a choice, did I?"

"No, but still. I hated not being able to tell you things, to have to pretend it was all about Peter."

"What was all about me?"

Oh crap. I hadn't planned on telling Peter about my stupid crush, ever, and particularly not in front of a whole audience. But the room's too small; there's nowhere to hide. And now that it's come out, I'm just so tired of lying. I slowly turn to him, trying to gather my thoughts.

"You've probably noticed I've been acting kind of emotional lately..."

"Really? No, I haven't noticed anything."

"Right. Well, a lot of it has been about Dad. But not all of it."

"Okay." He looks confused. Apparently all this crying has short-circuited my thought bubble or maybe he's just in massive denial about what I'm going to say. I suppose the plus side about having an audience here is that now everyone gets to feel awkward rather than just Peter and me, and we won't be left staring at each other after my bombshell goes ka-thud. We've got other people here and other crises to fry, so maybe we'll just be able to move on to the next one and get past the awkward awfulness of it all.

I look him in his wonderful chocolate brown eyes. "You've got to promise you'll forget this immediately after I tell you. You're my best friend in the entire world and I don't want to do anything to make that change."

"I'm not going anywhere, Gwen. I mean, where would I? I live just down the hall."

"Promise me."

"I promise I will forget everything you tell me."

"You too." I tell Mom and Not Dad. "I don't want to hear another word about it."

"My lips are sealed," Not Dad promises.

"And mine as well," Mom says.

Okay, this is it. I take a deep breath. I can't look Peter in the eyes because I can't bear the thought of what I might see there, so I fix my gaze straight ahead on his mile wide chest.

"I-know-I'm-a-complete-idiot-but-I-have-a-really-bad-crush-on-you." I blurt out.

I look up at him cautiously, my heart holding its breath along with the rest of me. But I can't read him.

"So, now you know how I feel," he finally says.

"I know, and that's why I wasn't going to tell you."

"I don't think you understand. Gwen, I feel the same..."

"...as you always have," I say finishing the sentence for him, knowing what he's going to say but not wanting to actually hear him say it. "I get that. And I don't want that to change."

Peter sighs, then looks up over my head at my mother who's still sitting behind me. "Mrs. Pendergrass, may I?"

I turn to see what's going on, but she's smiling, and gives him an expansive sweep of her arm. The kind that says, go ahead, be my guest.

I look back at Peter, confused. He takes my hands, gently holding them in his. "I've been wanting to do this for about as long as I can remember," he says quietly, then bends down and kisses me softly on the lips.

Oh.

His lips are so soft, his breath so warm that the feel of them linger on my lips long after he straightens, looking down at me, his eyes shining. But it was too short, too tender, too unexpected. I need to try again, and I need to feel his arms around me, and I need to keep my knees from collapsing under me. Fortunately, he's still holding both my hands in his, holding me up until my legs decide they can do it on their own.

However, I am also painfully aware of Mom and Not Dad staring at us, so I'm going to have to take one out of three. I let go of one hand and turn to face them, lacing my other hand's fingers in Peter's and gripping them as tightly as I can, with no intention of ever letting go.

"Show's over," I tell them. "Nothing to see."

"What did I say?" Mom asks, a huge smile on her face. "I told you to go talk to him."

"Shut up, Mom."

"I knew there was something between you two, the first day I met you," Not Dad adds. "Anyone could see it."

"Yeah, well apparently I'm not just anyone."

"Neither is your boy, Peter," Not Dad replies.

"He's not my boy."

"Okay, your man, Peter."

"I'm right here you know," Peter adds.

"Anyway," Not Dad goes on, "you want to know what he strong-armed me into doing today?"

"Do I?"

"You really do," Mom chimes in.

"Okay. So, what did he do?"

"He made me drive him all the way down to Connecticut."

"What's in Connecticut?"

Peter shrugs, a small smile on his face.

"Take my chair," Mom says getting up and patting the seat, "I think you may be the one who needs to sit." I reluctantly do so, though I stubbornly refuse to let go of Peter's hand.

Not Dad opens a laptop that's been sitting on the table this entire time. Yeah, sorry I didn't notice it before; I've been kind of distracted. When the screen wakes up, there's a video of a middle-aged women in a business suit frozen in mid-word. Not Dad hits the return to start button and then plays the video.

"Ms. Pendergrasses," the woman on screen says, putting an emphasis on the pluralization of our name. "I have just heard a remarkable story from a remarkable young man. At his request, I am making this video, but please call my office at your earliest convenience because I'll need to speak directly with Karen by end of business day this coming Tuesday, at the very latest."

Karen, of course, is my Mom, and this woman's voice is incredibly familiar. But I just can't place it.

"I talked on the phone with one of you just a few days ago, and based on Peter's explanation, I'm assuming it was Gwen,"

Oh my god! It's Mrs. van der Whoever, the Admissions department woman from Yale.

"Since I understand that you, Karen, have not been exactly kept in the loop, let me introduce myself. I am Mrs. van der Diem, director of admissions at Yale."

They went to Yale?!! I look up at Peter and he gives me an embarrassed smile.

"Before I go any further," Mrs. van der Whosen continues, "I should tell you that here at Yale, we take academic integrity quite seriously, and normally any candidate who falsified information on their application would be immediately disqualified for admission. However, as Peter has explained, in quite passionate and eloquent detail I might add..."

I squeeze Peter's hand, but my eyes are fixed on the screen.

"...this is a somewhat unique circumstance as it appears that the factual information in the elder Ms. Pendergrass's application is accurate and she truly was the author of the submitted writing sample which was the primary basis for her acceptance.

"According to Peter, all that was falsified was the authorship of the admission essay and the signature on the application. We will need confirmation of that, but if true and if the elder Ms. Pendergrass was not party to this deception, it does not seems reasonable to penalize her for actions that others made on her behalf. Particularly as her writing sample was unanimously considered by the committee to be the best one submitted to the program in this admissions cycle."

"You go, Mom," I whisper to her.

"I have talked to the department chair, and she has agreed that if Karen Pendergrass would submit her own admissions essay, then, assuming it is of the quality we expect, we will still extend to her the scholarship we'd previously offered.

"With two small changes.

"Gwen, Peter has proposed a somewhat unique argument. Since you wrote the admissions essay which in part got your mother accepted —and I must say as a side note that this is truly quite remarkable for a high school sophomore—your Peter has argued that Yale actually accepted both of you and should increase the scholarship to cover both of your living expenses."

No way...

But Mrs. van der Whosen goes on. "Unfortunately, the admissions process does not work that way, and the scholarship is a fixed amount, both in stipend and food allowance."

Yeah, I was right. No way.

"However, we do have some latitude on housing if the accepted applicant has a live-in spouse or partner. And although it's not normally done for live-in children, there are some precedents, and we should be able to change your supplied rooms to one in our couple's housing."

Oh, my god. But if they can't increase the money, and she can't work...

I look around at my Mom and Peter and Not Dad, but they're all smiling.

"They are not large," she goes on, "but I've been assured that this won't be a problem for you. However, even with this housing, we know that the scholarship will not provide sufficient funds for two people to live, nor is it expected to. And unfortunately, the requirement that Karen not work during the term of the scholarship is non-negotiable.

"That said, we do currently have a part-time opening at the school library, one that I believe would be compatible with a high school schedule. Gwen, if you take this job, then as an employee you would get a discount at any of the university dining halls and between your pay and that discount, you should be able to keep body and soul together.

"It won't be steak and caviar, mind you, but then again, I gather you aren't eating that now.

"Lastly, Gwen, while I admire your spunk and ingenuity and that of your friend Peter here, just because we are giving you what some might say amounts to a free pass does not mean we will accept any such behavior in the future. You are clearly a bright and creative young woman, but from here on, asking forgiveness will not be easier than asking permission, and your continued employment will depend on your complete honesty and integrity.

"I hope this will be an acceptable arrangement as we would be quite pleased to have you both as additions to the Yale community."

Not Dad stops the video.

I look at Mom. "Are we going to Yale?"

"We are going to Yale. Assuming you…"

"Are you kidding?! We're going to Yale!"

And we scream and hug and dance while Not Dad and Peter watch on. We're going to Yale! We are going to YALE!

Those five words keep running around and around in my head, but there's this strange, nagging feeling that I'm forgetting something. And whatever it is, it feels bad.

And suddenly it clicks. We are going to Yale. We are moving to Yale. And Peter's here.

I disentangle myself from Mom and walk to Peter. I guess my thought bubble is back on, as he looks at me with a sad smile.

"I guess you figured out the cloud's lead-lining," he says quietly.

"I can't believe you did all this."

"Anyone would have."

"No, no, they really wouldn't."

He shrugs. "If you love something, set it free…"

"But I don't want to be set free. I just found you."

"I've been here the entire time. And it's not until next fall… we have months and months."

"Until we don't."

"Until we don't," he reluctantly agrees. "But I'll come visit. It's only about two hours away by train."

"How will you afford it? It's got to be what, $150 or so, round-trip?"

"A little less. And there's a student discount."

"That's still a lot of money. I don't want to see you once every six months."

"That's why I'm taking a part time job with Not Dad. It's mostly filing and stuff, but he said he could also teach me the ropes."

"Really?"

Yes, yes, I know I just asked really. So, sue me. I don't want to get everything I dreamed of and lose everything I want... so forgive me if I need a little reassurance.

"Really," Peter says quietly. "I'm not letting you get away that easily."

Oh, the hell with it, I'm taking the other two out of three whether Mom's watching or not.

Chapter 39
In which... well, things are good.
Yeah, I know.

Though I can't believe I'm saying this, things really are good.

Mom called Mrs. van der Deim—hey, I got it right this time—and delivered her very own essay and met with the department and pretty much wowed 'em. At the same time, I met with Jeff, who runs the library and who is about the coolest librarian you've ever met. He looks like a biker but knows more about Jack Kerouac and the beat generation than most people know about anything. Not to mention he actually does ride a motorcycle which Mom has forbidden me from ever riding.

Still, I'm fairly sure I can wear her down before ever actually ends.

I'm not sure how much I wowed Jeff, but at least I passed muster and we're all set to start in the fall. My new high school is all shiny and new... and some of the teachers are too, actually having this strange quality of, um, what do you call it? Oh yeah, enthusiasm. Just unnatural, if you ask me.

I'm completely petrified of going there without Peter but I know I'll manage. Somehow. And not necessarily well. But I will. Somehow. Or at least I keep telling myself.

Mom, Peter, and I went back to Glenhaeven though I made them both read the book before I would let them go. It was good and it was terrible, sometimes both at the same time. Mom asked if there happened to be any video of Dad and they found some from his farewell party. We both pretty much lost it, but in some strange way, it was also cathartic. Dad was saying goodbye to the world, and at the same time it felt like we were saying goodbye to him as well.

As for Peter and me... well, get your own boyfriend and find it out for yourself.

He's mine and I'm not sharing.

On the other side of the coin, Mom and Not Dad never really clicked. I mean, they liked each other well enough, and still do, but at the end of the day, that's pretty much all there was to it. Fortunately, it was mutual. He still comes around now and again, usually dropping off

Peter after a stakeout or some such thing, but whenever he does he always says hi and they have a cup of coffee and catch up.

Still, not everything's perfect. Buddha's moved on to a better place. That is to say, Peter's apartment. Where Mitch pretty much treats him like a god.

We weren't going to be able to take Buddha with us because the apartment in New Haven has a strict no pets policy. Buddha apparently figured this out, because at about the same time we got the letter telling us this, he decided to move in with Peter, his Mom and Mitch.

Like Not Dad, Buddha comes around and visits now and again, but it's clear it's just for nostalgia's sake, checking in to see how the old neighborhood's getting on without him. Mom's still kind of baffled how Buddha knew to move, though if you ask Mitch, he'll go on for hours about how Buddha is psychic and how he's learning more from that cat about life than he has from anything since the publishing of <u>Zen and the Art of Motorcycle Maintenance</u>.

Me, I know the simple truth. That cat can read.

If you don't believe me, then answer me this. Just yesterday I was over at Peter's place and saw him ripping a label off the bottom of one of their kitchen chairs. He managed to industriously pull the whole thing down and then immediately started eating it.

Now I ask you, why in God's name would a cat go through all that effort to remove an old label and then **eat it?** The answer was clear, however, the moment I pulled the half-eaten label from him. For there, right at the bottom, in big block letters it said BY PENALTY OF LAW, NOT TO BE REMOVED EXCEPT BY THE CONSUMER.

Now, for all his faults, at his core, he's a good kitty. He's not going to violate the law. So really, once he pulled it down and read it, what choice did he have but to eat it?

And with that, I rest my case.

BOOK BLOOPERS & OUTTAKES
(or my murdered darlings)

This is what happens when you write yourself into a corner (or how to mess with your daughter when she's reading it chapter by chapter as it's being written)

Ginger asks if I want to see Bax's grave, but I don't think I can take it right now and she doesn't push it. Mr. Ink said he'd tell Chris to meet us at the dock and he's filling up the small motorboat when we arrive. Ginger gives me a big hug and we swap emails. She promises to write and I promise to respond so at least the ball is in her court.

I feel emotionally burned out. I'm just numb, resigned to my failure to find dad, my failure to salvage Yale, my failure to be truthful with Mom. I'm even numb to the icy spray that tries to soak me on the way back to the mainland. I'm so numb in fact, that when the water begins to swirl up my ankles and swamp the boat, I really don't care.

Out of the corner of my eye, I see Chris running around frantically, trying to bail out the quickly rising flood, but I don't really care. And when the water closes in over my head, in some ways it's a relief.

Sure, it was a short life, but at least it was mine. The End.

The Lost Greenpeace Saga

As I come into the lobby, I notice an envelope in the outgoing mail basket. It's really just an old metal basket someone nailed to the wall long before we arrived, but everyone dumps their outgoing mail into it. Right now, the basket has only one letter in it and something about it draws my attention.

As I get closer, I realize that it's got Mom's Greenpeace return-address sticker on it. Now I know you're probably wondering why Mom is donating to Greenpeace at all—or at least you should be if you've been paying any attention. Sure, baby seals are pretty darn cute, but since I was born, Mom's probably seen the Loch Ness monster more frequently than she has money that was not already allocated to some frivolous thing like food, clothing or rent.

But Greenpeace apparently didn't get the memo. A couple of years ago, for no apparent reason, they got it in their little green heads that Mom would be an excellent target for their guilt-based contribution drive, so they plied her with brightly colored return address labels pre-printed with her name, address and photos of unbearably cute baby animals on them.

However, since we have the disposable income of an indigent marmoset, she wrote them back a very nice letter saying that while she believed in their cause, she couldn't give them any money and they should save their resources by not sending her other solicitations. This, of course, only encouraged them, and a week later she received a very nice calendar with more baby animals on it.

She wanted to send it back but I pointed out that this would cost us several dollars in postage and they wouldn't be able to re-use it anyway. So she sent them yet another letter, this one even more forcefully telling them that the only way she could support their mission was by ensuring they didn't waste any more of their money trying to get some of her money as she didn't have any. So please stop sending her solicitations.

This time she got a tote bag. I was actually pretty encouraged by this trend and suggested she keep writing refusal letters until we got the really big swag, but she instead decided to send them a change of address notice using Greenpeace's own corporate address as our "new" address. She figured that by the time they realized they were sending pleas for money to themselves, our real address would be long wiped from their system and they'd just be forced to delete the entire database entry.

After that, we didn't receive any more mailings from them, though I do have this sneaking suspicion that somewhere out there, they are still asking themselves for money, and will be until the end of time. Still, the upshot of the whole deal is that on those rare occasions where she needs to send out a letter, she uses one of the Greenpeace return address stickers, which is why I noticed this one.

Alas, the birthday party that never was...

He doesn't say anything for a long moment, his hands continuing to torment the bread dough.

Or brick dough, depending on your acceptance of reality.

Finally, he places the dough into an old, heavy plastic bowl. It's got a large chip out of the 1970's floral pattern that encircles the lip, and if you believe Mitch, the event in which this chip occurred beggars the imagination. Needless to say, I don't personally believe a word of it, so I won't bother repeating it.

Peter lays a clean(-ish) dish towel on top of the bowl. The dish towel has rows of bright yellow happy faces printed across it, and two-thirds of the way down there's this one single happy face that's bright green with two angled, stereotypically "alien" eyes on it. He's told me it's a trophy from his seven year old birthday party when his parents decided at the last minute to move the entire party from Los Angeles to Roswell, New Mexico... but apparently neglected to tell the parents of the other kids who they took along.

Best birthday party ever, and Peter has assured me the kidnapping charges were eventually dropped, so no harm done. Plus, all the kids got little, identical dish towels as party favors along with a good dose of the kind of second-hand smoke that makes the miles just fly by.

The Belgian Government's Dark, Mischievous Streak

What is it with the Universe and me? For some inexplicable reason the Belgians appear to be running the show and they seem to think I'm France. It's the only rational explanation.

Well, it's rational in *my* world.

See, as you may or may not know, all the history textbook say Napoleon Bonaparte was defeated by the English and Prussian forces at the Battle of Waterloo in 1815. However, if there is any justice in the world, the next edition of all those textbooks will list Belgium as having won that battle, despite not even having been a country back in 1815.

Feel free to reread that paragraph as many times as you need; I'm just going to lie here and avoid dealing with things.

Okay, moving on. Belgium cares about this battle because it took place on what is now Belgian soil, though at that time it was part of the

United Kingdom of the Netherlands. Yeah, who knew? Well, other than Wikipedia, of course.

But the whole "it was on our land" thing is just their excuse. The real reason they care is simply because it's a great opportunity to tweak the French, who of course lost this battle. And, you have to understand that Belgium and France are very much like oil and vinegar, particularly if the oil mocked the vinegar and the vinegar made disparaging jokes about the oil's intelligence to which the oil responded by putting the vinegar on arguably some of the best frites in the world.

Or at least so I've heard.

Anyway, in 2015 Belgium innocently proposed the creation of a commemorative €2 coin to celebrate the 200th anniversary of the Battle of Waterloo. However, to their profound shock and surprise, France vetoed the plan, which you (and the French government) would probably have expected to have been the end of it. And it was, for about a week or two... until the Belgian government found an obscure loop-hole in the Eurozone rules that allows any EU country to issue their own coinage, *as long as it is not in a standard amount.*

And so the Belgian €2.50 coin was born, both gleefully celebrating Napoleon's defeat and, as I see it, fully winning the Battle of Waterloo in favor of the Belgians, some 200 years after it happened.

And last, but not least, the untold story of the oddest phone call Not-Dad ever got

"Well, there was the time this guy called me up and said he thought he'd accidentally killed himself during an episode of Lost, and now he couldn't get cable."

"Excuse me?"

"It's actually far less interesting than it sounds."

"We'll be the judge of that."

"Okay, so this guy calls me up..."

"Yeah, we got that part."

"And he tells me he'd been watching Lost... "

"Uh-huh, that was pretty much part of your setup."

"Right. So, the day he was watching it was end of a really close election cycle, so about every ten or fifteen minutes or so he'd get interrupted by some political phone call. He got so sick of it that he started telling them he was dead when they asked for him, just to get them off the phone."

"Why didn't he not answer, or take his phone off the hook?"

"He was on call at work, so he really couldn't. Anyway, a couple of days go by and he's pretty much forgotten about the whole thing until he tries to order some pay-per-view thing from the cable company, and they tell him they can't process his order because he's dead."

"So, he accidentally killed himself while he was watching Lost and now he can't get cable. Okay, I'll give you that one."

CPSIA information can be obtained
at www.ICGtesting.com
Printed in the USA
JSHW012153070723
44155JS00002B/55